Cornwall : the cultural construction of place

1872229271

**CORNWALL COUNTY COUNCIL
LIBRARIES AND ARTS DEPARTMENT**

GW00480689

CORNWALL
The Cultural Construction of Place

edited by
Ella Westland

The Patten Press
in association with the
Institute of Cornish Studies,
University of Exeter

ACKNOWLEDGEMENTS

The publisher and editor gratefully acknowledge grants in support of this book from South West Arts, from the University of Exeter's Research Fund and the Department of Continuing and Adult Education, and from the Institute of Cornish Studies.

INSTITUTE OF CORNISH STUDIES

Sardinia Pilchardus
(The Pilchard)

INVESTMENT
SOUTH WEST ARTS

CORNWALL
COUNTY COUNCIL

The Institute of Cornish Studies is part of the University of Exeter, and is funded jointly by the University and Cornwall County Council.

First published in Great Britain in 1997

by the Patten Press (Publishers)

The Old Post Office, Newmill, Penzance, Cornwall TR20 8XN

ISBN 1 872229 27 1

Typesetting in-house at the Patten Press
Printed and bound by the Cromwell Press, Broughton Gifford, Melksham, Wiltshire

5069

CONTENTS

INTRODUCTION

Place is no longer the province of geographers. Beyond the materiality of rocks and weather, plantlife and population, the landscapes we are now trying to understand are made in our minds. Cornwall, the subject of this study, turns out to be many places, as perceived by different people and at different times. The cultural construction of 'Cornwall', that imagined land beyond the River Tamar, is the concern of this book.

Our collective fantasies often focus on place: Welsh rugby crowds, Whitby holidaymakers, mass marketing images of Berkshire pastures or Brixton streets, all bear witness to our shared imaginings. The huge and expanding global industry of tourism depends on manipulating our responsiveness to particular clusters of signs, associating them with actual holiday destinations, and ensuring that our expectations are fulfilled on arrival: Lorna Doone and cream teas are marketed as attributes of a holiday in Devon, and the tourist industry works to ensure that we get them.

A place can become a symbol of patriotism or an object of derision. Place-names on their own -- Tolpuddle or Toxteth -- can function as complex historical or political labels that obscure other knowledge of the locality. Where various constructions of a place are available, they are likely to be put to particular uses. In 1991, when allegations of satanic child abuse in the Orkney Islands were being reported in the national press, rival images of the islands were promoted by the media in support of opposing interpretations of the evidence. Was the landscape idyllic and rural, supporting a community of hard-working and home-loving incomers seeking the good life, milking goats and baking bread, or wild and remote, harbouring a motley collection of weird and morally suspect dropouts who had withdrawn to the fringe of civilisation (Eldridge *et al* . 1996)? Ideas of place are persuasive ideological forces, bearing as they do the freight of so many feelings and values, and their prominent role in marketing and the media attests to their power.

It is not only outsiders who form and impose images of place. We all construct the places we inhabit, work in or remember; they are, to a large extent, imaginary. We invest a good deal in these mental and emotional constructs, indeed our self-definition and life choices may be bound up with them. A geographer of my acquaintance living upcountry found his vocation as a child by playing with a Great Western Railway jigsaw which pictured a desirable rural land. People with economic mobility find their decisions about careers inflected

1

by prejudices about location. North or south? Manchester or Milton Keynes? Cobb cottage or council house? Garden suburb or marina-side studio? Whether we live in such places, aspire to them or reject them, they are inextricably bound up with our sense of who we are.

So psychologists, sociologists, historians and critics of the arts are joining the geographers in the project of unpacking the meanings of places and the reasons why people of different communities and periods construct places as they do. Indeed geographers themselves are entering new lands and forming new alliances. Academic boundaries are being moved or crossed; if we are not quite ready to farm as a co-operative, at least we are borrowing each other's tools and acknowledging the work that is being done over the hedge.

The departmental structure of postwar western universities tended to militate against interdisciplinarity. In English departments, for example, literary critics occasionally studied place, but usually from within their own discipline (Hardy's Wessex) or with temporary help from a close neighbouring discipline like social history (to explain, say, pastoral writing in the context of urbanisation). In the 1960s and 1970s, English departments came under the influence of broader definitions of culture like those developed by Raymond Williams, a key figure in British thinking, and Edward Said, a Palestinian who was writing out of the States on colonial constructions of the East. At the same time, versions of feminism and marxian materialism were beginning to advance through universities, mingling with theories of history and discourse, ideas from anthropology and popular culture, and debates on the postmodern. Many departments across the humanities and social sciences were irreversibly affected by these systems of thought and their cross-disciplinary implications.

Out of this melting pot, distinct intellectual groupings have already emerged. Cultural geography is an eclectic new area in which, as the chapters by Chris Thomas and Philip Crang demonstrate, academics feel free to draw from a range of theories and disciplines. Regional studies -- formerly dominated by local history, economic geography and fieldwork -- is another area where traditional patterns of investigation are giving way to interest in cultural and conceptual definitions of place. The recent shift evident in Cornish Studies towards social sciences and the arts, and its readiness to engage with new theoretical discourses, mark a notable change in academic orientation in response to the broad movements I have outlined.

This book is proof that a 'new Cornish Studies' is already in existence. Its practitioners are not necessarily writing west of the Tamar; an increasing amount of research on Cornwall is being undertaken elsewhere (though the line between 'in' and 'out', as between native and incomer, is blurred by the personal and longstanding attachments that many researchers have to the county). However, a group of academics growing around the nucleus of the Institute of Cornish Studies -- represented in publications like the new series of the *Cornish Studies* journal and here by the contributions of Philip Payton, Bernard Deacon and Alan Kent -- are beginning to question the 'ownership' of

2

Cornish Studies, and asking whether a view *from* the periphery could, or indeed should be inherently different from a view *of* the periphery.

**

This book samples new writing about place using Cornwall as a case study. Differences in approach were inevitable and indeed encouraged. The chapters are mostly written by academics in a variety of analytical discourses, but other voices can be heard, from the lyrical to the practical. Contributors were asked to be explicit about their differences and provide a brief introduction for each chapter designed to acclimatise the reader for the experience offered in the pages ahead.

Many disciplines mingle in the first half of the book, which ostensibly covers historical and literary themes from the industrial revolution to the Second World War. Bernard Deacon's opening paper unpicks a crucial nexus of place studies: where constructions of place intersect with personal identity and a sense of being a people. Taking the period of industrialisation, a time of tremendous economic and cultural change in Cornwall as across Europe, he examines the relationship between the expanding mining base of the economy and the rise of mining as a symbol of Cornwall's status and a source of powerful imagery. In this account, insider and outsider views of Cornwall are complementary, with both groups adopting the dominant imagery of successful industrialisation. Philip Payton's analysis of the Celtic Revival complicates the insider/outsider model further, showing how one sector of the Cornish middle classes in the early twentieth century responded to Cornwall's post-industrial plight by fostering a cultural identity that looked back to the past. This reactionary image of Cornwall was to merge with strategies for tourism in a pragmatic alliance between the publicists of the Great Western Railway and the Cornish themselves.

Moving from history to literature, the book's next section introduces the poetry of the Victorian miner John Harris. John Hurst applies to Harris the model of a homegrown and primarily oral culture under invasion from a more organised and literary tradition: in Harris's case, the conflicting influences are those two vital shaping forces of early nineteenth-century Cornwall, mining and methodism. Alan Kent takes a more partial view of Cornish writing, situating a debate about romantic and realist representations of the china clay area of East Cornwall in his account of the wider Cornish literary tradition. Alan Kent grew up in the clay country, which became the setting and subject of his first novel *Clay* (1991). His voice is uncompromisingly *of* the Cornish periphery, a salutary reminder that every writer in the book, however apparently detached in stance and style, writes from a specific personal position.

The significance of a writer's gender, and the subtleties of gendering place, are revealed in the following chapters -- by Helen Hughes on Daphne du Maurier's romancing of Bodmin Moor, by Simon Trezise on the views of North Cornwall and romantic love held by Emma, Florence and Thomas Hardy, and by Su Reid in her interpretation of Virginia Woolf and St Ives. Judith Hubback's study of the multivalent symbolism of the coast has women at its heart, as she explores the shoreline that is such a prominent feature of the actual and romantically imagined Cornish landscape.

Where we know we are dealing with fictions, we can attempt to keep those imagined scenes conceptually apart from the 'real' Cornwall; the last section of the book, however, highlights the ultimate impossibility of separating the imaginary from the 'real'. Chris Thomas, a cultural geographer, describes a complex set of attitudes to Cornwall created from the outside by Great Western Railway publicity. GWR's influence on the national sense of the South West is unquestionable, but the cultural texts produced by the company -- guidebooks, slogans and posters -- do not yield simple messages, or tell us how those messages have been decoded from 1900 to now. These images of Cornwall from the beginning of the century have permeated the understanding of late twentieth-century emmets (the Cornish term for holidaymakers), of incomers taking up residence in a place of their own imagining, and even of indigenous Cornish people. Cornwall cannot be separated from the composite 'Cornwall' that partakes of many sources and is particular to each one of us.

Representations of Cornwall, in the end, often tell us more about the needs of the nation than about the people living west of the Tamar. Nickianne Moody, writing from a media studies department, considers the process whereby Winston Graham's postwar Poldark novels, mediated through BBC television and video in the 1970s and 1980s, became the cultural phenomenon of 'Poldark', performing a series of social functions for Britain in the post-1974 period. Harold Birks, taking his cue from tourism studies, explores Jamaica Inn on Bodmin Moor as a site for visitors to Cornwall, sampling the many kinds of nostalgia on offer and speculating on the level of consumer resistance. Behind the inn, local people at car boot sales reclaim their land.

Storytelling may strike us as a more traditional way in which local people can lay claim to their land -- that inextricable mixture of physical place, work and community -- however else it may be seen and understood by others. But Mike Dunstan's work in the china clay villages reveals the complications of oral art even in a clearly identifiable community, as local reminiscences intertwine with variants of widespread modern legends. Separating inside from outside becomes a demanding and ultimately meaningless task, since the most self-contained communities in the modern world are not sealed off and the least travelled people are far from being placebound. Philip Crang's concluding essay develops this argument by using a day in his own life to test one possible model of a region. In the weave of what he terms a 'regional tapestry', many of the threads found in the experience of any individual stretch well beyond the immediate locality, through travel, reading and hearsay or through the agency of such modern devices as telephones and television.

4

If Cornwall residents today have many connections with the rest of the world, contributors to the book living a long way off may have significant ties which connect them to Cornwall. They see themselves not as 'academic emmets', casual tourists in a place they temporarily appropriate for their own ends, but rather as individuals with some personal stake in the place and a right to commit themselves, if only from a distance and in the privacy of their research, to Cornwall. We put down our roots in many places; birthplace or habitation are not the only conditions of belonging.

This collection of essays ends in an enticing trail of Philip Crang's footnotes. Whether you wish to follow them into a cultural geography of the postmodern, or remain further back in the book, marvelling in John Harris's mine or playing on the shore of the psyche, is your choice as reader. But once our exploration has taken us into another's Cornwall, the possibility of returning 'home' to the Cornwall from which we started is no longer open to us. Whatever our levels of assent to the chapters of this book, our reading is bound to make us more aware of the meanings that we and others invest in places like Cornwall, and of the logic shaping those meanings that lies deep in our own personal politics and sense of social identity.

Ella Westland   University of Exeter

REFERENCE
Eldridge, J., J. Kitzinger and K. Williams, *The Mass Media and Power in Modern Britain*. Oxford University Press, 1996.

'The hollow jarring of the distant steam engines' : images of Cornwall between West Barbary and Delectable Duchy

Bernard Deacon

Recently, academic interest in the construction of places and in place identities has blossomed. (for a selection of recent work from a vast literature see Crick 1991; Jewell 1994; Keith and Pile 1993; Macdonald 1993; Rose 1995; Tindall 1991) The ways places are constructed and the form place identities take are clearly connected although the two are not identical. People construct places socially and people experience identification with places. But tracing the links between the construction and the experience is not an easy thing to do. Indeed, in work on Cornwall there has been an emphasis on the former at the expense of the latter. Attention has focused on the period after the 1870s, when the modernist search for an authentic world led to the dominant construction of Cornwall as a romanticised periphery. In such a construction Cornwall is a product of the gaze of artists and tourists, anthropologists and novelists. (Chapman 1992; Dodd 1986, 14-15; Foster 1995, 450) In this construction, and in the deconstruction of it, the voice of Cornish people themselves is rarely heard. The Cornish are constructed; they have little role in the construction.

My contribution to this volume adopts a different vantage point. Turning to the period between the 1770s and the 1860s I argue that insiders had an important role in constructing both 'Cornwall' and its identity. In making this claim I am both re-asserting the importance of the view from the 'margin' (Shields 1991, 278) and re-emphasising the role of 'native scholarship'. (Marshall 1981, 225) To pursue these themes I borrow from two theoretical approaches. First the converging work of some economic historians and historical geographers helps to contextualise Cornwall, one of Europe's early industrial regions. Langton (1984) and Hudson (1989, 1992) argue that industrialisation produced distinct place identities as economic specialisation increased the differences between places at the same time as they were being inserted into an emerging global economy. Industrial regions thus gave rise to cultural regions. However, this approach emphasises material structures over discourses and images of regions, the economic over the cultural. To balance this I therefore combine this model of industrial regions with the work of Paasi (1986, 1991) who brings together material factors and discursive representations in a model of regional identity formation which stresses the role of both insiders and outsiders in the construction of identities and that of social institutions in the reproduction of those identities over time.

'Remote areas', wrote the social anthropologist Edwin Ardener, are the 'very crucibles of the creation of identity.' (1987, 50) But the people who live in these 'remote areas' are not necessarily the ones who supply the raw materials melted in the crucibles. Indeed, another anthropologist, Malcolm Chapman, has devoted a comprehensive text to the argument that the centre 'colludes' and even 'initiates' the construction of minority, peripheral identities in opposition to the dominant central identity. Chapman argues that the identities of the modern 'Celts' have been constructed through the categories of people in England; these romanticise and glamorise the 'Celt' as 'the Other', within a model where cultural fashions move outwards from the centre to the periphery. Once the periphery is reached such features cease to be seen as normal but become 'traditions' to be rescued or saved, more often than not by the educated middle classes from the centre. Chapman's deconstruction of the 'Celts' alerts us to the undeniable fact that some powerful images of Cornwall owe much to attitudes and processes in the centre, to travel writers, visitors, painters, novelists and poets who have 'discovered' Cornwall. Once discovered, Cornwall is then reconstructed through outsiders' images, these being, since the eighteenth century, heavily imbued with romanticism (Chapman 1992, 138-209 and Macdonald 1989, for similar points about Brittany).

However, the message of Chapman's text, that outsiders were the main actors in constructing the identities of the Celtic peripheries of Britain, identities which are then used by insiders as their own self-definition, can be challenged. I intend to argue here that this model, while shedding useful light on metropolitan views of the 'Celts', fails to capture the actual historical changes of image and identity in one 'Celtic' periphery in the early nineteenth century. In contrast, I shall suggest that, while representations of Cornwall before the late eighteenth century and since the 1870s may have been, to a large extent, created outside Cornwall, there was a period, between the 1770s and the 1860s, when insider representations were at least equally important in constructing 'Cornwall' and its identity (cf. Lowerson, 1994).

'A peculiar people'
In 1877 Bishop Benson, relatively recently installed as the Bishop of the new Cornish diocese, wrote: ' the Cornish are never weary of saying, 'Since they are a most peculiar people': it is quite the truest thing which I have heard them say.' (Morrish 1983, 256) The dominant meaning of 'peculiar' was, up to this time, 'particular', 'independent' and 'special', although it may be wondered whether Benson was alluding to the modern connotations of 'odd' in his observation. Anthropologists could no doubt see this 'peculiarity' as an aspect of 'Otherness' created by outsiders. Nevertheless there are problems with this view. Most obviously, it tends to ignore the role of individuals and groups in Cornwall itself. People do not just passively adopt and accommodate structures and processes imposed from outside. There is, instead, a constant process of negotiation, mediation and resistance (Hall 1992; Giddens 1991). This role of agents suggests that the model used by Chapman may blind us to the active participation of people in the margins in the creation of a set of images about themselves and the place they inhabit. They may indeed borrow from dominant

8

discourses but the content of the resulting identities cannot simply be 'read off' from such discourses.

Furthermore, while anthropologists are at home in the cultural world of meanings, they seem less aware of other, more material factors. Their approach can be contrasted, for example, with the work of historical geographers and economic historians who have recently been re-evaluating the history of industrialisation in late eighteenth/early nineteenth century Britain and the relationship to the emergence of regional identities. Turning the previous view of this relationship on its head, John Langton argues that industrialisation, far from destroying regional distinctiveness in England, actually reinforced it. Specialised production regions stimulated the rise of regional cultural identities as people began consciously to identify themselves with the regions in which they lived (Langton 1984). Regional economics led to regional cultures. The economic historian Pat Hudson has joined Langton in arguing that the industrial revolution was a period when regional integration and identities were stimulated (Hudson 1989 and 1992, 101-132. And see Gregory 1988).

Yet, while the anthropological view of identity formation emphasises culture and fails to locate it within material processes, the Langton/Hudson view somewhat vaguely reduces the production of a distinct cultural identity to economic change. To understand the formation of regional identities fully, we have to grasp the point that there are two processes at work. First, there are the structures of everyday life, including such things as settlement patterns, nature of work, religious allegiances and cultural observances. All this operates at a very local face-to-face level, helping to create the texture of local life. But these economic and social structures do not directly cause or create a regional identity, which also depends on ideas and images about particular places, the people who inhabit those places and their past. As societies become more literate, these representations and meanings produce texts of particular places that allow people to imagine themselves and their places through imagery and metaphor. The texts in turn become ritualised over time and may be detached from day-to-day structures (see Daniels 1992 for the 'textual turn' in the social sciences).

We can combine these two aspects following the approach of theorists like Anssi Paasi (1986 and 1991). He argues that the material factors of economics and culture make up the 'factual identity', based on face-to-face relationships. Meanwhile the ideas and images that people hold about places and their inhabitants can be termed 'imagined identities'. Both factual and imagined identities are created and reproduced by insiders and outsiders through a variety of social institutions ranging from the family to the nation state. Place identities are produced through both these processes. But there is no simple cause-effect relationship, each component varying in importance over space and time, although it may be the case that imagined identities become more important as modernisation proceeds.

While Chapman makes use of the concept of centre and periphery we must also note that centres and peripheries are not necessarily fixed over time. The 'centre' of one era can be relegated to 'periphery' in the next and *vice versa* (Richards 1993). The late eighteenth century was one period when the centre-periphery system was shaken up as industrialisation began to transform certain

European regions. During this phase, some peripheries became centres of economic change and technological innovation. Insiders in these places were much more likely to make their own images than insiders in places that remained firmly stuck on the periphery. One of the places moving from periphery to a more central position in the eighteenth century was Cornwall. Sidney Pollard has identified Cornwall as one of his ten early British industrial regions:

> it was tin and copper mining and smelting which formed the basis of one of the most advanced engineering centres in the world to the 1840s, and of a complex industrial society exhibiting early developments of banking and risk-sharing to deal with the particular needs of local industry as well as a remarkable attempt to cartelize copper in the 1780s. (1981, 14)

At such a time the feeling of what it meant to be 'Cornish' was transformed in the crucible of industrialisation. The Cornish people were more actively constructing images of themselves and their place, a construction that reached a high point in the campaign for a separate diocese that ultimately introduced Bishop Benson to his 'peculiar' people.

Industrialisation and tradition : the new and the old in insider images
By the late eighteenth century there were two possible representations of Cornwall and the Cornish population in circulation. One was Cornwall as 'West Barbary', a lurid and dramatic place populated by food rioters (such riots occurred regularly from the end of the seventeenth century through to 1847) and heavy drinking roisterers who lived most of their lives underground. According to one visitor from London in 1775, 'natives' of Cornwall were happiest when:

> they can sit down to a furze blaze, wringing their shirts and pouring the mud and water out of their boots. But the common people here are very strange kind of beings, half savages at the best. Many thousands of them live entirely underground, where they burrow and breed like rabbits. They are as rough as bears, selfish as swine, obstinate as mules, and hard as the native iron. (Cited in Hamilton Jenkin 1925, 13)

In their spare time these troglodytes presumably sallied forth to lure innocent mariners onto the rocks of their inhospitable land. In this representation of the primitive periphery by the civilised centre, Cornwall was indeed 'the Other', populated by a barbarian tribe.

Yet at the same time a less dramatic, more reflective representation was in the making. Pococke observed in 1750 that, while parish feasts were still kept with 'great prophaneness and debauchery', the 'common people are much polished and ready to do all kind offices, which I observed more especially among the tinners' (Pearse Chope 1967, 209). This prefigured the dominant representation of the mining population and soon, by extension, the Cornish people as a whole, that had supplanted the West Barbary representation by the 1820s.

It was really no contest when it came to which representation the Cornish themselves would adopt. Indeed, Cornwall as West Barbary was hardly an image easily adopted by insiders; it was always restricted to a voyeuristic metropolitan market, fascinated by news from the peripheries. The global process of industrial capitalism had presented Cornish people living through the economic and social upheavals of the eighteenth century with another possible representation of themselves. They adopted it with some enthusiasm and in doing so also adopted, in retrospect, the image of West Barbary as a binary opposition. In the late eighteenth century the preferred myth became one of progress from darkness to light, from West Barbary to Industrial Civilisation. This narrative of achievement both fitted the rationalist, science-based discourses of technical progress that were dominant in industrialising Cornwall and was encouraged by Methodism, which claimed for itself the credit for this moral revolution. (For the importance of myths, both individual and collective, see Samuel and Thompson 1990, 9. For the culture of industrialisation in Cornwall see Payton 1992, 77 and Todd 1967.) And in the re-telling of this myth in the nineteenth and twentieth centuries West Barbary became more barbarian and industrial civilisation more civilised.

Of course, this myth of Industrial Civilisation was found in other early industrialising regions as well as in Cornwall. It was a generalised representation in the same way as the representation of the remoter 'provinces' as barbarian 'others' was or the representation of 'Celtic Britain' was later to become. However, there is a crucial difference. These other myths can be accommodated within a simple centre-periphery framework where people in the centre busily construct representations of the peripheries. And the centre in this context was and is London and the South East of England. But during the late eighteenth and early nineteenth centuries the process of industrialisation was producing multiple and dispersed 'centres'. For a short period the cultural hegemony of the South East was challenged. In such a context spaces opened up for insiders in the various dynamic industrial regions to negotiate their own versions of the myth of Industrial Civilisation, a myth that had no single centre.

By the 1800s Cornwall was a society dominated by the dynamism of the mining industry. At its peak in the early 1860s mining and quarrying employed 30% of all adult men and 10% of waged women in Cornwall (Lee 1979. For the economic history of Cornwall in this period see Buckley 1992; Payton 73-98; Rowe 1953). Representations of this society were, not surprisingly, over-determined by images of mining and landscapes of mining. Mining had metamorphosed Cornwall, helping to destroy old differences and create new ones. For some the process of destroying the old was more apparent than that of creating the new. Daniel Webb noted on a visit in 1810 that 'the people are here enriched by the mines and fisheries. Their manners bear no striking difference from those of large towns in general, arising from the influx of strangers and the facility of travelling' (1812, 132). This suggests a tension; in one way Cornwall and the Cornish were different from other places because of the economic specialisation in mining, but the spirit of industry was erasing differences. As late as the 1850s writers were still noting 'differences' and welcoming or lamenting the extinction of them:

11

anomalies of this kind do substantially act as so many obstacles, so much unnecessary friction, in the way of the machinery of civilisation ... the power of combined action on the one hand, the power of human thought itself on the other, will gain enormously by their entire removal. (Merivale 1857, 328)

Yet the machinery of civilisation was proving remarkably slow in its task of creating uniformity, mainly because, partly in a reaction against it, people themselves were clinging to and even inventing differences.

Indeed, the parallel growth of regional self-assertiveness accompanying industrialisation led to the appropriation of new symbols of 'peculiarity', new banners around which the 'imagined Cornish community' could be proclaimed as somehow different from others. The differences were sometimes real, sometimes invented. This distinction is not perhaps as important as it might seem, as both real and invented differences gave meaning to the experience of living in a particular place at a time of profound change. Dellheim (1986) has shown how, by the 1860s, writers in Lancashire and Yorkshire had, in a similar way, evolved a discourse about their counties that allowed them to express a county pride. In this discourse, differentiation was stressed, differentiation from southerners in general and (in the case of Lancashire and Yorkshire) from each other in particular.

This discourse of differentiation had already emerged in Cornwall by the 1820s. To some extent it was a result of Cornwall's economic specialisation as a mining region and the 'factual identity' this had given rise to, in relatively socially homogenous communities bound together by Methodism (Deacon and Payton 1993 and Deacon 1993). But it also rested on a growing desire on the part of the local literate classes to define their place and its people as different. Thus a local writer on 'the habits and manners of the Cornish' in 1828 could claim that 'the general character of the Cornish is strongly marked with features so peculiarly its own, as to distinguish it from every other county in the kingdom; it exhibits lights and shades which can be discovered nowhere else.' (Godolphin 1828)

The discourse of difference deepened during the first decades of the nineteenth century. In 1806, the antiquarian, Reverend Richard Polwhele, with his roots firmly in the small gentry class, concluded that, because of its 'intercourse with other provinces, if (the manners) of the Cornish were in any way peculiar, it could only have been in former ages'. (Polwhele 1806, 133) Yet, thirty years later, Polwhele was busy pinpointing Cornish peculiarities, from a supposed adherence to superstitions to a predilection for saffron buns. Moreover, the superstitions of Cornwall, he argued, 'assimilate in a surprising manner' to those of Scotland, Ireland and Wales (Polwhele 1836, volume 1, 112 and volume 2, 163 and 8). In this Polwhele was anticipating the Anglican, Tory Celticists of the early twentieth-century Cornish Revival.

For others, more centrally located in the industrial mainstream of Cornish life, local peculiarities were more prosaic. Samuel Drew, a farmer and tin streamer's son from near St.Austell, who had begun work at eight years old as a buddle boy in a local streamworks, emphasised in the 1820s the 'proud spirit of independence' of the Cornish. For Drew the miners in particular and the Cornish in general were an example to others 'in the scale of intellect, and in the improvements that have been made ... which have resulted from mental cultivation.' They were 'highly intelligent, compassionate, hospitable, industrious, speculative and brave.' Here we again have the representation of the Cornish miners as paragons of industrialisation. Even their regular resort to food rioting could be re-interpreted by Drew as a result of their 'warmth and ardour' (Hitchins and Drew 1824, 710, 717, 727).

However, the expansion of mining had not occurred in a vacuum. It took place within a pre-existing society with its own historical legacy. Hatcher has pointed out how mining had been an important component in the creation of an early constellation of 'independent' attributes (Hatcher 1970, 1974). The presence of stream tinning from before the thirteenth century created a class of mobile, peasant farmer-tinners. Their mobility was both encouraged and reflected by a conventionary land tenure system which had become common by the fourteenth century together with the relative absence of manorialism and customary services. The 'independence' of the tinners, the maintenance of which was crucial for royal revenues via the coinage duty on tin, was institutionalised through the emergence of Stannary law, which in the medieval period gave certain legal rights and privileges to tinners as a group (Payton 1992, 50-52). Well into the seventeenth century, the tinners were still regarded as a group apart by many outsiders. Although by the end of the eighteenth century the machinery of the Stannaries was clearly creaking as Cornish mines turned to the more heavily capitalised deep copper mining, these traces of former times helped to give a particularly local and unique dimension to the structures and meanings of mining and Cornwall. For insiders, the food riots of the eighteenth century, although arising from a different context, could be interpreted as providing an element of continuity with those turbulent and 'independent' tinners of earlier centuries.

Another relic of pre-modernity that helped structure insider images of Cornwall in its industrial period was the Cornish language. Cornish had been used as a vernacular throughout the early modern period to the end of the eighteenth century, although since the mid-seventeenth century it had been marginalised both socially and geographically. By the early 1700s it was restricted to the coastal parishes of West Penwith and the Lizard, the poor and the older generation. Outsiders writing about Cornwall in the late eighteenth and early nineteenth centuries would often give it a mention and note the consequences of its loss. As Warner wrote in the 1800s, 'with the disappearance of their language, the Cornish have lost almost all those provincial peculiarities in customs and amusements, which distinguished them from the inhabitants of other English counties' (Warner 1809, 359. For the decline of the language see Pool 1975). However, the Cornish language could not simply be ignored by antiquarians and writers in Cornwall in the later eighteenth century. It remained important in two ways.

Insiders like William Pryce, while clearly mesmerised by the distinctiveness of deep metal mining, included a list of Cornish language terms in an appendix to his largely technical treatise *Mineralogia Cornubiensis*, the publication of which was itself a tribute to the role of mining in Cornish society. He did this:

as the idioms and terms of Cornish miners are mostly derived from the ancient Cornish British dialect, and therefore not easily intelligible to gentlemen unaccustomed to Mining, who may have occasion to converse or correspond with them. (1778, i)

Three decades earlier than Pryce's compilation of Cornish mining terms, William Borlase, in pursuing the explanation of the antiquities of Cornwall, had also found it necessary, for equally instrumental reasons, to acquaint himself with the meanings of placenames. The fact that over 80% of place-names in Cornwall, more in the west, were in the Cornish language meant that the death of the spoken language did not erase its memory (for Cornish placenames see Padel 1988). In addition, the starting point for nineteenth century writers on Cornwall, especially indigenous writers, was often Carew's *Survey of Cornwall* (1602). Yet this had been written at the very end of the sixteenth century, at a time when Cornish was still spoken widely in mid and west Cornwall and, although not himself a Cornish speaker, Carew had devoted a section of his book to the language (Carew 1811, 150ff). Later writers, both plagiarists and non-plagiarists alike, were therefore introduced to the existence of the language, which retained the potential to be employed as a factor of differentiation.

The second way the language remained important was less instrumental. For example, in 1748/49 Borlase wrote that 'it will be a kind of duty in us Cornishmen to gather together the remains of our departed language.' (Pool 1986, 118) There is more than a hint here of the later injunction by the cultural revivalist Morton Nance to Old Cornwall Societies almost 200 years later to 'cuntelleugh an brewyon us gesys na vo kellys travyth' [collect the fragments that remain so that none might be lost]. (Nance 1925, 3) And it was hardly for instrumental reasons that such an enthusiast for the new industrial age as Davies Gilbert arranged a series of Cornish placenames in alternate rhyming stanzas in 1828. As a writer in the *Cornish Magazine* commented, the sounds of the placenames, even though the meanings had largely been lost, 'cannot fail to affect a Cornish heart with that peculiar sort of pleasing melancholy which is excited by the portrait of a dear departed friend' (anon. 1828). For insiders the language was thus taking on a symbolic meaning almost as soon as it had been detached from its social base.

So, by the 1820s at the latest, for insiders mining and associated images such as the steam engine were the dominant representations of Cornwall. But these images interacted with other 'peculiarities', for example the 'tradition' associated with metal mining and the Cornish language, the demise of which was too recent to be ignored and which helped make Cornwall distinct. Here then was the production of a complex set of images that could still act as a symbol of 'difference' for future generations. Thus it was the drive of insiders to assert their regional identity, either as a reflection of Cornwall's status as one of Europe's first industrial regions, or as a reaction against perceived threats from outside produced by that same process of industrialisation, that fixed these images within the regional identity.

Landscapes of fire : outsider images
For most visitors in the eighteenth and early nineteenth centuries Cornwall was a dismal place. Caesar Thomas Gooch wrote back to his family in Norfolk in 1754 that:

> I have now seen a great deal of Cornwall and think it upon the whole a dismal country to live in ... the inland dwellings are a vast distance from neighbours, everywhere surrounded with rocky mountains, and the prospects chiefly over barren lands. (1962, 60)

Later, another East Anglian visitor, Thomas Preston, summed up the country from Bodmin to Truro as

> the most dreary possible, a complete moor with scarce a dwelling visible, you may travel for miles over a swamp and see nothing but a few men at work at what is called 'stream work'. (1972, 481)

While inland Cornwall seemed to be a desolate waste, the fishing villages on the coast were to be avoided as far as possible. John Wesley found their attractions marred by 'the perfume' of pilchards and conger-eels (1864, 327). In these examples the Cornish landscape was not being read as picturesque despite the emergence of romanticism during the later eighteenth century.

This is not to say that visitors did not come to Cornwall to seek and find the picturesque and the romantic. Early in the nineteenth century tourist guides began to be published and these drew attention to 'picturesque', usually coastal, locations such as Kynance Cove and Lands End. (Paris 1806) Perhaps the best example of this romantic reading during Cornwall's industrial phase was written by an exiled Cornishman, Cyrus Redding. He could conclude that 'Cornwall is the land of the wild, the picturesque and the imaginative.' (1842, 3) Nevertheless, while picturesque readings were increasingly available by the 1840s, they were in competition with other interpretations. As Westland has pointed out, 'at this stage Cornwall's image in the eyes of the rest of Britain was more likely to have been formed by ideas about maritime activity and the mining industry than by any notions of glorious solitude.' (1995, 155) The words of the Reverend Warner offer a very different representation of the Cornish landscape: 'however valuable it may be in a commercial point of view, it can offer no claim to the praise of the picturesque or beautiful.' (1809, 346)   In stark contrast to the emerging view of pastoral rurality in South East England, the most commonly remarked landscape feature in Cornwall was that created by its industry. On a visit in the 1760s Thomas Kitchen observed that 'as the county abounds in mines, the air is filled with mineral vapours.' (Kitchen 1764, 89) In fact, Cornwall as a whole did not 'abound in mines'. Mining in the eighteenth century was still relatively localised; the bulk of copper ore production was accounted for by just seven parishes from Gwennap in the east to Gwinear in the west, and John Rowe has claimed that 'practically the entire mining region was within eight miles of the summit of Carn Brea'. (1953, 66) While it is true that tin mining was more widely spread, until the late eighteenth century there was not much underground mining east of Truro. Already, however, we can see 'Cornwall' being represented by mining, the dynamic factor in the landscape.

This was because the mining districts of Cornwall left outsiders with their most vivid impressions. An intrepid visitor to Redruth in the 1790s found that 'it is in a cloud of smoke, which was the reason we did not breakfast'. (Spreadbury 1971, 11) In the same decade William Maton described the appearance of the towans near Hayle as 'truly dismal':

> The immense volumes of smoke that roll over it, proceeding from the copper houses, increase its cheerless effect, while the hollow jarring of the distant steam engines remind us of the labours of the Cyclops in the entrails of Mt. Etna. (1797, 235)

The volcanic metaphor also crops up in the writings of Warner. Travelling on the edge of the mining country to the north west of Penryn, he described it as 'a district filled with extinguished volcanoes, which, having exhausted their fury, could now only be traced in the universal desolation they had occasioned'. For Warner, this was the 'remarkable feature of Cornwall'. (Warner 106) These landscapes of fire fascinated the visitor unused to the impact of industrialisation.

> The dismal scene of whims, suffering mules, and hillocks of cinders, extends for miles. Huge iron engines, creaking and groaning, invented by Watt, and tall chimneys, smoking and fuming, that seem to belong to 'Old Nicholas's' abode, diversify the prospect

wrote a visitor to the Consolidated Mines at Gwennap during the 1790s. (*Mining Journal*, 22 February 1840) It was the mining landscape that, for outsiders, made Cornwall different. That jaded traveller, George Lipscomb, who meandered across southern England in the 1790s, in an increasingly frustrated search for the 'interesting', finally found it at Polgooth Mine near St.Austell: 'Now we had arrived at a spot which was truly interesting -- at a kind of new country of which we had previously formed no tolerable idea'. (1799, 249) Here, finally, was a landscape markedly different from those he had seen to the east.

The significance of the mining landscape is that it coloured representations of Cornwall as a whole. As early as the 1760s the dominant representation of Cornwall was being derived from its mining sector. Later writers went further, interpreting the rest of Cornwall in relation to mining. When William Maton was still in the 'bleak country' between Looe and Fowey he began to fancy himself 'already arrived in the mining country, and that we had bid adieu to fertility and picturesque beauty' (137). The non-mining landscapes of Cornwall were being read with reference to the mining landscapes. In a similar fashion, Robert Fraser, in his *General View of the County of Cornwall*, prepared for the Board of Agriculture, discussed the mines of Cornwall before the ostensible subject of his treatise, farming. For him it was the mines, 'to which so great a part of its capital and industry is directed,' that were central for understanding

Cornwall (1794, 14). The farmer, by the 1790s, was playing second fiddle to the miner in representations of Cornwall.

It was the industrial landscape that most impressed outsiders, just as industrial society impressed insiders. And although outsiders tended to focus on the landscape rather than its inhabitants, thus beginning a process that continues to the present day, it was not only the mining landscape that intrigued visitors by its difference. When they were noticed at all, the people who inhabited that landscape were also invested with distinct characteristics. These characteristics, however, owed little to notions of 'Celticity'. While some outsiders were defining the Cornish people as 'Celtic' by the 1800s, this was not the dominant representation of this periphery, although both insiders and outsiders would occasionally use the term. (For examples of the use of the term 'Celtic' to describe the Cornish see Borlase 1769 and Warner 1809).

In the 1760s the mining population was defined as 'in many respects a community distinct from the other inhabitants of the County'. (Kitchen 108) This was echoed later by Lipscomb, who focused in the 1790s on the miners as:

a race of men distinct from the common class of British subjects; they are governed by laws and customs almost exclusively their own ... they are separated from the manners of modern improvement, and resemble the primitive possessors of an uncultivated soil, rather than kindred brethren of a great and enlightened nation. (1799, 262)

Lipscomb was still leaning towards West Barbary imagery here. But his view of the miners as a distinct class was supported by Warner in 1808:

We observed a few circumstances in their character as a body, which appeared to distinguish them from all other tribes of workmen that had fallen under our notice. These peculiarities naturally arise from the nature of their employment, which is altogether unlike that of the labouring classes in general throughout the kingdom. (297-298)

But to Warner what was noticeable was the miners' progressive and industrial spirit; the system of wage payments in the mines, relying as it did on an element of contracting between miners and adventurers (shareholders) 'keeps their spirits in an agreeable agitation, renders their minds lively and alert, and prevents that dullness which generally characterises the English labourer.' He went further. The positive attributes of the mining population were by the early nineteenth century being projected onto the Cornish working class as a whole. Impressed by the mining population, Warner's approbations spilt over into more general praise for Cornish people generally. The inhabitants of Cornwall generally were all 'marked by peculiar features of character. Its men are sturdy and bold, honest and sagacious; its women lovely and modest, courteous and unaffected' (Warner 1809, 348).

These new peculiarities were, unlike those of 'West Barbary', much more acceptable to the bourgeois visitor. Indeed, the Cornish working class had become the shock troops of wage labour, paragons of industrialisation, ingenious, inventive, civil, well mannered and alert. Representations of the miners as a barbarian race of primitives had been exchanged for an equally overdrawn picture. Furthermore, the effects of mining suffused the whole of Cornish society. According to Thomas Preston, by 1821:

the mines of Cornwall occupy the attention of the principal inhabitants. As you advance to the west, so you hear them more and more talked about till you arrive at Truro; there their whole ideas are immersed in the value of the shares of such and such a mine; if you go to Redruth, then it is the weight of a piece of ore or the quality of what was raised or dug up yesterday. (1972, 489)

While exaggerated and, in its own way, as romanticised as West Barbary or 'Celtic Cornwall' imageries, these representations were, by the 1820s, echoing and echoed by insider representations. Thus outsider and insider representations had effectively converged by the second quarter of the nineteenth century to be closer together than probably at any time since.

The flowering of the Cornish identity
By the 1850s the continued growth of the Cornish economy had produced a mature industrial society in which a number of institutions reproduced an assertive Cornish identity. 'County' institutions like the Cornwall Agricultural Society and the three 'royal' literary institutions at Penzance, Truro and Falmouth reproduced landed and middle class views of Cornwall (Crook 1990, 13 and 48; Riddle 1993, 3). These societies, purporting to serve the whole territory of Cornwall, helped to encourage a Cornwall-wide dimension in the realm of ideas. And, by the 1800s, a wider reading public was emerging to consume these ideas. This market was also served by newspapers and magazines which again took their sphere of interest to be Cornwall as a whole. The *Royal Cornwall Gazette* had already begun publishing in 1801 and was followed in 1810 by the *West Briton*. Both papers, one Tory and the other Whig/Liberal, were published in Truro but both had evolved by the 1850s into Cornish newspapers providing news coverage of all parts of Cornwall. Both, too, provided a platform for regional pride; a letter writer to the *Royal Cornwall Gazette* in 1811 wrote:

I have been highly gratified (in common, no doubt, with every Cornishman who is alive to the honour of his native county) at perusing in your late papers the substance of the scientific lectures of our excellent countryman Dr [Humphrey] Davy. (*Royal Cornwall Gazette*, 16 March)

Magazines such as the short lived *Cornish Magazine* of the late 1820s and later ventures such as *Netherton's Cornish Almanack*, published annually from 1854, also reinforced this local patriotism and encouraged readers to imagine themselves as members of a wider Cornish community.

These institutions also help to explain why a regional identity emerged based on the territory of Cornwall and not some area either larger (such as Cornwall and Devon) or smaller (industrial West Cornwall). Ideas of local allegiance among the gentry and middle classes were institutionalised on a Cornwall-wide

18

basis, this in turn reflecting the earlier administrative history of Cornwall as a county and aspects of the image of the place, such as the Cornish language, which 'belonged', or had once belonged, to virtually all parts of the territory. However, this is only part of the equation. At one level elite ideas about Cornwall are just another local example of the gentry county communities that were common in England. (For the notion of county communities generally see Everitt 1979.) But the ideas of these classes were also influenced by and reacted with the fact of local industrialisation. This, entirely located in Cornwall, remained the dynamic core of ideas of Cornishness. Significantly, both the Royal Geological Society and the Royal Cornwall Polytechnic Society were actively concerned in their earlier years with Cornish mining, although there were relatively few practical spin-offs from their activities at first (Crook 33). It was this merger of the 'county' identity of the landed class and the pride in the industrial region found among sections of the urban middle classes, that produced the assertive sense of pride based on Cornwall's technical prowess. This literate, energetic form of the Cornish identity was articulated most keenly by the middle classes and resembled the regional identities of northern England or (later) South Wales more closely than they did the socially conservative county identities of the English shires.

To some extent the ideas generated by the institutions and classes already discussed would have penetrated into the working class. According to Samuel Drew, 'almost all classes are much addicted to reading; and in proportion to the extent of its population, there is probably no county in England in which so many volumes are read, as in this' (Hitchins and Drew 727). However, working people were not just passive recipients of ideas generated by their social 'betters'. Other social institutions were themselves already reproducing a distinctive regional collective identity, one experienced as much as a 'factual identity' than as an 'imaginary' one. Herman Merivale, a percipient Devonian and lawyer who had lived in West Cornwall in the 1840s, observed in the 1850s that:

> if any political partisan were to seek to rouse the passions of the western population, he would find his purpose much better answered by enlisting in his cause a few Methodist teachers and a few mining 'captains' than through the gentry of the district. (306)

By gentry Merivale might have included the urban-based county literary societies where the non-conformist presence was surprisingly muted (Crook i). The social institutions most crucial in reproducing the working class identity were, instead, the chapel, the workplace and the family.

Cornish Methodism produced its own institutions in the nineteenth century -- literary institutions (as at Camborne), magazines (for example the *Cornish Banner*) and later even schools for its middle class (as at Penzance, Truro and Launceston). It also had its own regional peculiarities, gaining members through periodic and vigorous mass revivals which began in a major way in the 1780s in the west and continued to the early 1860s. This revivalist aspect, together with the 'democratic' flavour of Cornish Methodism, helped produce a local Methodism that was seen as distinctive by outsiders. (For an example of this, a Wesleyan minister described the Cornish as 'the mob of Methodism ...

19

rude and refractory', see Drew 1834, 491). In addition, Methodism had become the 'established' religion in the majority of Cornish communities by the 1820s; in 1833 a Cornish vicar lamented that 'in a few words, we have lost the people. The religion of the masses is become Wesleyan Methodist'. (Cited in Rule 1971, 262.)

According to Luker, Methodism in Cornwall, based on 'community' and household, was a means through which traditions, perception and culture were preserved. It acted as a 'badge of regionalism in the face of encroaching external forces' (1987, xv). Luker also claims that there was a division in late eighteenth and early nineteenth century Cornish Methodism between 'insider' congregations and lay preachers and 'outsider' pastorate. There was also 'an increasingly articulated regional sensitivity on the part of the Cornish which fuelled an exaggerated identification of Methodism as "theirs".' (322 and 290) This is illustrated by the self-confident declaration at Redruth by fifty leading Cornish laymen on John Wesley's death in 1791, emphasising lay control and local autonomy, and by the series of secessions in Cornish Methodism after 1815. (Rowe 1993, 262ff.)

To some extent, Methodism was an alternative focus of loyalty to the workplace. The mining workplace reinforced notions of independence and economic enterprise while, at the same time, buttressing informal co-operation among work groups often bound by kinship. The particular mix of community that had emerged by the 1820s -- small scale, close-knit, Methodist, with a strong sense of 'moral economy' that found expression in periodic food rioting -- was also seen as particularly 'Cornish'. It was most visible in the rural-industrial areas around the significantly named 'central' mining district of Camborne-Redruth. The identification of the mining communities in particular and West Cornwall in general as being most 'Cornish' is well illustrated by John Allen's description of the migration of miners from mid and west Cornwall to the Liskeard district in the 1840s: 'the dialect of the people grew more provincial and Cornish than before'. (1856, 398)

Ideas about Cornwall were therefore being articulated by the intelligentsia, local antiquarians and the middle classes, and these ideas, interlocking with the 'factual identity' that had emerged in Cornwall's mining districts, provided symbols and images that could be appropriated both by the contemporary working class and by later generations. The working class form of Cornish identity, a more defensive reaction to the economic changes brought about by industrialisation, intersected with a pro-active pride on the part of the middle classes in Cornwall's industrial prowess. The result was a vigorous regional identity. This was in turn reproduced by 'county' institutions, newspapers and, later, novels among the middle class and in the chapels, workplaces and homes of the working class.

By the 1840s and 1850s then, a regional identity had been produced based on Cornwall's experience as a mining region. Merivale noted the 'profound attachment professed for [Cornwall] by its own children.' There was a pride, even arrogance, among the Cornish:

The thorough Cornishman's respect for his own shrewdness and that of his clan is unbounded, or only equalled by his profound contempt for 'foreigners' from the east ... this feeling increases ludicrously in intensity as we advance further west.(289 and 316)

This geography of meanings reflected the geography of mining, which supplied the dominant images of place in Cornwall. Moreover, this identity of an industrial region overlaid other, perhaps older, aspects. This older, proto-national identification was not lost on outsiders. Wilkie Collins in 1850 observed that 'a man speaks of himself as Cornish in much the same spirit as a Welshman speaks of himself as Welsh'. (1861, 70)

The regional identity flowered briefly in the middle of the nineteenth century. The successful campaign for the separate diocese that gave Bishop Benson his Bishopric in 1877 was backed up by claims that the Cornish were a people 'with their own peculiar needs and feelings' and can be seen as symbolic of its heyday (Morrish 246-247). But after the 1870s de-industrialisation began to undermine the economic basis of this identity and sapped the confidence of earlier years. By the 1890s new occupations and new images were appearing. While the working class continued to look to older certainties and to their 'Cousin Jacks and Jennies' as a refuge from the storms of economic change caused by the flight of capital from Cornwall, both outsider and some insider members of the middle classes sought out new, more romantic images. This restructuring of elements of the Cornish identity is closer to the model proposed by Chapman, as outsider images re-imposed themselves, at least in the representations adopted by both the guide book industry and the 'Celtic Revival'. (Of course, some insiders also played a considerable role in creating these images! The obvious example is Quiller-Couch, 1893.) This time, though, the images were less in harmony with popular insider consciousness as Cornwall set course on another transformation, from Industrial Civilisation to 'Delectable Duchy', from a narrative of achievement to 'Vanishing Cornwall'.

BIBLIOGRAPHY
Anon. The Cornish cantata. The Cornish Magazine 3 (1828): 199.
Allen, John. History of the Borough of Liskeard. Liskeard: W.F. Cash, 1856.
Ardener, Edwin. 'Remote areas': some theoretical considerations. Ed. Anthony Jackson. Anthropology at Home. London: Tavistock, 1987. 38-54.
Borlase, William. Antiquities, Historical and Monumental of the County of Cornwall 1754. London: W.Bowyer and J.Nichols, 1769.
Buckley, Allen. The Cornish Mining Industry: a brief history. Penryn: Tor Mark, 1992.
Carew, Richard. Survey of Cornwall 1602; London: J.Fauldner, 1811.
Chapman, Malcolm. The Celts: the construction of a myth. London: Macmillan, 1992.
Collins, Wilkie. Rambles beyond railways. London: Richard Bentley, 1861.
Crafts, Nick. British Economic Growth during the Industrial Revolution. Oxford: Blackwell, 1985.
Crick, Bernard. National Identities: the construction of the United Kingdom. Oxford: Political Quarterly/Blackwell, 1991.
Crook, Denise.The early history of the Royal Geological Society of Cornwall, 1814-1850. Unpublished PhD thesis, Open University, 1990.

Daniels, Stephen. Place and the geographical imagination. *Geography* 77 (1992) : 310-322.

Deacon, Bernard. And shall Trelawny die? The Cornish identity. Ed. Philip Payton. *Cornwall Since the War*. Redruth: Institute of Cornish Studies and Dyllansow Truran, 1993. 200-223.

Deacon, Bernard and Philip Payton. Re-inventing Cornwall: culture change on the European periphery. *Cornish Studies* 1 (1993): 62-79.

Dellheim, Charles. Imagining England: Victorian views of the North. *Northern History* 22 (1986): 216-230.

Dodd, Philip.Englishness and the national culture. Eds. Robert Colls and Philip Dodd. *Englishness: Politics and Culture 1880-1920*. London: Croom Helm, 1986.

Drew, J.H. *The Life, Character and Literary Labours of Samuel Drew*. London: Longman, Rees, Orme, Brown, Green and Longman, 1834.

Everitt, Alan. Country, county and town: patterns of regional evolution in England. *Transactions of the Royal Historical Society* 5th series, 29 (1979): 79-108.

Jeremy Foster, Imagining nations. *Ecumene* 2.4 (1995): 449-453

Fraser, Robert. *General View of the County of Cornwall*. London: C.Macrae, 1794.

Giddens, Anthony. *Modernity and Self-identity: self and society in the Late Modern Age*. Cambridge: Polity, 1991.

Godolphin, Godfrey. On descriptions of the habits and manners of the Cornish. *The Cornish Magazine* 3 (1828): 93.

Gooch, Caesar Thomas. A journey to Cornwall in 1754. *Old Cornwall* 6 (1962): 58-61.

Gregory, Derek. The production of regions in England's Industrial Revolution. *Journal of Historical Geography* 14 (1988): 50-58.

Hall, Stuart.The question of cultural identity. Eds. Stuart Hall, David Held and Tony McGrew. *Modernity and Its Futures*. Cambridge: Polity, 1992. 273-316.

Hamilton Jenkin, A.K.Cornish mines and miners. *Old Cornwall* 1.1 (1925): 9-18.

Hatcher, John. Non-manorialism in medieval Cornwall. *Agricultural History Review* 18 (1970): 1-16.

_____. Myths, miners and agricultural communities. *Agricultural History Review* 22 (1974): 54-61.

Hitchins, Fortescue and Samuel Drew. *The History of Cornwall*. Volume 1. Helston: William Penaluna, 1824.

Hudson, Pat. The Regional Perspective. Ed. Pat Hudson, *Regions and Industries: a perspective on the industrial revolution in Britain*. Cambridge University Press, 1989. 5-38.

_____. *The Industrial Revolution*. London: Edward Arnold, 1992.

Jewell, Helen. *The North-South Divide: the origins of Northern consciousness in England*. Manchester University Press, 1994.

Keith, Michael and Steve Pile. *Place and the Politics of Identity*. London: Routledge, 1993.

Kitchen, Thomas. *England Illustrated: Cornwall*. London : R. and J. Dodsley, 1764.

Langton, John. The industrial revolution and the regional geography of England. *Transactions of the Institute of British Geographers* NS9 (1984): 145-167.

Lee, C.H. *British employment statistics 1841-1971*. Cambridge University Press, 1979.

Lipscomb, George. *A Journey into Cornwall*. Warwick : K.Sharp, 1799.

Lowerson, John. Celtic tourism - some recent magnets. *Cornish Studies* 2 (1994): 128-137.

Luker, D.H. Cornish Methodism, revivalism and popular belief, c.1780-1870. Unpublished PhD thesis, Oxford University, 1987.

Macdonald, Maryon. 'We are not French!': language, culture and identity in Brittany. London: Routledge, 1989.

Macdonald, Sharon. *Inside European Identities: ethnography in Western Europe.* Oxford: Berg, 1993.

Marshall, J.D.The study of local and regional 'communities': some problems and possibilities. *Northern History* 17 (1981) : 203-230.

Maton, William. *Observations on the Western Counties of England.* Volume 1. Salisbury: J.Easton, 1797.

Merivale, Herman. Cornwall. *The Quarterly Review* 102 (1857): 289-329.

MORI. *Community Identity in Cornwall.* London : HMSO, 1993.

Morrish, P.S. History, Celticism and propaganda in the formation of the Diocese of Truro. *Southern History* 5 (1983): 238-266.

Nance, R.Morton. What we stand for. *Old Cornwall* 1.1 (1925): 3-6.

Paasi, Anssi.The institutionalization of regions: a theoretical framework for understanding the emergence of regions and the constitution of regional identity. *Fennia* 164 (1986): 105-146.

_____. Deconstructing regions: notes on the scales of spatial life. *Environment and Planning A* 23 (1991): 239-256.

Padel, Oliver. *A Popular Dictionary of Cornish Place-names.* Penzance : Alison Hodge, 1988.

Paris. *Guide to Mount's Bay.* Penzance, 1806.

Payton, Philip. *The Making of Modern Cornwall.* Redruth : Dyllansow Truran, 1992.

Pearse Chope, R. *Early Tours in Devon and Cornwall.* 1918; Newton Abbot: David and Charles, 1967.

Pollard, Sidney. *Peaceful Conquest: the industrialisation of Europe 1760-1970.* Oxford University Press, 1981.

Polwhele, Richard. *The History of Cornwall.* Volume 7. London: Cadell and Davies, 1806.

_____. *Reminiscences in Prose and Verse.* Volumes 1 and 2. London : J.B.Nichols, 1836.

Pool, P.A.S. *The Death of Cornish.* Penzance : Cornish Language Board, 1975.

_____. *William Borlase.* Truro : Royal Institution of Cornwall, 1986.

Preston, Thomas.A Cornish tour : the diary of Thomas Preston of Norfolk, 1821. *Old Cornwall* 7 (1972): 481-490.

Pryce, William. *Mineralogia Cornubiensis.* London: James Phillips, 1778.

Quiller-Couch, Arthur. *Delectable Duchy.* London: Cassell, 1893.

Redding, Cyrus. *An Illustrated Itinerary of the County of Cornwall.* London, 1842.

Richards, Eric. Margins of the industrial revolution. Eds. Patrick O'Brien and Roland Quinault. *The Industrial Revolution and British Society.* Cambridge University Press, 1993. 203-228.

Riddle, Christopher. 'So useful an undertaking': a history of the Royal Cornwall Show 1793-1993. Wadebridge: Royal Cornwall Agricultural Association, 1993.

Rose, Gillian.Place and identity : a sense of place. Eds. Doreen Massey and Pat Jess. *A Place in the World? ; places, cultures and globalization.* Oxford University Press/Open University, 1995. 87-118.

Rowe, John. *Cornwall in the Age of the Industrial Revolution.* Liverpool University Press, 1953. 2nd Ed. St.Austell : Cornish Hillside Publications, 1993.

Rule, John. The labouring miner in Cornwall, c.1740-1870. Unpublished PhD thesis, University of Warwick, 1971.

Samuel, Raphael and Paul Thompson. *The Myths We Live By.* London: Routledge, 1990.

Shields, Rob. *Places on the Margin: alternative geographies of modernity.* London: Routledge, 1991.

Spreadbury, I.D. *Impressions of the Old Duchy: Book 1, Through Cornwall by Coach.* Mevagissey : Kingston, 1971.

Tindall, G. *Countries of the Mind: the meaning of place to writers.* London: Hogarth, 1991.

Todd, A.C. *Beyond the Blaze: a biography of Davies Gilbert.* Truro: Bradford Barton, 1967.

Warner, Richard. *A Tour through Cornwall in the Autumn of 1808*. London : Wilkie and Robinson, 1809.

Webb, Daniel Carless. *Observations and Remarks During Four Excursions Made to Various Parts of Great Britain*. London : Allen, 1812.

Wesley, John. *Journal*. Volume 3. London : Wesleyan Conference Office, 1864.

Westland, Ella. The passionate periphery: Cornwall and romantic fiction. Ed. Ian A. Bell. *Peripheral Visions*. Cardiff : University of Wales Press, 1995. 153-72.

Paralysis and Revival: the reconstruction of Celtic-Catholic Cornwall 1890-1945

Philip Payton

This chapter draws upon the model of a centre-periphery relationship (first postulated by Sidney Tarrow, with his notion of 'Older' and 'Second' peripheralisms) to suggest that the reconstruction of Celtic-Catholic Cornwall in the period 1890- 1945 was a function of the rapid de-industrialisation experienced by a flawed Cornish economy. This, in turn, is developed from The Making of Modern Cornwall *(1992) where I suggest that the Revival was an integral part of a project designed to construct a post- industrial economy and culture in late nineteenth-century, early twentieth-century Cornwall. The essay 'Re-inventing Cornwall: culture change on the European periphery' by Bernard Deacon and Philip Payton (1993) has sketched the process of transformation from industrial to Revivalist culture in modern Cornwall, but this chapter takes the discussion further to describe the manner in which the Revival became institutionally acceptable and informed the images of Cornwall constructed by the Great Western Railway in this period.*

For the student of cultural change, modern Cornwall is an enigma. Despite centuries of apparent incorporation into the English state, there remain not only the remnants of distinct constitutional identity (embodied now in the institution of the Duchy of Cornwall) but a popular sense of 'difference' which, at its most acute, claims nothing less than separate nationality. To those who stress the powerful assimilatory mechanisms of the modern state, this stubborn survival is a surprise (Deacon 260), and yet a reading of Cornish history (Payton 1992) indicates that such survival is not merely residual but reflects a dynamic process of cultural 're-invention' in response to continual socio-economic change (Deacon and Payton). Although for some commentators the articulation in this century of an apparently renewed sense of Cornish nationality is 'a truly astonishing rebirth' (Berresford Ellis 1985, 148), while for others it represents the impact of externally-generated images of Celtic 'Otherness' (Chapman), the dynamics of culture change in modern Cornwall are best understood in the context of a centre-periphery model. (Payton 1992) Here an enduring relationship between an 'English' centre and a 'Cornish' periphery has perpetuated Cornish 'difference' over time. In other words, Cornwall has remained 'different' because of (rather than despite) its historical experience.

The fall from grace
But peripherality is itself a dynamic condition, so that although the centre-periphery relationship might remain constant, its determining and consequential characteristics may alter radically from one era to another. Thus, for example, the experience of industrialisation in the peripheries of modern western states both perpetuated and re-defined the qualities of their peripheral condition. As Sidney Tarrow has argued, an 'Older Peripheralism' of territorial and cultural isolation was disturbed at length by the modernising impact of industrialisation. This served to 're-invent' the peripheral condition, precipitating a 'Second Peripheralism' of economic and social marginality. (Tarrow 16)

In Cornwall's case, the applicability of Tarrow's analysis is not hard to see. It is certainly possible to identify a Cornish 'Older Peripheralism' of territorial and cultural isolation, disturbed ultimately by the intrusions of the Tudor and Cromwellian States, and superseded by a 'Second Peripheralism' of socio-economic marginality where -- notwithstanding Cornwall's early and prominent role in the Industrial Revolution (Rowe 1953 and 1993) -- its experience of industrialisation was imperfect, over-specialised and incomplete. The paradox is that, while for a time Cornwall led the world in the development of steam engineering and deep mining, which in turn created a vibrant Cornish industrial culture, the basis of that industrialisation was structurally flawed. By the second half of the nineteenth century, indeed, in the face of an inability to diversify, the Cornish economy was already experiencing the onset of de-industrialisation. The crash of Cornish copper in the 1860s and the tin crisis of 1870s signalled Cornwall's fall from grace, and one consequence was a massive 'Great Emigration' which robbed Cornwall of the younger, more energetic, better skilled elements of its population. In the history of British (and world) industrialisation, social and economic marginality came early to Cornwall.

The effects of this fall from grace were traumatic. Socially and economically, Cornwall was plunged into an all-pervading sense of resignation and hopelessness, a fatalism and paralysis which would last until after the Second World War. Culturally, the trauma was at least as great. As Bernard Deacon has argued in the previous chapter of this book, the Cornish identity of the late eighteenth and nineteenth centuries represented not the lingering attributes of an 'Older Peripheralism' but rather an assertive self-confidence founded upon Cornwall's early place in industrial development, a sense of industrial prowess and technological superiority. This, in turn, begat the myth of 'Cousin Jack', the replication on the international stage of a Cornish identity based on industrial prowess where Cornish ethnicity was deliberately enhanced as an economic device. To be a Cousin Jack was to be sought after as an innate inheritor of mining expertise . (James)

As early as 1756, in deference to this emerging sense of Cornish self-importance, Elizabeth Montagu had written ironically of 'the large continent of Cornwall' (Aspinall-Oglander 224), while even ten years earlier the Lord Lieutenant had complained of the excessive local patriotism of his Cornish militias: 'They all express great readiness to defend their country, but they mean their county'. (Colley 81) Samuel Johnson was similarly impressed (Rowse 1986, 297-301), noting with feeling in a skit on the equally preposterous claims of Cornish and American independence, that 'Every Cornishman is a free man.' By 1839, at the height of Cornwall's industrial prowess, Thomas Lean could point with pride to the central role played by Cornwall and the Cornish in developing the steam engine:

The very existence of its [Cornwall's] deepest, most extensive, and most productive mines, is owing, not merely to the invention of the steam en- gine, but to the state of great perfection to which that machine has been in that county ... the improvements which the engine has, for many years re- ceived, are due to native [Cornish] engineers; whose skill and watchful care, maintain it in its present state, or add continually still further im- provements ... (Barton 1)

Twenty years later George Henwood could add: 'The Cornish are remarkable for their sanguine temperament, their indomitable perseverence, their ardent hope in adventure, and their desire for discovery and novelty ... .' As Henwood concluded, '... to this very fact has science to boast so many brilliant ornaments who claim Cornwall as their birthplace.' (Burt 232)

With Cornwall's identity bound so closely to the characteristics of a self-confident industrial society, the impact of rapid de-industrialisation created a cultural crisis of cataclysmic proportions. The Cornish response was twofold. One reaction was for society to turn in on itself, the hitherto out- going identity becoming increasingly a private affair as communities sought to come to terms with their socio-economic plight. In an atmosphere of fatalism and resignation, quiet stoicism in the face of adversity became a virtue, part of a culture of 'making do' (Deacon and Payton 68-70) in which the elements of popular culture such as Methodism, rugby football and brass bands were no longer vigorous icons of an assertive identity but had become introverted expressions of a 'fossilising' way of life.

A second response was an attempt to meet this crisis head on, to confront the economic and cultural paralysis in which Cornish society now found itself. One method, paradoxically, was to insist that there was no crisis, or that at least the crisis was only temporary. Throughout the first half half of this century and beyond, stubborn adherence to the notion of a Cornwall whose *raison d'etre* was industrial prowess led sections of the educated middle class to assert that the resurgence of the Cornish mining and engineering industries was not only inevitable but imminent (Burt 1989). Despite the evidence of dereliction and depopulation that was plain for all to see (John Rowe recalls that 'Harrowing tales have been told of the distress prevalent in Cornish mining districts during 1921 and 1922' (Rowe 1986)), the ability of Holmans (the Camborne engin- eering firm) to survive the sweep of de-industrialisation by turning its attentions to new markets seemed to tell a different story:

For Holmans the inter-war years were a period of exceptional progress and prosperity. The new rock-drills and compressors won high praise in every mining camp, on almost every public works and contracting job; and the new venture, the Pneumatic Tools Department, proved a great success. By 1939 the firm was in its heyday. (Hollowood 77)

However, the experience of Holmans was at best atypical (as the reversal of its fortunes in the post-1945 era was to confirm), and the inability of Cornish mining to deliver its much-vaunted revival caused even some of its staunchest supporters to conclude sadly that Cornwall must look elsewhere for its salvation. Sir Arthur Quiller-Couch agonised and argued but decided eventually that, as the great days of mining were unlikely to come again, Cornwall should turn its attentions to the creation of a post-industrial economy by responding to an emerging tourist industry that had already begun to make itself felt by the turn of the century (Payton 1992, 125-128).

The real descendents of the Celts?

Significantly, this move towards the creation of a post- industrial economy was matched by a similar (perhaps congruent) attempt by one section of the Cornish middle class to construct a post-industrial cultural identity. Here the project was nothing less than a determination to look back over the debris of the industrial period to a pre-Reformation medieval Celtic-Catholic Cornwall, a Cornwall which was Cornish-speaking and unequivocally 'Cornish' in all its cultural attributes, a re-assuring model for those wishing to escape the paralysis of the late nineteenth, early twentieth centuries. Ambitious in the extreme, this project sought not only to convince Cornish society that notions of a cultural identity based upon industrial prowess were no longer tenable but depended for its success in persuading sufficiently large (or at least influential) sections of that society to embrace the concept of 'Celtic Cornwall'.

This appeal to 'Celtic Cornwall' was a calculated co-option of elements of a wider 'Celtic Revival' that had already by the late nineteenth century made a significant impact in Scotland, Ireland, Wales and Brittany. Although the Breton model was to become increasingly important for Cornish Revivalists, at first it was the experience elsewhere in the British Isles that caught Cornish attention. And here the evidence was conflicting.

In Scotland, the Revival had been directed at the creation of a 'Celtic Scotland', a means of rehabilitating the Highlands and Islands in the post-Jacobite era and a device for bridging the Highland-Lowland divide. This addressed the alienation of Highland society as well as co-opting Highland symbolism (the kilt, the tartan, and so on) in the interests of a unified Scotland, Britain and Empire. In Ireland, however, the Celtic Revival was altogether more threatening to the British polity. In the aftermath of the Famine, Celtic symbolism was increasingly adopted as a focus for anti-English activity, its deployment in everyday life designed to emphasise a popular culture that was inherently un-English. The Gaelic language and 'Gaelic sport' were visible signs of separate identity, and in largely Catholic Ireland the appeal to a Celticity founded on the Age of Saints and the early Celtic Church had a ready appeal. In Wales, largely Nonconformist in contrast to Ireland and industrialised on a scale that the Cornish could appreciate, the Revival nonetheless also had a nationalist edge. It too was bound up with language and was associated increasingly with a Radical Liberalism that was embracing Home Rule for Wales as a political objective.

28

In its nationalist guise the Celtic Revival was of course echoing the imperatives of the wider nineteenth-century European movement from which it had sprung, the Romantic Movement which had assigned the right of self-government and territorial unity and independence to the multiplicity of European peoples, and had identified language as the principal badge of nationality and ethnic kinship. German, Italian, Slav and other nationalisms emerged from this ideology, creating or bringing down empires and building or disintegrating nation-states. Thus those who wished to bring the Celtic Revival to Cornwall brought in their wake not only the diverse experiences of Scotland, Wales and Ireland but also a wider ideological agenda focussed on the issue of nationality. To be successful in Cornwall, they had to tread carefully.

Although we may trace the antecedents of what was to become the 'Cornish-Celtic Revival' back as far as Robert Stephen Hawker (vicar of Morwenstow from 1824 to 1874) or even to Richard Polwhele in the early 1800s, the Anglican, Tory, anti-industrial predilections of a Hawker or a Polwhele were in fact out of tune with the utilitarian, technological, Liberal Nonconformist character of nineteenth-century Cornwall. Even the antiquarian enthusiasms of Davies Gilbert ('the Cornish Philosopher') represented curiosity rather than nostalgia or regret for the passing of former times. For Gilbert was the archetypal Cornishman of his age, and in the introduction of his 1826 edition of the medieval Cornish language passion poem 'Pascon agan Arluth' (Passion of Our Lord) he emphasised that 'No one more sincerely rejoices than does the editor of this ancient mystery that the Cornish dialect of the Celtic or Gaelic languages has ceased altogether from being used by the inhabitants of Cornwall' (Berresford Ellis 1974, 132). Cornish would have been an impediment in an English-speaking industrial world, an obstacle to improvement and enlightenment, a view shared by Matthew Arnold (Cornish on his mother's side) who -- despite his enthusiasm for Celtic literature -- also favoured the demise of Cornish and other Celtic languages (Durkacz 201-203).

Arnold was opposed to Irish Home Rule for similar reasons, and could no more accept the arguments of those who proposed a self-governing Ireland 'than I should believe them if they assured me that Scotland, Wales, or Cornwall were fatally and irresistably drifting to a miserable separation from England'. (Rowse 1976, 153) As Arnold intimated, relief at the passing of the Cornish language represented not only faith in the triumph of an English-speaking industrial world but also a darker contempt for all that was 'Celtic'. Arnold's father (Dr Thomas Arnold of Rugby) was himself, as Moynihan has claimed, 'an inveterate Celt-hater', and Matthew recalled that

when I was young, I was taught to think of Celt as separated by an impossible gulf from Teuton: my father in particular, was never weary of contrasting them; he insisted much often on the separation between us and them than on the separation between us and any other race in the world. (Moynihan 124)

As Moynihan has remarked, 'Dr Arnold's strenuously reiterated views gain an added dimension of brutality when the information is supplied that Mrs Arnold, Matthew's mother, was a Cornishwoman'. (Moynihan 125)

And yet, even in Cornwall itself such views were not uncommon. In March 1848 Sir John Trelawny, the Cornish MP, pondered the Irish situation and -- despite the undisguisable evidence of his own name and his reputation as a radical Liberal -- could claim 'the superiority of the Saxon over the Celtic race' (Jenkins 338). His position was perhaps not unlike that of Sir Charles Trevelyan, who in the 1840s, with his equally unmistakable Celtic surname, combined his governmental responsibilities as Assistant Secretary at the Treasury with his religious duty as a member of the evangelical 'Clapham Sect' to condemn the indolence and racial inferiority of the Scottish Highlanders. He believed that only through prolonged improving contact with Anglo-Saxon society could the feckless Celts become truly civilised and learn the thrift and responsibility of 'practical men'. As Devine has observed, Trevelyan 'regarded himself as being the result of such a process of improvement because his family belonged to the class of reformed Cornish Celts who had benefitted by close and long contact with Anglo-Saxon civilisation'.(Devine 164) It was a view echoed by the chairman of the West Cornwall Railway in Truro in May 1859, who in welcoming the construction of the Royal Albert railway bridge that now connected Cornwall to the rest of Britain, explained with considerable relief that hitherto Cornwall was 'neither within nor without the borders -- but now we are part of England (cheers)'. (Corin 20)

Others, perhaps, were less ready to admit their racial failings and their gratitude to the improving influence of the English, but even in overseas communities, where emigrant Cousin Jacks were anxious to stress their ethnic distinctiveness, Cornish 'Celticity' was something to be explained and qualified. At the Burra Burra mine in South Australia in 1859, the Reverend Charles Colwell could tell his Cornish Wesleyan chapel-goers that they were the 'real descendents of the Celts' (Payton 1984, 71), a claim made in contradistinction to the local Irish who deployed 'Celticity' as a means of asserting an identity that was both non-British and anti-British. For the emigrant Cornish, to be 'Celtic' was to be more British than the English, to be descendents of those 'Ancient Britons' (the name of a Burra pub in the 1850s!) who in the emerging iconography of British Imperialism were almost proto-Anglo-Saxon in their quest for justice, greatness and freedom. In 1900 Marie Trevelyan (that name again!) published her *Britain's Greatness Foretold,* the story of Boadicea in which Trevelyan traced the origins of 'our present freedoms' and the glories of the British Empire back to the struggle of the Ancient Britons against the Romans (Fraser 299).

In nineteenth-century Cornwall, then, notions of 'Celticity' were ambiguous and complex in the extreme. Industrial prowess underpinned claims to separate (even superior) Cornish identity but this identity was based on the apparent triumph of an English-speaking Nonconformist industrial society which, in the estimation of commentators such as Trelawny and Trevelyan, drew upon the improving influence of England and had ameliorated the worst excesses of the Celtic inheritance. And yet, notions of Celticity were important, not least overseas where the emigrant Cornish asserted separate identity both as an economic strategy to emphasise their status as 'superior' colonists (Cousin Jacks) and as a device to negate the competing claims of the 'inferior' Irish. To this was added, at home and abroad, the status of the Cornish as 'Ancient

Britons', a subtle construction which admitted Celtic provenance and yet established the Cornish as progenitors of Anglo-Saxon virtue in the pageant of Britain's greatness.

Securing the Cornish Revival

Although the project to 're-invent' or revive Celtic-Catholic Cornwall was founded on the premise that Cornwall was by now (c1900) moving firmly into a post-industrial existence, in which a Cornish identity based on industrial prowess would indeed be untenable, there was in the concept of Ancient Briton (with its emphasis on British greatness) a link of sorts between this new Celtic Revival and the Cornish identity of the recent industrial past. It was, perhaps, an ideological bridge which assisted the early Revivalists in wedding their Celtic Revivalist agenda to a potentially hostile middle-class constituency in Cornwall. This may help to explain the readiness of elements of the Cornish establishment to embrace the Celtic Revival, Lieutenant-Colonel C. J. H. Mead (who served with distinction in the Royal Marines in the Great War) supplying a telling synthesis:

> Cornwall is not England, and its people are Celtic and Brythonic. Isolated from England almost entirely by the River Tamar, with its other three sides bounded by the sea, this, together with its native mineral wealth, has caused the Cornishman from earliest times to seek his living on the water or underground. A hardy race of seafarers and renowned throughout the world as miners and engineers, their Celtic temperament and isolated geographical position have given them very definite hall marks. (Mead 234)

Perhaps significantly, the early Cornish-Celtic Revivalists, notably Henry Jenner and L. C. Duncombe Jewell, projected an Anglican, Tory view of Revivalist culture, a conservatism calculated not to offend establishment sensibilities. Jenner went so far as to become a Tridentine Catholic and actively cultivated an enthusiasm for a romantic Jacobitism, perhaps not appealing traits to a partly Nonconformist Cornish establishment, but in his determination to ensure that the Revival remained firmly apolitical he struck a Cornish chord. By and large, Cornish political opinion had been opposed to Irish Home Rule, largely on religious and strategic grounds, a conviction that had led many Cornish Liberals into the (anti-Home Rule) Liberal Unionist camp as it emerged in the years after 1880 (Pelling 164). When the Celtic Conference was held in Birkenhead in September 1917, with the Great War as yet unresolved and with the Easter Rising still fresh in memory, Welsh and Irish delegates felt that 'The time for Celtic re-union and re-assertion of their primal power was surely at hand' (Phillips 13-14), for if nothing else the War was about the rights of small nations, but their call for a 'Celtic Union' was met with a guarded response from from Henry Jenner: 'I am sure that if it keeps clear of all traits of politics, and I am confident it will, Cornwall will be happy to join in, in spite of the loss of our language'. (Phillips 114) A few years later, in 1924, it was reported in one newspaper that although Jenner considered that Cornwall had as much right to call itself a nation as had Scotland, Wales, and England ... he was not advocating Cornish independence or even 'Cornish Home Rule', nor did he wish to translate the Irish words Sinn Fein into Cornish -- their version of them was 'One and All', a better motto. (*People's Weekly*, 23 August 1924)

Certainly, Jenner would have been aware of a degree of suspicion in some areas of the Cornish academic establishment. For example, Thurstan Peter, author of a historical survey of Cornwall and President of the Royal Institution of Cornwall during the Great War, had made the equivocal comment:

at the Pan-Celtic congress of 1904 Cornwall was accepted as a separate nation. If the study of the language can be revived so as to enable us more fully to appreciate the few [sic] remains of its literature it will be very desirable, but we have no desire to see Cornwall aping the larger countries of Ireland, Wales and Brittany in their efforts after what they mistakenly suppose will lead to home rule. (Peter 202)

Jenner's political conservatism was matched by a modest estimation of what the Revival might achieve in Cornwall. Although he assured delegates at Birkenhead that 'Cornwall is not unmindful of its Celtic past,' he opined that 'Cornish will not be revived as a spoken language, nor will there ever again be a Cornish literature'.(Phillips 97) However, behind these public utterances was a Jenner more committed to a Revivalist agenda than his ambivalent statements might have had contemporary observers believe. After all, Jenner had . made a conscious decision to be 'Cornish'. Although born in 1848 in St Columb Major in the heart of Cornwall, he was not of Cornish descent and was in fact of English and Scottish parentage. It was, as Robert Morton Nance was to note, open to him 'to choose any of three nationalities. He chose from the first to be Cornish' (*Old Cornwall*, 2:8, Winter 1934, 1). Commitment to the Revival was thus an expression of personal identity.

Similarly, as early as 1904 Jenner had published his *Handbook of the Cornish Language*, a guide to the history and structure of the language but also a handbook for those who might wish to try to learn it. In the same year, he secured Cornwall's membership of the Celtic Congress, at once gaining recognition from other countries of Cornwall's status as a Celtic nation and subscribing to the Pan-Celtic movement. It appears, then, that Jenner was deliberately modest in his public advocacy of Cornish Revivalism while behind the scenes he pursued a more focussed agenda. This, perhaps, was part of strategy to woo the Cornish middle class. Certainly, he was aware of the need to co-opt rather than alienate the existing Cornish learned institutions. The Royal Institution of Cornwall, the Royal Cornwall Polytechnic Society, the Royal Geological Society of Cornwall and the Morrab Library were all products of the scientific and literary flowering of Cornwall's industrial era, powerful expressions of that Cornish identity that the Revivalists now proposed to supplant. As Jenner explained to his Celtic colleagues, 'These societies cannot be called especially Celtic societies, but they are certainly Cornish in all their local sympathies and endeavours ...'(Phillips 100) It was best, therefore, to work within these institutions to achieve the aims of the Revival. Jenner did this with great success, especially within the Royal Institution of Cornwall. In 1909, for example, it was reported that 'Mr Jenner represented the institution at the Celtic gathering in London' (JRIC 17,1910-1911,51). Jenner went on to become President of the Institution, and in 1936, two years after Jenner's death, the Institution's Council had struck a 'Jenner Medal' which was to be awarded to individuals who had made an outstanding contribution to areas of study pursued by Henry Jenner. The first award was made to A. S. D. Smith, the language Revivalist who had founded the magazine *Kernow*. In the following year the recipient of the medal was the Reverend Canon G. H. Doble whose work on Cornish Saints had made him 'a cultural link uniting Cornwall … with Wales and Brittany' and who had 'helped to maintain the Inter-Celtic relations which Mr Jenner himself felt to be so valuable' (JRIC 25,1937-38,53).

Jenner's strategy of 'Celticising' the Royal Institution was embraced by other Revivalists, so that, for example, its AGM in 1924 received a report from Robert Morton Nance detailing his trip to Brittany in the company of the Cornish scholars Charles Henderson and Canon Doble to attend the Celtic Congress at Quimper. Doble considered that 'even yet Cornwall has more to contribute to the Celtic cause' (JRIC 21,1925,451-454). Later, the Royal Institution was to play host to the Congress when it visited Cornwall. However, in parallel with this strategy of influencing and co-opting existing institutions was a determination to create new organisations whose agendas would be more firmly Revivalist. In 1901 Jenner had founded his Cowethas Kelto-Kernuak (the Cornish-Celtic Society). It folded during the Great War but in 1920 he and Nance launched a new Old Cornwall movement, an initiative designed to bring the Revival closer to ordinary people across Cornwall by establishing a federated network of Old Cornwall Societies in Cornish towns and villages.

In 1928 one of the long-term aims of the Cornish revival was at last realised, the creation of a Cornish Gorsedd (Gorseth Kernow) modelled on the revived Gorseddau of Wales and Brittany. Membership of the Gorsedd was open by invitation to anyone who had made an outstanding contribution to the Celtic spirit of Cornwall or who had demonstrated competence in the Cornish language. Bards thus elected were expected to work for the good of Cornwall in their chosen fields, and annually they met in Open Gorsedd (usually at a stone circle or some other place of historical association) to enact their Gorsedd ceremony. Borrowing heavily from the Welsh and Breton models, this ceremony was nevertheless a synthesis of the symbolism that had come to characterise Cornish-Celtic Revivalism.

Within its Christian framework (of hymn and prayers) there was also in the Gorsedd ceremony a hint of pantheism (anticipating, perhaps, the 'Celtic paganism' of the post-1945 era) and the accommodation of the notion that King Arthur was not dead but had assumed the form of a Cornish chough, echoing the belief that Arthur would return to restore the nationhood of Cornwall. This heavy emphasis on Arthurianism reflected one of the chief preoccupations of the early Revivalists, not least of J. Hambly Rowe (a founder of the Arthurian Congress) and Sir John Langdon Bonython who in the 1930s became both Bard of the Gorsedd and President of the Royal Institution of Cornwall. Other Revivalist preoccupations were 'the mystic Celtic temperament' (*Old Cornwall* 2:8, Winter 1934, 5) and 'the Celtic Church, which survived and flourished in Wales and Cornwall when most of Britain had relapsed into paganism' (*Old Cornwall* 2:10, Winter 1935, 4), but the over-riding concern was to legitimise the 'Celticity' of Cornwall. Thus when the Celtic Congress visited Cornwall in 1932, Jenner spoke on the 'Awakening of Celtic Cornwall', with one observer declaring that 'no intelligent person can remain utterly ignorant of his or her Celtic nationality'. (*Old Cornwall* 2:4, Winter 1932, 22)

The most Celtic thing in Cornwall is the Kernewek
Increasingly, the Cornish language was seen by the Revivalists as the central feature of this Celticity. In 1926 W. D. Watson wrote that 'Today a great renewal of Celtic thought and feeling is taking place, and although we Cornish have but relics of our language, and are small in numbers, yet we have our part to play in the movement'(*Old Cornwall* 1:3, April 1926, 5). Five years later a more confident assertion could insist that 'The Cornish language is more and more taking its place as the chief token of Celtic nationality in Cornwall' (*Old Cornwall* 2:2, Winter 1931, 33), while in 1932 it was claimed that 'the most Cornish thing in Cornwall is the Kernewek'(*Old Cornwall* 2:4, Winter 1932, 22). When *Tyr ha Tavas* (Land and Language), a Revivalist movement aimed at inspiring youth, was launched in 1933 a principal objective was 'to utilise the Cornish Language, both as an outward and visible sign of nationality and as a means of helping Cornish people to realise their essential kinship with other Celtic Races' (*Old Cornwall* 2:5, Summer 1933, 29). It was no surprise when in 1928 it was decided that the newly-established Gorsedd would conduct its annual ceremony entirely in the Cornish language.

Although Henry Jenner had appeared pessimistic about reviving Cornish as a spoken language, his enthusiasm for Cornish had inspired other Revivalists such as Robert Morton Nance and A. S. D. Smith to attempt such a project with verve and determination. Nance decided to abandon Jenner's early concentration on Late Cornish, the language as it had last been spoken, and, in a manner consistent with the Revival's appeal to a pre-Reformation medieval Celtic-Catholic Cornwall, he looked back beyond the industrial era to the period of Middle Cornish. Middle Cornish was the language of the surviving literary texts of the fourteenth to early sixteenth centuries, the Cornish of the Miracle Plays and Passion Poem. These works were agreeably medieval in ambience (an important consideration for those harking back to the culture of pre-industrial Cornwall) and provided a wealth of linguistic material from which the language might be reconstructed for modern use. However, there were inconsistencies in usage and gaps in both vocabulary and grammar, so Nance had to use techniques of internal analogy and to borrow from Welsh and Breton, as well as standardising and synthesising as he went along. The result was his so-called 'Unified' Cornish, based on Middle Cornish but reflecting Nance's own methods and objectives.

Nance's colleagues were delighted, Smith writing that Unified was 'a compact medieval language ... and little likely to undergo any further change'. (Smith 20) Thus constituted, Unified Cornish proved the vehicle for language revival in the years before the Second World War. Nance's *Cornish for All* was

34

published in 1929, and other publications such as *Lessons in Spoken Cornish* (1931) and *Cornish Simplified* (1939), together with English-Cornish and Cornish-English dictionaries, appeared as aids for the would-be learner. But although Unified Cornish was successful in bringing the existence of a Cornish language to a much wider public and did indeed create a small band of habitual users, there was some disappointment at the relatively slow generation of fluent speakers. The Second World War, of course, disrupted the work of the Revivalists and in 1947 Smith complained that the Revival 'has not yet produced many speakers of Cornish. More are badly needed'. (Smith 8)

Elsewhere in the Revival there was also some disquiet. Although the Revival had captured the attention of at least elements of the Cornish middle class, influencing the activities of organisations such as the Royal Institution of Cornwall and founding its own bodies such as the Old Cornwall movement, attempts to penetrate the increasingly 'fossilised' popular culture had proved largely unsuccessful. In 1937 one correspondent to a local newspaper lamented: 'If we are quite truthful we have to admit that the revival of the Gorsedd has scarcely touched the lives of the common people in Cornwall.' (Miners 31) Politically, the Revival had, largely under Jenner's influence, refrained from intervention in an increasingly distinctive Cornish politics at a time of socioeconomic crisis, foregoing one possible avenue for penetrating popular consciousness. Even when *Tyr Ha Tavas* was formed in 1933, its vague political posturing hardly engaged with the real political issues of the day (Payton 1992, 135). Oddly enough, where there was political concern expressed by the Cornish Revivalists, it was for the Breton language which 'thanks to an over-centralised government, is still a proscribed one in the Breton schools' (*JRIC* 21,1925,454). Later, during the War, this concern was translated into support for Bretons fighting with the Free French and Allied forces, support which 'marked a further stage in the development of closer relations between the two Celtic peoples of Cornwall and Brittany' (*Old Cornwall* 3:12,Winter 1942,514).

The identification of the Revival with Anglicanism, particularly the Anglo-Catholic movement (which had much in common with the Revival, not least in its appeal to a pre- Methodist Cornwall of Saints and Celtic Christianity), while perhaps striking a chord with elements of the Truro establishment, was again hardly likely to engage with popular culture. The completion of Truro Cathedral (with its deliberate Breton ambience) had encouraged the Anglo-Catholic movement and its links with the Cornish Revival. The scholarship of Canon Doble had rediscovered the multiplicity of Cornish-Breton religious connections, smoothing the way for W. Tregonning Hooper in his establishment of 'Inter-Celtic' links between Cornish and Breton wrestling associations (the distinctive style of Cornish and Breton wrestling was seen as important evidence of cultural commonality between Cornwall and Brittany), and by 1933 the Anglican Church in Cornwall had accommodated the liturgical observance of the principal Cornish-Celtic Saints. (Miles Brown 119)

However, in perhaps the only overt confrontation between Celtic Revivalism and the 'fossilising' culture it was designed to supplant, the increasing confidence of the Anglo-Catholic movement provoked a Nonconformist backlash. Bernard Walke, who had been curate of Polruan in the early years of the century, had risen to fame as the Anglo-Catholic vicar of St Hilary and had turned St Hilary church into something of a shrine for the movement, writing that until the impact of Anglo-Catholicism in Cornwall: 'There was nothing here to kindle the faith that gave to Cornwall so many saints or to light again the fire that burnt so fiercely in the day of John Wesley.' (Walke 33) However, in 1929 one critic complained that 'The steady rise of the Anglo- Catholic movement has inevitably tended to harden denominational distinctions' and that 'When incense is burnt in Truro Cathedral and confessions are heard there ... when the validity of the sacraments is made to depend on episcopal ordination and apostolic succession, then, by implication ... the Methodists and all Free Churchmen are unchurched' (Hamilton Jenkin 199-200). This tension came to a head in 1932 when a Kensitite (fundamentalist Nonconformist) mob, mainly from outside Cornwall but encouraged from within, raided St Hilary and laid waste the church, smashing its candles and pictures and carrying off its statues.

The Cornish Riviera
As noted earlier, the attempts by the Cornish Revivalists to create a post-industrial cultural identity were matched by a similar (perhaps identical) attempt to build a post-industrial economy. The backbone of this economy was to be, as Quiller-Couch foresaw, the burgeoning phenomenon of tourism. By the 1890s tourists were already being attracted to Cornwall by its alleged 'Mediterranean' qualities, and in the early twentieth century the Great Western Railway turned its attention to the potential of the Cornish holiday market when it invented the 'Cornish Riviera'. Although the initial focus continued to be on the 'Mediterranean' and the 'exotic', the introduction in 1905 of the 'Cornish Riviera Limited' train heralded an increasing reliance by the Great Western on the symbolic repertoire of the Cornish-Celtic Revival. In short, there was a high degree of collaboration, sometimes overt, between the image-makers of the Great Western Railway and the architects of the Cornish-Celtic Revival, in which a significant section of Cornish society colluded in the creation of touristic imaginings of Cornwall (Payton and Thornton 1995).

Ironically, in contrast to the difficulty experienced by the Revivalists in penetrating popular culture at home, the Great Western-Revivalist nexus became the predominant influence on the new external constructions of Cornwall that emerged in the period before 1945. S. P. B. Mais, who was soon established as the foremost Great Western iconographer, went out of his way to consult the Revivalists and to listen to their advice, writing in 1934 in the third edition of his book *The Cornish Riviera* that 'Owing to the kindness of the Cornish Association, the Rev. G. H. Doble, Vicar of Wendron, Mr Trelawney Roberts, and other correspondents I have been able to rectify a few inaccuracies. Such help is invaluable and will, I hope, be continued'. (Mais 7)

The Cornish Riviera was, indeed, the classic exposition of the Great Western's image of Cornwall, especially commissioned and first published by the company in 1924 as part of a massive marketing campaign that ranged from the evocative naming of locomotives (such as 'Chough' and 'Tregeagle') to production of thousands of posters illustrating the delights of Newlyn, Newquay, Looe and elsewhere. Mais's intention was to paint a pen-portrait of

Cornwall as the land of 'difference'. Thus Cornwall was 'a Duchy which is in every respect un-English ... Cornish people are not English people' (Mais 9) and, harking back to Celtic-Catholic Cornwall and beyond: 'in the Duchy medievalism still exists, the candle lit by the early saints still burns'. (Mais 7) North Cornwall was 'The country sacred to King Arthur' (Mais 141), while 'The musical placenames make etymologists of us all ... [they] are not to be passed without enquiry into the language that gave them birth'. (Mais 6)

The Great Western's reward for this unequivocal embrace of Revivalist imagery was a significant increase in Cornish tourist traffic in the inter-War period, as the seeds of mass tourism were sown. Not to be left behind, the London and South Western Railway (after 1922, the Southern) adopted a similar strategy, so that its North Cornwall route became 'King Arthur's Land', its King Arthur class locomotives sporting names such as 'Merlin' and 'Lyonesse'. Between them, the Great Western and the Southern popularised an image of Cornwall that, for better or worse, caught the imagination of a generation in Britain.

Conclusion
Paradoxically, then, the area of apparent unqualified success for the Cornish-Celtic Revival in its reconstruction of Celtic-Catholic Cornwall was in the realms of tourism. The desire to create a post-industrial culture and to build a post-industrial economy had developed hand-in-hand. It represented not only a determination by elements of the Cornish middle class to come to terms with the socio-economic and cultural crisis in which they found themselves but was also a deliberate collaborative effort between these Cornish 'insiders' and external 'outsiders' anxious to market Cornish 'difference'.

And yet, despite its inability to impact upon a popular indigenous culture still locked in the paralysis precipitated by rapid de-industrialisation, the Cornish-Celtic Revival had successfully wooed the opinion-makers of the Cornish establishment. They had for the most part been persuaded to abandon notions of a Cornish identity based on industrial prowess and, despite deep-seated Nonconformist industrialist suspicion of Celtic 'indolence' and 'backwardness' as exemplified hitherto in Ireland or the Highlands, had been assured that Cornish Celticity -- the heritage of Ancient Britons -- represented neither a threat to the British polity nor a challenge to Cornish institutions.

For Cornwall, the reconstruction of this Celtic-Catholic identity was a rational response to to the trauma of rapid de-industrialisation. In a society that had so recently experienced the triumph of industrial culture and yet had so quickly succumbed to the social and economic marginality of a 'Second Peripheralism', the Cornish-Celtic Revival had given meaning and dignity to those who understood the enormity of the situation in which they found themselves and sought still to be Cornish.

BIBLIOGRAPHY

Aspinall-Oglander, Cecil. *Admiral's Wife. Being the life and letters of Hon Mrs Edward Boscawen from 1719 to 1761.* London: 1940; cited in Ed. Michael Duffy. *Parameters of British Naval Power 1650-1850.* Exeter: University of Exeter Press, 1992.

Barton, D.B. *On the Steam Engines in Cornwall* 1839. Truro: Bradford Barton, 1969.

Brown, H. Miles. *A Century for Cornwall: the Diocese of Truro 1877-1977.* Truro: Oscar Blackford, 1976.

Burt, Roger. Ed. *Cornwall's Mines and Miners.* Truro: Bradford Barton, 1972.

_____. Ed. John H. Trounson. *The Cornish Mineral Industry: past performance and future prospects 1937-1951.* Exeter: University of Exeter Press, 1989.

Chapman, Malcolm. *The Celts: The Construction of a Myth.* London: St Martins Press, 1993.

Colley, Linda. *Britons: Forging the Nation 1707-1837.* New Haven: Yale University Press, 1992.

Corin, John. *Fishermen's Conflict: the story of Newlyn.* Newton Abbot: David and Charles, 1988.

Deacon, Bernard. 'Is Cornwall an Internal Colony?' Ed. Cathal O'Luain. *For A Celtic Future.* Dublin: Celtic League, 1983.

Deacon, Bernard and Philip Payton. 'Re-inventing Cornwall: culture change on the European periphery'. *Cornish Studies* 1 (1993).

Devine, T.M. *Clanship to Crofters' War: The social transformation of the Scottish Highlands.* Manchester University Press, 1994.

Durkacz, Victor Edward. *The Decline of the Celtic Languages.* Edinburgh: John Donald, 1983.

Ellis, P. Berresford. *The Cornish Language and Its Literature.* London: Routledge & Kegan Paul, 1974.

_____. *The Celtic Revolution: A Study in Anti- Imperialism.* Talybont, Y Lolfa, 1985.

Fraser, Antonia. *The Warrior Queens: Boadicea's Chariot.* Weidenfeld and Nicolson, 1988.

Hollowood, Bernard. *Cornish Engineers.* Camborne: Holmans, 1951.

James, Ronald M. 'Defining the Group: nineteenth-century Cornish on the North American Frontier'. *Cornish Studies* 2 (1994).

Jenkin, A.K. Hamilton. *The Cornish Miner* . 1927; Newton Abbot: David and Charles, 1972.

Jenkins, T.A. 'The Parliamentary Diary of Sir John Trelawny'. *Camden Miscellany XXXII;* Camden Fifth Series. Volume 3. London: Royal Historical Society, 1994.

Jenner, Henry. *A Handbook of the Cornish Language.* London: David Nutt, 1904.

Journal of the Royal Institution of Cornwall (JRIC), (various).

Mais, S.P.B. *The Cornish Riviera.* London: Great Western Railway, 1934.

Mead, C.J.H. *Cornwall's Royal Engineers.* Plymouth: Underhill, nd.

Miners, Hugh. *Gorseth Kernow: the first fifty years.* Penzance: Gorseth Kernow, 1978.

Moynihan, Julian. 'Lawrence, Women and the Celtic Fringe'. Ed. Anne Smith. *Lawrence and Women.* London: Vision/Barnes and Noble, 1978.

Nance, Henry Morton. *Cornish For All.* St Ives: Federation of Old Cornwall Societies, 1929.

Old Cornwall (Journal of the Federation of Old Cornwall Societies), (various).

Payton, Philip. *The Cornish Miner in Australia: Cousin Jack Down Under.* Redruth: Dyllansow Truran, 1984.

_____. *The Making of Modern Cornwall: historical experience and the persistence of 'difference'.* Redruth: Dyllansow Truran, 1992.

Payton, Philip and Paul Thornton. 'The Great Western Railway and the Cornish-Celtic Revival'. *Cornish Studies* 3 (1995).

Pelling, Henry. *Social Geography of British Elections 1885-1910*. London: Macmillan, 1962.

Peter, Thurstan C. *A Compendium of the History and Geography of Cornwall*. London: Houlston, 1906.

Phillips, D. Rhys. Ed. *The Celtic Conference, 1917: report of the meetings held at Birkenhead, September 3-5*. Perth: Milne, Tannahill and Methven, 1918.

People's Weekly, 23 August 1924 (Moonta, South Australia).

Rowe, John. *Cornwall in the Age of the Industrial Revolution*. Liverpool University Press, 1953; St Austell: Cornish Hillside Publications, 1993.

_____ . 'Cornish Mining Crisis in the 1920s'. *Cornish Banner*: August 1986.

Rowse, A.L. *Matthew Arnold: Poet and Prophet*. London: Thames and Hudson, 1976.

_____ . *The Little Land of Cornwall*. Gloucester: Alan Sutton, 1986.

Smith, A.S.D. *How to Learn Cornish*. Arundell: Smith, 1947.

Tarrow, Sidney. *Between Centre and Periphery: grassroots politicians in Italy and France*. New Haven: Yale University Press, 1977.

Walke, Bernard. *Twenty Years at St Hilary* 1935; London: Anthony Mott, 1982.

Mine, Moor and Chapel: the poetry of John Harris

John Hurst

There is always an element of inscrutability in the emergence at a particular point and place in time of a vigorous artistic culture. Likewise there would appear to be an element of the random, or at best the unpredictable, in the particular aspects of an individual creator's experience which, through the processes of the creative imagination, produce works of art which establish a validity both in their own and subsequent times.

Those processes can be studied in a particularly striking and accessible manner when a society, or a section of that society, is moving into artistic expression, or to a form of artistic expression new to it. The observations of the Hungarian writer and sociologist Gyula Illyes on the factors being brought to bear on the traditional peasant culture of Hungary, and the range of experiences to which the Cornish poet John Harris was exposed, provide templates of the processes of cultural change and artistic 'take-off' which are both markedly similar and yet strikingly different. Illyes's classic analysis provides a starting point for an examination of the process of cultural 'take-off' in nineteenth-century Cornwall after the literary silence in the county for two hundred years since the publication of Carew's Survey of Cornwall *in 1602. This chapter outlines the characteristics of the work of John Harris (1820-84), particularly the extremes of quality to be found within his work and noted by all writers on it.*

In his classic study of Hungarian peasant life *The People of the Puszta* (1936), Gyula Illyes speculates with a mixture of wonder and distress about the impact of a limited level of literacy on peasant society, and on the mechanisms within that situation for the dissemination of ideas. The issues that he identifies, even arising as they do from a comparatively remote context, bear remarkable similarities to the world of nineteenth-century Britain in general and of Cornwall in particular -- to the world in which John Harris grew up and grew to be a poet.

European culture filters in. It is something of a mystery how... since newspapers are not taken in peasants' dwellings. The drivers... occasionally read a copy and this is passed round. Otherwise print arrives only in the form of wrapping- paper and almanacs. (Illyes 213)

The effect of this inadequate, and in Illyes's view corrupted and corrupting diet is that it has 'obscured, confused and finally killed the culture of a whole stratum of society'. (213) It is, he believes, arguable that the peasants were more educated when they had never heard of printing, for this area of Southern Hungary was one which had 'poured forth a stream of folk art as rich and inexhaustible as the geysers in Iceland'. (213) Indeed, he asserts: 'the press has disseminated among the farm servants far more numerous and dangerous superstitions about the world and society than any old witch with her peering glance'. (214)

An essential feature of the life of the puszta as Illyes portrays it is a role for poetry that is assumed and accepted.

> On every puszta... there can be found at least one poem.... They write on little bits of paper -- if indeed they have any paper at all... They call themselves poet-reporters... They are tranquil folk, who work normally but while they are doing it they think up poems... Of course there was a lot of dross in their efforts... But they would produce... with practice... something of undoubted value. (215)

The parallels of much of this with life in nineteenth-century Cornwall are striking.

As late as 1870 when Thomas Hardy made his first visit to St Juliot, Emma Hardy tells us that newspapers were a rarity even in the professionally literate context of a rural Rectory. They would have been more readily available in the Camborne in which John Harris grew up in the 1820s and '30s, but their penetration into the houses of the poor must have been limited at that early date. Harris does not speak of newspapers as one of the narrow range of formative influences available to him. The shortage of writing materials and the importance of wrapping paper is, moreover, a striking feature in common. For the young Harris it was -- more than a conveyor of concepts, however rudimentary -- the material for writing itself. 'I used the clean side of cast-off labelled tea-wrappers, which my mother brought from the shop'. (*Songs* 4) Harris tells, too, that his verses came to him even in the middle of the hard toil of the mine or the field. 'I used to put pencil and paper on the grass a few feet in advance of me, then hoe away, making my poetry at every hack, and when I came up to the sheet write down my verses'.(9)

It is clear that one role played by the Hungarian peasant poets was closely akin to that filled by the creators of the broadsheets in British writing. They regarded themselves as 'poet-reporters' carrying on a news service, 'hawk-eyed sociologists', according to Illyes, 'who got right to the heart of the matter... on the most trifling local incidents'.(124) There is a good deal of evidence that there were parallel figures in Cornish culture -- particularly in the Western half of the county. There was, for instance, Henry Quick of Zennor, who hawked his somewhat maudlin doggerel around the parishes in the 1830s and '40s. And he was not without rivals, such as 'Blind Dick' Williams of Sennen, and Billy Foss of Sancreed. In addition Cornwall had the 'wandering droll tellers' of whom Hunt gives a brief insight in the Introduction to *Popular Romances of the West Country*, last representatives of a tradition known in Carew's time and, according to Hunt, only 'become extinct within the last twenty years'.(5) Hunt's comments are enlightening: 'As the newspaper gradually found its way into this western county... the occupation of this representative of the bards was taken away.' Traditional ballads formed the staple of the droll-tellers, often modified for local circumstances, and often with a strong admixture of the supernatural. Offerings were carefully adapted to audience. Anthony James of Cury, for instance, 'had The Babes in the Wood for religious folks [i.e. Anglicans]; but he avoided the "conorums", as he called the Methodists'. (Hunt 27)

Anthony James's wariness of the Methodist community is of particular importance for our present purposes. All commentators are agreed in two basic assertions about the work of John Harris. First, dominating factors in his driven creativity were his direct and powerful response to the natural, his experience of work in the mine, and his deeply felt Christianity in its Methodist form. Second, a variability of quality in his work so marked that it is possible for him to move, almost from one line to the next, from the sublime and the sensitive to the trite and the bathetic. It is the central argument of this essay that this lack of 'quality control' relates not merely to his self-taught status but also to fundamental ambiguities within Methodism about its position within the changing pattern of British society and its relationship to British culture, using that term both in its sociological and its artistic sense. Harris can be seen, therefore, as in a sense sharing with Illyes's Hungarian peasants the same disadvantages of education and opportunity, but as having been moved forward, to a degree, beyond their experience by the shaping forces involved in the dynamic of Methodism. It was a feature of that dynamic that it can be seen as both an enlargement and a limitation.

The enlargement offered by Methodism to the working classes is obvious. It was a prime spur to literacy and to leadership through its twin emphases on the importance of direct access to the Bible and of the role of the lay Methodist in preaching the sacred text. It brought with it, too, its own repository of poetry in the hymns of John and Charles Wesley assembled under John Wesley's editorial hand in the Collection of Hymns for the Use of the People Called Methodists in 1780 and which continued to be used within Methodism, with some additions in 1831, for nearly a century. The language of the Authorized Version and the theological fervency of the Methodist hymnody together provided a potent starting point. These gifts, however, were so potent that they inevitably provoke questions about the character and quality of life in the community before they were freely and directly available to working people.

The situation was almost certainly particularly acute in Cornwall. Though there were small and rather isolated communities of Presbyterians, Independents and Baptists, and a brief flowering of Quakerism, Cornwall had been little touched by that kaleidoscope of radical religious movements which had agitated much of the country through the period of the Reformation and Commonwealth. As Tom Shaw says, 'even during the Commonwealth the English Nonconformists had failed to capture the allegiance of the Cornish'.(14) Though it is easy to overlook the work and presence of conscientious incumbents throughout the period, Harris was no doubt expressing a view widely held among Cornish Methodists about the time before the coming of the Wesleys:

Oh what a cloud of Blackness hung o'er thee
In thy young morn, my Cornwall! Men lived on
Almost as prayerless as those callous crags.
No Sabbath schools were planted on those wilds,
Which now hang thickly mid rejoicing hills.
'T was rare to find a Bible anywhere;
It now adorns the hut of every hind.
And if a good man turn'd his face this way,
He walk'd an angel in the realm of sin.
But good men came; a Christian poet came
And stood upon this 'narrow neck of land',
And tun'd his lyre where rock o'er rock frowns throned,
And pray'd among those song-inspiring things,
That the good Spirit of the Lord would come
And make this wilderness a fruitful field;
Then went his way, leaving his name behind.

Both John and Charles Wesley visited Land's End, John in 1743, 1757, and finally at the age of 82 in 1785. Charles came in 1743 and composed there the hymn 'Come, Divine Immanuel, Come' which calls on the Lord to

Carry on thy victory,
Spread thy rule from sea to sea.

The Christian poet is, therefore, presumably Charles Wesley; but the essential point is clear. From a Methodist perspective, though good men there may have been, before the coming of Methodism Cornwall's history is one of Blackness. That rejection of the old ways which the 'droll-teller' Anthony James found among the 'conorums' is, therefore, consistent with a worked-out and defined theological stance on their part. Moreover, though they maintained a firm belief in the supernatural as shown by divine intervention in history they were equally firm in their rejection of the superstitious.

Harris makes this very clear in his *Autobiography*: 'The district in which my boyhood was spent was famous for its harvest of ghost stories...But I set my face against it all.' (39) He goes on to recount a particular incident in which he calculatedly acts against the influence of a necromancer whose activities were influential in the area, by 'defying the enchanter on his own ground' and visibly living to tell the tale. 'This incident,' he drily comments, 'was not without its moral on the minds of my companions'.(45)

This uncompromising and single-minded stance contrasts strikingly with the approach hinted at by Illyes -- that, though the pervasiveness of superstition may well be an indication of an undeveloped society and a narrow world view, it may be less damaging in human terms than some of the influences which replace it. Harris's stance, on the other hand, renders him incapable of using incidents of the superstitious creatively, because the only approach possible for the witnessing Methodist is from the moral high ground. Similarly his rejection of the Cornish world of 'blackness' leads to a failure to use material lying to hand, and a reliance upon a somewhat faded and 'literary' device in his prettification of the Cornish landscape with a ubiquitous bevy of fairies, as in the opening section of the otherwise admirable 'Kynance Cove':

I've been to fairyland, and seen the fays
Unvested in their workshop...
Hail, fairy-featured, beautiful Kynance!
A loving smile is ever on thy face
And Beauty revels mid thy gold arcades. (*Songs* 66)

Again Hunts's evidence is interesting. He points to the prevalence of belief in fairies in Cornwall and West Devon in the early years of the nineteenth century, but to a breed very different in character to the decorative creatures who inhabit the more cultivated lands to the East of Dartmoor where

the curiously wild and distinguishing superstitions of the Cornwallers fade away, and we have those which are common to... the more fertile counties of mid-England... The darker shades in the character of the Cornish fairy... belong to an older family... (79-80)

It is these more sinister and less benevolent beings who are used effectively and dramatically by Crosbie Garstin in *The Owl's House* (1923). Harris, on the other hand, distances himself from the texture of the local scene by embracing an external and literary apparatus. The matter is, however, more complex than it may so far seem.

The vividness of Harris's response to the natural scene in Cornwall is beyond question, whether to the scenes of his childhood in the neighbourhood of Carn Brea, or to the keenly experienced visits in his mid-thirties to Land's End and Kynance. Within a most restricted pattern of life he is, nevertheless, able to live at a level of intensity that comes near to being disturbing.

I walked the storm-swept, heather-hung Land's End
And mused within its sea-wash'd galleries,
Whose granite arches mock the range of Time...
I treasured up the lore the seagulls taught
Which in white clouds were cooing to the breeze
I quaff'd the music of this granite grove
And read rude cantos in the book of crags
Stretching me in the theatre of heath,
When morn was breaking, and the light-house seem'd
An angel in the water, and the rocks
Rang to the music of a thousand throats. (*Songs* 78)

Side by side with this direct response to the natural there is also developing an awareness of the sweep of Cornish history, which though it is inevitably coloured by the rejection of the earlier 'blackness' nevertheless betrays a genuine and direct fascination with that past. It is clear, for instance, that he became aware of and had access to Borlase's *Antiquities of Cornwall*, Gilbert's

Parochial History of Cornwall, Smith's *Religion of Ancient Britain* and, indeed to Hunt's *Popular Romances of the West Country*. All these provide background material for the strange poem written in 1868, *Luda: a Tale of the Druids*. Where he had access to these volumes is not clear -- perhaps in the Library of the Royal Cornwall Polytechnic Society in Falmouth? -- but elsewhere in the volume which contains *Luda*, in an essay on the eighteenth-century ploughboy poet Robert Bloomfield, he comments enthusiastically on the much greater accessibility of books than that which obtained in Bloomfield's time, or, indeed, in his own boyhood:

> Surrounded as you now are with the wealth of many minds, with libraries and institutions... Books and schools now fill the land almost like trees the forest... the works of our great Shakespeare can now be obtained for a shilling, Lord Byron for 7d and dear John Bunyan's *Pilgrim's Progress* for a penny.(203)

The strength of feeling that Harris brought to his growing awareness of Cornwall's past is shown particularly clearly in his poem on a celebrated conservation scandal of the 1860s, the destruction by quarrying of the Tolmen at Constantine:

> Much I feel
> To lose a boulder from my native moors,
> As if a sister perished. Ye who love
> The poetry of the mountains, guard, o guard
> Our curious cromlechs! Let no hand of man
> Destroy these stony prophets which the Lord
> Has placed upon the tarns and sounding downs
> With tones for distant ages. (*Songs* 119)

That Harris was by no means alone among Cornish Methodists in his interest in what would then have been termed 'antiquities' is indicated from a somewhat later but nevertheless very relevant source. W. Gregory Harris's *Trengwith: a Chronicle of Clerical and Social Life in West Cornwall* (1928), though at times clumsily written, provides fascinating insights into the traditional approaches and varying perspectives of the Methodist community in Penwith in the 1920s. On the one side there are those prominent members of the chapel community who distrust any activity which is not directly concerned with the promulgation of the Gospel. On the other there are those who have developed significant musical or literary gifts, who are actively involved in the early days of the Old Cornwall Society, and are happy to participate in the presentation of a suitably bowdlerised version of the old Cornish droll *Lady Lovell's Courtship* -- as adapted from Hunt's *Popular Romances*. It is clear that, with whatever reservations and with whatever ambiguities, Harris was of those within Methodism who wished to know and to further knowledge of Cornwall's past.

In doing so it had, nevertheless, to be from that high moral ground which we have seen directing his attitudes to local folk belief. *Luda*, for instance, in its theme concerns the death throes of Cornish paganism when the local Druid

45

community -- the details of Druid practice being liberally cross-referenced to Borlase -- engages in battle with the Christian prince, Arthur. Harris is thus able simultaneously to display his fascination with and knowledge of Cornwall's past, engage in the anti-war propaganda which came increasingly to concern him in his later years, and present the triumph of the Gospel, as embodied by Arthur, over the paganism of the Druids. This structuring of the poem is worthy of remark, for Harris was openly critical of those Victorian writers such as Tennyson who turned their attention to the revival of the Arthurian stories rather than the evocation of contemporary heroism, of which he felt there were examples lying to hand. Nor is the poem very satisfactory, not least because the four-stress line lacks the gravitas of the pentameter which he uses so forcefully in such narrative poems as 'A Story of Carn Brea' and 'The Land's End'. And it is hard not to feel that the Christian ending is largely the fig-leaf placed upon the narrative, the chief purpose of which is the evocation of that remote and alien past.

Harris is not alone within Cornish Methodism in his distrust of the medievalising tendencies of much in the writing that relates to Cornwall, and particularly of the cultivation of Arthurian and pagan themes. Jack Clemo has expressed similar reservations and, like Harris, has sought to direct his attention and creative energies to contemporary figures and modern spirit and experience. For both, too, a major catalyst of their poetry springs from the ambiguity within their attitude to the mine and the clay-pit. And both feel driven to give a moral overlay to the directness of their perceptions. The point is clearly seen if one looks at one of the most celebrated and powerful passages in Harris's work, the evocation of the mine in its context within the poem 'Christian Heroism' (*Lays* 1856), where it stands out like a precious stone within a lode of country rock. Though, like many other Cornish Methodists in the period before the Second Reform Bill, John Harris was markedly apolitical that does not imply that he was unaware of social injustice. Indeed, if the evidence of the autobiographical poem *Monro* (1879) is to be believed, such an awareness was inculcated by his mother at an early age, as he listened to her tell of

> those who left their much loved home retreat
> To walk this selfish world to preach and pray
> Of hope expiring under long delay
> Of genius hidden in some reedy cell
> Of virtue trodden in the public way
> Of good men clothed in rags... (Book I)

Rather, however, than seek involvement in extra-parliamentary agitation such as Chartism -- the reaction of Cornish Methodism to those Chartists who came to Cornwall was by no means universally supportive (Jenkin) -- Harris as a writer sought rather to offer positive images of working men, often in declared contra-distinction to the defects of those who were better placed. Indeed he would attract to the ranks of virtuous working men some unlikely candidates -- Shakespeare no less. In the poem which won him the Shakespeare Prize in April 1864 he writes:

46

This greatly gifted one
Was labour's noblest son...
The glory of the soil
The towering prince of toil. (1866, 134)

Nearer to home, however, he was powerfully moved by the story of the
Callington miner -- and Methodist -- Michael Verran, who attracted nation-
wide publicity for his heroism in allowing a fellow miner to escape first from an
impending accident. Contrary to all expectation Verran survived the explosion,
and his story drew the attention of Carlyle and his friend John Sterling and their
influential Cornish connections the Foxes of Falmouth. Caroline Fox became
the administrator of the national fund which was set up to aid and reward
Verran. It is Verran whose story is told in 'Christian Heroism', though Harris
returns to it in the short poem 'The True Hero', and in a more extended passage
in Monro (Book 1). 'The True Hero' is the least effective of these, for its purpose
is solely to point the moral. Both the passage in Monro and that in 'Christian
Heroism' provide Harris with the opportunity to evoke the world of the mine,
which he does in language of striking power and directness:

Hast ever seen a mine? ...
Hast ever, by the glimmer of the lamp,
Or the fast-waning taper, gone down, down
Toward the earth's dread centre ...
Hast ever heard within this prison-house,
The startling hoof of Fear? the eternal flow
Of some dread meaning whispering to thy soul?

The passage is full of Miltonic and Worsdworthian echoes. It shows, as it
develops, more than a nodding acquaintance with the theories of the vulcano-
logists (where, one asks, does this come from?); but more than all, the passage
is a highly crafted response to the experience of splendour and terror that the
mine presses on him. The mine is too overwhelming to be the subject of
moralising. Not so, however, the story of Michael Verran. Speaking of the
'butcher-czar' of his time:

I take him with his soul besmeared in gore
And place him crown'd and worshipped and adored
Beside the Christian miner, who to save
His comrade's life, sat to be blown to death.
I take them, and I place them side by side
Upon the world's great platform, and I ask
'Which of them is the hero?'

It is in writing of another working class hero, Samuel Westlake, the railway
driver who by prompt and self-endangering action averted a major crash, that
he speaks of how

Gone is the age of knighthood
The palfrey and the squire
And he who would revive it
But overstrains his lyre
Yet there are other heroes...

Harris, then, rejects much in the past of Cornwall's culture while displaying both love of and fascination with its people and the broad sweep of its history. At the same time he rejects much in the contemporary presentation of that past as displayed in the medievalising of such poets from outside Cornwall as Tennyson and Swinburne and, from within the county, as Hawker, the distinguished and eccentric Vicar of Morwenstow. Where then are the positive features which, while rejecting the traditions available to him in the Cornwall of his boyhood, nurtured him as a poet?

He appears from the start to have had an innate and unstructured response to the natural of remarkable vividness:

No teacher taught him on his native moor
For it is vain to guide the true-born bard. (*Monro* Book II)

Moreover, even when the riches and stimulus became available to him -- and he speaks of these in terms almost extravagant -- the priority of the natural remains unquestioned:

The holy silence of the universe
Was more to him than...
    volume of sweet verse
Inscribed of old by some immortal pen. (*op.cit.*)

That intensity of response is focused on his passionate apprehension of Cornwall. It is Cornwall which is his theme, that which he knew and came to discover. (It is to be remembered that, such were the limitations of his experience, he did not stand on the sea-shore until he was in his 'teens, though living within sight of a distant sea, and he did not visit Land's End and Kynance until in his thirties.)

His native Cornwall which his heart has worn
Like some bright crystal in the waters clear...
Is yet to Monro like a daughter dear.
Her hills and glens in softened light appear
And all her waters have a liquid sound
Like that which fell upon his youthful ear
When first his harp among the hills he found. (*Monro* Book X)

The view may be a retrospective one; but he is in no doubt that, though his perceptions may have modified, his experience of the nature of Cornwall is a seamless whole, fully bearing out the Wordsworthian hope that 'the child is father to the man.'

In that process of modification, the books to which he had such sparing access as a child and young man manifestly formed his mode of address. The language of the Authorized Version is omni-present. Equally influential -- and Harris's Augustanism is often mentioned -- must have been the formalised emotionalism of the Wesleys' hymns:

> Those dear tokens of His passion
> Still His dazzling body bears;
> Cause of endless exultation
> To his ransomed worshippers;
> With what rapture
> Gaze we on those glorious scars.
> (From 'Lo, he comes with clouds descending'.)

If Harris's mode of expression may often seem excessive, it is all of a piece with the intensity of the language with which he became familiar Sunday by Sunday. To a naturally fervent nature the literary experiences to which he was gradually exposed -- Bunyan, Defoe, Burns, Byron, Shakespeare -- came as successive revelations, embraced despite a prevailing Methodist prejudice against some of them. He speaks of how a 'middle-aged matron', seeing that he was reading Burns exclaimed:

> You ought to be ashamed of yourself. You a local preacher, and reading Burns'... but no strictures of hers could induce me to shut up this fountain of pure melody. (*Songs* 10-11)

His response to his first reading of Shakespeare, in his late twenties, was similarly uninhibited. The play was *Romeo and Juliet.*

> The delight I experienced was beyond words to describe...The bitters of life changed to sweetness in my cup... Some times I cried, sometimes I shouted for joy, and over the genii-peopled heights a new world burst into view. (*op.cit.*)

In speaking of Shakespeare, again he manages to rise above the limiting claim to him as a working-class hero to seize on more essential attributes:

> The magic wielder of the mightiest quill
> Who read the human heart with royal skill,
> And from the fields of fancy called a train
> Of passing pageants, subject to his will,
> The good, the brave, the vicious and the vain. (*Monro* Book VIII)

Yet one wonders how he might have responded to so tangled a moral dilemma as that posed within, say, *Measure for Measure?* It is here, in fact, that one comes close to the central dilemma about Harris himself.

49

Harris knew directly extremes of privation through his work in the mine and his impoverished childhood, and of personal sorrow in the death of his daughter Lucretia. He knew the range of depravity -- increasingly as the years passed in his work as a Bible reader in Falmouth. He is capable, as a poet, of speaking with moving directness that is nevertheless carefully and skilfully crafted, of his daughter's death:

> Ah! thou were like a rose,
> Dropped by an angel on earth's feverish clime,
>   To bloom full lovely, till December's winds
> Blasted thy beauty in its morning prime
> Ere it had half unclosed. (*Songs* 103)

Though it lacks the masterly compression of Shakespeare, this is of a piece with:

> Death lies on her like an untimely frost
> Upon the sweetest flower of all the field
>   (*Romeo and Juliet* IV.v. 28-29).

And yet he is capable of reducing the profound to the trivial, as in the verses on Leonardo da Vinci (*Monro* 1879, 94).

It has often been suggested that the remarkable tendency to fall into the trite that Harris displays relates to the extent to which he was both self-taught and lacked friends who could act as sensitive critics. There may be ways in which this is true, though in his later days, from which much of the tritest work proceeds, he was in close touch with the cultured circle which spread outwards from the Foxes and the Royal Cornwall Polytechnic Society. It might seem, rather, not that he lacked critics, but that he had a fatal sense that he did not need criticism. Firstly because he was aware from earliest days that he had a poetic gift:

> He sang because the sounds he could not stay (*Monro* Book II)

and as already quoted:

> No teacher taught him on his native moor
> For it is vain to guide the true-born bard. (*op.cit.*)

Linked with that, there was the dangerous sense that, living under the newly recovered dispensation of Methodism, much of what lay to hand was under 'a cloud of Blackness'. This led, therefore, perhaps to an almost fatal self-confidence and to an ability, even a duty, to adopt a mode of bardic self-assertion.

In turning his back on the folk tradition of his immediate Cornish past Harris was, however, in no way moving into a total cultural impoverishment. Full of variety and interest though the records show the culture of the South West to have been, it is clear that by the 1820s that culture was long past its peak. Nor, in comparison with the unusual situation in Hungary, may it ever have displayed the remarkable range to be found in Central Europe. By reasons of geographical and ethnic accident, several streams of musical activity and creativity in the crafts coalesced in the area about which Illyes writes, and to which the researches of Bartok and Kodaly bear remarkable witness. There is nothing in the British tradition which quite parallels this, though at their height some Celtic cultures produced a similar folk richness. And even that was long gone. There is, therefore, a sense in which Harris's loss was a personal rejection of a tradition nearing its end, not the abandonment of an immensely vital and still viable cultural inheritance. Secondly, while Illyes portrays the move into a media-oriented and capitalist-inspired culture as providing for his people a development that was almost wholly loss, this is far from the case for Harris. For if the moralistic cast which spreads over Harris from his association with the ethos of Methodism is damaging, there is far more that is positive in the effect of Methodism on his work. While there is in his less inspired verses dreary and negative concerns with the demon drink and the evils of the Church of Rome, there is much of joyous praise. For he was, essentially, a praise-maker, as in the extraordinary flight of eloquence towards the end of Book II of 'A Story of Carn Brea':

> More, more of thee my Saviour - though the winds
> Howl, and the waves rise higher than the land;
> Though poverty come rushing like a blast,
> Or persecution meet me on the way,
> Or pain or weakness; Saviour more of Thee (*Songs* 34)

-- a passage which needs to be encountered at its full extent for the full onrush of its eloquence to be appreciated.

It is a confidence, too, which enables him to take head on the most profound theological themes from which more widely and systematically educated poets might have turned aside in caution; as in the remarkable passage, mixing naivety and grandeur in equal proportions, on the Crucifixion:

> The startled sun grew dark at fervid noon
> The great hills rocked like boulders in their bed
> The cattle lowed to be called home too soon
> And thunder spoke to thunder overhead...
> The temple's veil was rent like slender thread,
> And those who in the Saviour's death combine
> Confessed with burning lips He was the King Divine. (*Monro* Book II)

This has all the confidence and much of the verbal skill of Charles Wesley's great hymn 'Wrestling Jacob', which likewise tackles directly a great moment of Biblical narrative.

John Harris can be seen, then, as the first Cornish writer since the late sixteenth century to achieve a strong and personal poetic voice and a substantial body of work of poetic quality. That voice finds its fullest expression when he is able to bring into balance the positive features of his faith, his responses to the natural, unmediated by second-hand literary devices, and his love for his native county, unclouded by his rejection of her past: when his tradition can find an authentic voice.

Jack Clemo's words form the best valediction. Speaking of the 'incongruous treasure' of Harris's art, he says:

Holier here than in Burns or Clare
The peasant fibre kindled by poetry.
Chaste and sober, faithful in Wesley's fold
He grew as saint and rhymer,
His mine-sharpened vision, Bible drill...
Raising among the Redruth slag-tips
An unstained simple testament. (Clemo 1993, 28)

BIBLIOGRAPHY

Borlase, William. *Observations on the Antiquities, Historical and Monumental, of the County of Cornwall.* Oxford: W.Jackson, 1754.

Carew, Richard. *The Survey of Cornwall* (1602). Ed. F.E.Halliday. *Richard Carew of Antony.* London: Melrose, 1953.

Clemo, Jack. *Approach to Murano.* Newcastle-on-Tyne: Bloodaxe, 1993.

Garstin, Crosbie. *The Owl's House.* London: Heinemann, 1923; London, Heinemann, 1928.

Gilbert, Davies. *The Parochial History of Cornwall.* 4 Vols. London,1838.

Hardy, Emma. *Some Recollections.* Ed. R. Gittings. Oxford University Press, 1961.

Harris, John. *Lays from the Mine, the Moor and the Mountain.* London: Alexander Heylin, 1853. 2nd edition with additional poems. London: Simpkin, Marshall & Co., 1856.

_____. *The Land's End, Kynance Cove and other poems.* London: Alexander Heylin, 1858.

_____. *Shakespeare's Shrine.* London: Hamilton Adams & Co, 1866.

_____. *Luda.* London: Hamilton Adams & Co, 1868.

_____. *Bulo.* London: Hamilton Adams & Co, 1871.

_____. *Monro.* London: Hamilton Adams & Co, 1879.

_____. *My Autobiography.* London: Hamilton Adams & Co, 1882. [Selection in *Songs.* Ed. D. M. Thomas.]

_____. *Songs from the Earth: Selected Poems of John Harris, Cornish Miner 1920-84.* Ed. D.M. Thomas. Padstow: Lodenek Press, 1977.

Harris, W. Gregory. *Trengwith: a chronicle of clerical and social life in West Cornwall.* London: Bodley Head, 1928.

Hunt, R. *Popular Romances of the West Country.* London: Chatto & Windus, 1865. 3rd ed. (revised), 1881.

Illyes, Gyula. *The People of the Puszta.* Tr. G.F.Cushing. Budapest: Corvina Press, 1967. [Originally published in Hungarian, 1936.]

Jenkin, A. *The Cornish Chartists. Journal of the Royal Institution of Cornwall* (1982): 53-80.

Newman, Paul. *The Meads of Love.* Redruth: Dyllansow Truran, 1994.

Shaw, T. *A History of Cornish Methodism.* Truro: Bradford Barton, 1967.

Smith, G. *Religion of Ancient Britain.* 2nd ed. London: Longmans, Green, 1846.

The Cornish Alps: resisting romance in the clay country

Alan M. Kent

The literary act has roots in the historical struggle men and women are engaged in at all levels in their attempt to make sense of the contradictions of the material world. As an academic I cannot hold with the nineteenth-century notion of literature as transcending the utilitarian organisation of society, an idea which to some extent still remains today. Literature was believed to be the product of mysterious forces working through the creative genius, whose vision soars above material conditions, place, society and politics. This was never better demonstrated than in English literature's reductive view of Cornish literature, which at worst fails to understand it at all by accentuating Cornwall as merely a 'timeless land', and at best offers a bland tolerance.

In fact Cornish literature, like all others, emerges out of the signifying conditions of its own time. It is concerned with the particular, the actual, the intricate human contexts (physical, spatial, temporal, psychological, sensate), and thus demands a placing in history and in cultural space. This chapter attempts to locate the literature which has emerged from the china clay mining region of mid-Cornwall. It focuses on that literature's complementary and contradictory facets of realism and romance, whilst contextualising its development within the wider context of Cornish literature and the historical struggle of the Cornish.

The starting point for this examination of romantic construction of the china clay mining region of Cornwall arose in a discussion with the Cornish novelist N.R. Phillips, who once put it to the author that the china clay landscape of the Hensbarrow Downs region in the east of the county had the potential to burst forth a range of historical romance equivalent to that about Penwith in the west, as outlined by Denys Val Baker in *A View from Land's End* (1982). Val Baker argued that in the mid-twentieth century, West Cornwall offered an ideal landscape for the projection of this fiction. It was a region rich in industrial and maritime heritage, crammed with folklore and myth, and appeared to offer a uniquely Cornish sensibility. However, by the late-twentieth century, many novelists constructing Cornwall have become frustrated with this traditional setting and location, and actively decided to foreground other regions of Cornwall: Sheila Reddicliffe's novel *The Cornish Mistress* (1992) has for its location the banks of the River Tamar whilst David Hillier's *Trevanion* (1994) shifts to Helston. Yet it is in the china clay landscape of mid-Cornwall that we are beginning to witness an unprecedented but significant emergence of the historical romantic tradition in a newer industrial landscape. Both indigenous writers and non-indigenous writers are now starting to explore in different ways than Jack Clemo -- poet of the clay/prydyth an pry -- the landscape, history and people of Hensbarrow Downs and the china clay mining region. This chapter offers an introductory account of the development of such a literature in relation to the cultural reconstruction of that region.

Cornish Literature

To understand this recent development we need to consider the Cornish literary tradition and how it directly affects the construction of 'clay' literature. How we see literature, or a continuing cultural tradition, or even our own identity, depends upon an act of perception and hence of selection on our part. Different periods will make different selections from the available evidence according to the spirit of the times. Indeed, the music, literature and arts of the past are truly alive only because our understanding of them has to change in this way -- from generation to generation, or even during the course of a single life. Literary and cultural history is especially fluid, because persuasive theories, let us say about what 'being Cornish' is or about 'what constitutes clay area ideology', begin to influence how people think of themselves and hence how writers express themselves.

Certainly Cornwall has expended enough effort over the centuries defending and defining a sense of identity which has somehow refused to succumb to political and cultural pressures from her larger and more powerful neighbour to the east, always remaining an inconvenient periphery and always demon-strating its difference and independence. This process actually started as long ago as Athelstan's 'cleansing' of the Cornish from Exeter in the 10th century. The fruits of Cornwall's unique identity, its close links with Brittany, Wales and Ireland, and the flowering of Cornish came to full season in the miracle plays, the saints' plays (saints' stories -- in particular of St. Austell on Hensbar-row Downs and St. Michael at Roche Rock -- remain active in the clay area) and passion poetry of the medieval period. A unique national identity seemed to be assured, not least because it was largely taken for granted, at the height of literary production in pre-Reformation and pre-industrial Cornwall.

The first revival of interest in Cornish culture came during the Reformation when Nicholas Roscarrock (Orme 1992) first began to collect the lives of the saints and their folklore, realising that these figures had had a tremendous impact on the culture of Cornwall, and whilst the community-generated miracle and saints' plays stopped being performed, new Renaissance men like Richard Carew (Halliday 1953) -- aware of a flourishing 'English' poetic tradition -- extolled the virtues of the soldier, lover and courtier, in so doing moving literature away from relics and cults to embrace what he termed 'the excellency of the English tongue'. Carew was part of a differential cultural process which culminated in the virtual shut-down of literary production in Cornwall, apparently whilst the writers recovered from the dislocation of the loss of Cornish and its replacement with English. The state of confusion and catastrophe was to last for over one hundred years. This shut-down occurs at broadly the same time as the clay industry first begins in mid-Cornwall.

The next most impressive period of Cornish cultural history was the industrial revolution of the eighteenth and nineteenth centuries. It too came from native stock going back to the best of the Cornish Methodist intellectual tradition that had always valued the primacy of education, law and religion. This period produced figures of important literary standing such as R.M. Ballantyne, J.F. Cobb and Edward Bosanketh and a wealth of talent in innovation, in mining, in engineering and in the physical sciences, very often among men who rose from humble backgrounds. It was this period which was to later form the dominant literary construction of Cornwall.

Clearly Cornwall was flourishing and yet, paradoxically, it was the industrial revolution and the success of that revolution in Cornwall that knocked the final nails in the coffin of Cornish literature, whilst ironically an Anglo-Cornish literature flourished. The latter end of the eighteenth century had seen a brief revival of literature in Cornish by Nicholas Bosun, John Keigwin and William Gwavas, but it was Anglo-Cornish poetry which came to a new vernacular strength in the nineteenth century in Robert Stephen Hawker, John Harris and James Dryden Hosken. Antiquarians like William Borlase, Robert Hunt and William Bottrell began to 'gather the fragments' of a culture apparently disappearing by the minute, and they collected tales and drolls from the folk tradition, as a different 'Doric' inheritance just as valuable as the intellectualism of an age of 'Athenian' enlightenment.

The voice of common people was heard and in part redefined by the individual work of Silas Kitto Hocking, Joseph Hocking, Walter Besant and Arthur Quiller-Couch, near creating a 'Cornish School'. Yet this unified mode was liable to decay and by the end of the century even its more important practitioners had slipped into Victorian sentimentality, rural parochialism and 'dialect-in-aspic' stereotypes.

So the 'Cornish Revival' happened again at the beginning of the twentieth century, led by L.C. Duncombe Jewell, Henry Jenner and Robert Morton Nance, as a united political and critical effort to re-establish the native heritage in a country which too many politicians, university professors, writers and journalists were coming to regard just as being part of the 'West Country' and England. There was a growing feeling, too, that wider economic forces and the mass media were actually eroding everything that was most distinctive and hence of most value in all minority cultures in the modern world. Thus it was that the twentieth-century Cornish revival contained a 'new' factor, for it realised that for Cornwall to maintain its identity it needed to revive Cornish language and literature.

As always, twentieth-century Cornish literature would have been all the unifiably poorer without the talents of very different indigenous writers such as A.L. Rowse, Jack Clemo, Charles Causley or D.M. Thomas -- all of whom have considered the clay industry significant to greater or lesser extents -- but non-indigenous writers have played an important part too in asserting a construction of Cornwall -- amongst them, Charles Lee, John Betjeman, Daphne du Maurier, Winston Graham, Susan Howatch and E.V. Thompson. All of these writers have tried to define what might be called a national psychology or at least national habits of expression, as they had appeared in Cornish culture over the centuries. The Cornish sensibility appeared to be characteristically extreme, containing a combination of opposite tendencies which manifests itself in a delight in domestic realism and the accumulation of small details on the one hand, and love of excess and wild and uncontrolled Celtic flights of fancy on the other. This 'Cornish muse' was often welcomed as an ally against the nineteenth-century conception of the Cornishman as a canny, world-wide technophile. The two are often combined in the early historical romances of Graham and Thompson, and are now repeated in the emerging romances of the clay.

Our contemporary understanding of the construction of Cornish literature owes much to the work of N.R. Phillips, Alan M. Kent, Myrna Combellack and Bert Biscoe, whose work critiques the dominant ideological and cultural forces under which Cornwall is forced to live. Their work is a vigorous polemic against the earlier themes either by using fragmentary narrative or by forging a radical new poetic. On the Cornish front most recently, Richard Gendall, Tony Snell, Tim Saunders and Pol Hodge have been the first to develop a progressive and provocative poetic which the earlier revivalists would never have dared to write. Their work can be seen in the context of the recent academic work by Lee, Bell, Ludwig and Fietz, who have all identified issues of Cornish cultural nationalism in contemporary British fiction and poetry.

Any construction of Cornish literature is deeply problematical. There are good reasons for this statement: the main one being that the Cornish went through a profound shift in cultural orientation in surrendering one language for another -- Cornish for English -- culminating in its temporal extinction at the end of the eighteenth century (Murdoch 1-18). A secondary factor is the division between the politics of identity of those indigenous to the place, and those outside Cornwall who have enforced their construct upon it (Hardie 7-12). Cornwall has been at the receiving end of this kind of construct for some time now. On occasions this construction has been correct; at other times, it has been very wrong, and taken an altogether incorrect view of Cornwall to Cornish readers and to those beyond the River Tamar. The division is completed by an often false yet, to the outside world at least, convincing romanticisation of place. My aim here, is to demonstrate how the shaping process of literature in the field of historical romantic fiction developing from Cornwall since 1945 -- broadly and usually linked to tin and copper mining -- now mirrors a new, emerging process of cultural production related to the china clay mining region of mid-Cornwall.

The White Mountains
Located in what A.L. Rowse calls the 'Higher quarter' (16), the china clay industry, which dominates the Hensbarrow Downs area around St Austell with mountainous white sandtips, chutes, settling tanks and drying plants, resulted from the experiments of William Cookworthy, a Plymouth chemist, who in 1748 found chinastone in St Stephen-in-Brannel, Carclaze and other mines, and began to work clay as well as tin. Production doubled from 1850 to 1867, reaching 130,000 tons. Although fewer than forty pits are working today, some are enormous concerns, about four hundred feet deep, producing half a million tons of clay annually. The industry is still the largest single employer in Cornwall, with a workforce of over six thousand.

Local Cornish people already feel passionately about the power and mystique of the mountainous-looking china clay tips (locally known as 'burras') of the mid-Cornwall region. Successive attempts by the major china clay producer, English China Clays International, to flatten the older pyramidal tips into more sanitised longitudinal 'blobs' of sand waste are always greeted with much objection and lamenting for the older, if more unstable form. A landscape has, over time, been constructed, weathered, endured, played in, loved in, walked upon, and it should not be changed according to the whims of the contemporary industry. When one realises that from 1900 until relatively recently, whole lives were bound up with particular clay-works (Arthur 34-51), one can understand the sympathy and sentimentality which has evolved around such a seemingly bleak landscape and lifestyle. The azure pools (caused by residual copper deposits), which complement lupin and heather-strewn tips, make for a remarkably beautiful sight, as appropriate a signifier for the mid-Cornwall region as any engine house or mine stack for Penwith and Kerrier. Alongside this the landscape and industry have created their own living and vibrant folk culture.

The heritage of the area -- itself a miniature cosmography -- is preserved and developed by the Wheal Martyn China Clay Heritage Centre at Ruddlemoor, near St. Austell, where the architecture, working processes, tools and lifestyles of the industry have been maintained for future generations. Formerly a museum, it now concerns itself with 'Heritage', in its literature promoting the production of china clay as a '200 year saga' (4). 'Cornwall of Mine', a company specialising in industrial safaris, offers coach trips to ferry visitors to two key sites of industrial activity: the tin and copper mines of Penwith and those of the interior Redruth/Camborne region. Now, in addition, one can visit the china clay mining area, whereas not so long ago the Cornwall Tourist Board was unhappy for visitors even to see the 'wasteland' from the A30, deeming it to be of no interest to the tourist and perhaps reflecting the extremities of Jack Clemo's early austere and heavy poetic of the region:

Near the white gashed cliff where the orchard
Held its brave menaced fruit
You crouched and were tortured
By the clang on the thrusting rails
Watching the iron lines encroach,
Hearing the clash of the buffers
That signalled my fate's approach,
The grimy burdens rumbling through the clay.
  'Goonvean Claywork Farm' in Clemo (1988), 39

Such poetry exemplifies the hard lifestyle of those people who lived and worked in the region, but times have changed. As John Lowerson points out, Cornwall now offers new tourist magnets (128-135) and the Borough of Restormel, where the clay industry is situated, now promotes, as part of its green tourism programme, the 'Cornish Alps Experience' (Summertime Specials leaflet, 1996). The landscape is seen as being worthy of visitors; the old working methods are of interest and importance. The earliest way of clay working was to dig claybearing ground from such a 'gashed cliff' using hand tools and take it to an area where it was worked with a stream of water. Clay and sand produced a milky suspension. The clay was refined in a series of settling pits and thickened in shallow pans before drying naturally in crude shelters called air dries (Thurlow 4-13).

At the end of the nineteenth century and at the beginning of the twentieth, mining for china clay was an activity as fraught with danger as that of the tin-miner, facing blasting accidents, harsh working conditions, long hours, badly guarded machinery and dangerous working practice. An example of such circumstances is found in Jack Clemo's *Wilding Graft* (1948) where Seth Spragg is described as having to walk 'with a limp, never having recovered from an accident on Retew claywork two years ago when his leg was crushed by a skip wagon'. (17) Similarly, in the preface to *The Shadowed Bed* -- published in 1986, but originally drafted in 1950 -- Clemo explains how this work also 'embodies the primitive clay-bed mysticism... in the gritty region of Cornwall which I describe'. (vii) This novel is the drama of one village, Carn Veor, in which an almost medieval imagination haunts a weird patch of the modern clay industry. Sinister occult forces are seemingly at work amongst the villagers, when the village is cut off from the outside world by a dangerous landslide. Clearing that landslide is Joe Gool, the protagonist of the novel; Gool's characteristics exemplify the qualities of what would become the typical clay region hero:

Joe Gool, who was working on the dam early in the afternoon, was not a paid labourer. He had come to the site when these men left it, and yielded to a whim, seeking some exertion before he met Bronwen Cundy. He was a tall gaunt fellow in his late twenties, obviously a native. The stark grey background suited him; he looked upon the general mess with stolid enjoyment as he added boulder, whitened gorse twigs and frayed clotted hazel boughs to the structure. His pale face had something of the wrenched, warped perversity of the landscape; he seemed to commune with the coldly volcanic clay world, knowing its vagaries and loving them. (11)

Female characters also feel the same presence of the artificially constructed landscape, as in 'The Clay Dump' (1951), a short story concerning the frustrated and paralysed life of Lucy Gribble, where landscape and emotional poverty are inextricably linked:

The side of the Gribbles' home stood nearest the dump -- so near that one side of the white pyramid loomed up from the garden hedge. Mrs Gribble had eyed it strangely during the last few days that she spent in the house, and Lucy too became fascinated, aroused to a certain identification of the gravelly dune with the heaping up of afflictions in her life. All of her hope of enjoyment had been like the flowers that pushed out so pitifully through the turf fringing the dump's base -- soon to be burst and flattened and buried by the descending vomit of sand and stone. (1976, 12)

Diseases such as clay-lung, resulting from sustained and unprotected contact with finely powdered clays, are as frequent as those felt by coal miners. There is pain, sorrow and heartache. There is danger on a day-to-day basis. The white mountains are a landscape charged with emotion and energy, and as historical romance has emerged elsewhere in Britain -- out of the Liverpool docks and the shipbuilding yards of north-east England -- so it has in this region of Cornwall.

A landscape ready for mining

The clay industry mirrors almost exactly the earlier decline of the tin and copper mining industries and its romanticisation into the the kind of tin and copper dynasty novels which form the backbone of popular historical romantic fiction about Cornwall. In a process which is already beginning -- only a few years into the next century -- a similar rationalisation of mineral extraction will surely occur in mid-Cornwall; the industry yielding to cheaper clay sources outside Europe, in the United States and South America.

Already the industry has been streamlined with new production methods reducing staffing levels. In 1945, it took approximately one hundred men to manage and work one mining operation. Now, that same operation, greatly expanded, is worked in one shift by just ten workers (Thurlow 8). Automation and new techniques have brought about a reverence for the old -- and it is at this interface between what is carried in the folk memory of the region and the new, that the romanticisation begins.

Other similarities can easily be noted. Like copper and tin mining, in the early years of the nineteenth century, local Cornish adventurers took over the small pits and opened new ones. There was bitter rivalry and much profit to be made. A brief survey of pre-Clemo literature demonstrates this. The popular novelist Joseph Hocking is interesting here. One of his most successful novels, *What Shall it Profit a Man?* (1924), concerns the rivalry between two families over the mining rights to a piece of mineral-rich land known as 'Pisky's Gully'. Gabriel Poldhu is so determined to make a success of mining exploration to gain revenge on the local squirearchy, that he sends his son to South Africa to receive some of the best mining training he can muster. A bitter feud follows as Poldhu senior contrives to gain access to the Gully. Typically -- like other indigenous Cornish popular fiction written in this period -- Poldhu junior falls in love with the daughter of the rival to his father. The novel, as was standard, ends happily with Poldhu junior's marriage and the father realising the error of his greed. It stands as one of the earliest romantic constructs of the china clay mid-Cornwall region, but points very well to some of its direct descendents.

Another relatively early novel is A.W. Holmes's *Out of this Fury* (1944), which charts the life of Harry Smithers and his wife Peggy. Smithers is evacuated to the china clay mining region, while his wife remains in London, the text being a 'faction', since Holmes himself came to Cornwall to manage Great Longstones claywork and dry. Much of the action takes place outside Cornwall, though the novel conveys something of the struggle of clayworkers' lives. It is also highly critical of the Cornish. Early on, Smithers criticises them 'for eating pasties,' curses them 'for the gallons of tea they drank,' and dislikes them for speaking 'incorrect English'. (5) His struggle is to manage a workforce ravaged by war with its best workers away fighting; certainly the reader senses Smithers' frustration with this landscape and the distance between himself and his wife, which resulted in the anti-Cornish feeling. The establishment of the clay landscape as hostile is to be repeated again, as is the separation of lovers whose lives are intimately connected with the clay.

Other emergent potential plots are freely available to the historical novelist. In 1858, there were 89 pits operated by 42 different companies or partnerships. These great families and partnerships, always alluded to in the tin-mining novels, have been dealt with in a more limited fashion in clay-mining fiction. The potential for conflict and high drama is massive however, as, say, the Martyn Brothers take on Old Gomm Clayworks, and the West of England China Clay Company buy out good clay-bearing land of the Carthews. Also undeveloped are the links that these families and prospectors had with some of the great potteries which were emerging in Plymouth and in the north of England. The grand pottery and exquisite porcelain produced by these great emporiums from the harsh kaolinised granite of Cornwall could surely be symbols of some Cornishman's refinement by an external source; or one can imagine metaphors about the heroine's white and beautiful complexion being compared to the 'porcelain earth'.

Photographic evidence from the clay region's past is now frequently displayed and freely available; where once the air dries and settling tanks spoke of the landscape's ruination, now a pervading sense of reminiscence and sentimentality is brought back by them. Bowler-hatted cap'ns (the foremen of the clay industry), standing dapperly dressed in white quarries, alongside miners with gaiters, neckerchiefs and braces, all curiously contribute to a construct of something lost -- and a range of narratives which need to be written. Sandy deserts of men working mica drags bring back an era of full employment, of hardship, yet ironically somehow of a satisfying and healthy lifestyle. Certainly, what could be more romantic than the bonnet-clad Bal maidens (women who scraped sand and dirt from clay blocks after months of drying) working beside imposing slip kilns? The bare backs of the Cornish shovel-wielding pan-kiln workers are the new stock figures for a developing genre. Horse-drawn wagons laden with processed kaolin and early locomotives pulling trucks appeal to our nostalgic sense of the industrial and rural still somehow in happy union. The 1995 and 1996 environmental conflicts between English China Clays International and clay villages such as St. Dennis and St. Stephen-in-Brannel over the expansion of tipping and exploration are seemingly a world away.

One can, of course, fire the warning shots now, just as commentators have deplored the romanticisation of the tin and copper mines (Hodge 61; Kent 1995, 7), but the process will not be halted. Once the region has its established emotional geography, it becomes harder and harder to resist. That is why our bookshops and libraries are already stocked with eighteenth and nineteenth-century mining sagas set in Cornwall. On the evidence of these texts, a gap of about a century, it would seem, is sufficient for writers to romanticise a place, for even the evils of exploitation to be dispersed.

The Cornish Alps have another card to play, however, in this process of romanticisation. Such fiction allows the opportunity for lovers to cavort in an incredible moonscape, with twisted, gullied heaps of sand, huge masses of derelict ground falling sharply to dangerous flooded pits. Such a harsh world is bound to make any romantic affair harsh and problematic.

Romancing the clay
With his stark, evangelical Nonconformity expressed through his early poetry and fiction, Jack Clemo brought world attention to bear upon the clay region. Clemo's powerful *Wilding Graft* (1948) is now regarded as the first narrative to be concerned with the clay industry. In the primitive and ingrown community of the novel, Garth Joslin, the novel's hero, finds himself falling in love with Irma, a young woman from London. For Clemo, the love they feel has to be symbolically matched by some measure of salvation, but if we remove Clemo's Calvinist edge, the novel is a perfect blueprint for the romantic fiction that is to follow. Clemo is indeed the master of gritty clayland realism. However, even he saw the potential for a romantic construct. *The Bouncing Hills* (c.1979), his collection of dialect tales and light verse, features a cover of a dancing girl, joyous in an industrial landscape. The tales, too, reflect the cheerful aura of village life in the china clay country as it was fifty years ago. Thus Clemo, too, contributed to the romancing process.

The romanticisation has already started; not quite an avalanche but at least a rumbling in the higher peaks. Rumer Godden's 1961 novel *China Court* described the responses of one rich family to the new industrialisation. Rowena Summers's *Killigrew Clay* (1986) focuses on the early development of the industry, with a plot -- and book cover -- borrowed from the tin sagas, only here the requisite stack house is transformed into the Cornish Alps. The raven-haired, shawl-wrapped heroine remains the same. Set in the St. Austell area, the novel follows the fortunes of the Killigrew family, in particular Charles Killigrew, the owner of a clay works. It is from the toil of his employees that Charles is able to give his son, Ben, the education he himself had never had. The clay fortune allows Ben a passport to an apparently better way of life, but Charles does not realise that his son is his own master. Summers presents Ben as young, virile and handsome in a manner not too distantly removed from the heroes of Joseph Hocking's novels. He falls in love with Morwen Tremayne (a Cornish name if ever there was one!), the beautiful daughter of a clayworker of lower status. Then, as this polarity is set up, it is further enhanced by a clayworkers' strike. Morwen must then decide where her loyalties lie.

During the novel, conventions of romance are used to maximum effect. In this sequence, used as a prologue, we learn how Ben and Morwen meet at midnight by the Larnie Stone (a fictional version of the Longstone). This marvellously chimerical section epitomises Cornwall's importance in historical romance as as place of difference, mystery and unconventional behaviour:

He pulled her to him, furious to be playing this idiotic game. He was not in-experienced, but he was at a loss in handling this delicious young woman with the looks of an innocent and a wanton at the same time, especially since all the differences between them decreed that they should stay worlds apart. But they were not worlds apart. They were here, beneath a great yellow moon, beside a standing stone with magic powers. A trysting place... and this was Cornwall, where anything was possible. And ancient ways were stronger than the laws of etiquette at that moment... (1986, i)

61

It is hard to remember that this is not West Cornwall but the clayland. Typically, landscape is central to the novel. After a visit to the clayey, waggon-cluttered streets of St. Austell, Morwen retreats to Hensbarrow Downs itself:

> Above her were the huddles of the clayworker's cottages, built in short rows of fours, all adjoining one another and set at angles to give a higgle-piggledly appearance... Beyond and around the clayworkers' cottages, rose the pale mounds of the spoil heaps, made eerily beautiful by moonlight, and as much a landmark for a returning clayworker in his cups as any standing stone on the moor. In sunlight, the spoil heaps glinted with the discarded small mineral deposits... The exhilaration of the day had whipped up more colour in Morwen's cheeks. She untied her bonnet, letting the breeze spin through her hair, and loved the wild freedom of it. (6)

With the strike quelled and the father's rage abated, Morwen and Ben are united and begin a 'new dynasty' (281), yet 'Fate's not done with them yet' (1987,i). In the sequel *Clay Country* (1987), Morwen is now mistress of Killigrew House in the heart of the industry, but there are problems: her love for Ben is just as strong as his for her, but she is unable to give him a son. In an incredible final chapter, the birth of Morwen and Ben's son occurs on the same night as the end of the Crimean war. The clay people's Celtic otherness is again expressed:

> The celebration fires still burned brightly as dusk began to enhance the moorland scene. The flames leapt skywards, and townspeople far below stood outside houses and taverns and looked upwards to enjoy the spec-tacle. And many wished they had been born with the same lack of inhibi-tions as the clay folk. (1987, 310)

The most recent manifestation of the romancing of the clay country comes from E.V. Thompson, a popular and prolific writer who lives just outside the area. In *Ruddlemoor* (1995), he switches from the concerns of his earlier fiction (Bodmin Moor, smuggling, fishing and tin or copper mining) to the clay industry. *Ruddlemoor* marks a shift in the saga of the Retallick family which began with *Chase the Wind* (1977), and is likely to become the first of a fresh series of novels following the fortunes of the Retallick family in the clay region. It contains all the conventions of romanticisation which I have outlined in this chapter. Josh Retallick and his wife, Miriam, take on a new challenge when they become owners of Ruddlemoor china clay works (in the locale of the Wheal Martyn China Clay Heritage Centre), but Josh has to leave to attend to a family tragedy in South Africa. When he returns it is in the knowledge that his youngest grandson, Ben Retallick, will follow him in the family business. An established clay narrative then develops. Ben's arrival rocks the local com-munity and rival clay owners see him as an unwelcome threat. He then encounters a stock set of female clay icons. Deirdre Tresillian is a member of the landed gentry and takes advantage of Ben's naivety, whilst Jo, a poverty-stricken young widow, brings out his protective instincts. Ben can have the pick of the clayland women -- but he eventually chooses the humble maid Lily. All this happens as Ruddlemoor enters troubled times, and the clayworkers plan to strike over pay and conditions. *Ruddlemoor* clearly epitomises the depiction of the china clay region in contemporary historical romance.

Pyramids on the box
The process of reconstructing the clay country in popular forms has not been restricted to fiction. The landscape was frequently used in the 1970s for science-fiction television programmes such as *Dr. Who* and *Blake's 7* (Haining 1983), which exploited its surreal features. A not dissimilar view put to a very different purpose was presented in the BBC drama documentary on Jack Clemo, *A Different Drummer*, televised in 1980 with Robert Duncan in the leading role. The drama, set in the 1920s and 1930s, explored the difficulties of the blind and deaf poet, following Clemo's life from his childhood and his encounters with teenage sweethearts, to his intermittent and then permanent blindness. Both the news of Jack's father's death in the opening sequences and the scenes in the schoolhouse took us intimately into Clemo's early life. The overriding image was of a strange and powerful figure crouched in a wild landscape. The weird scenery pervaded the whole drama, reinforcing Clemo's own physical disabilities, and leaving the viewer in no doubt as to why Clemo was forced -- in the words of Thoreau -- to follow 'a different drummer'. However, good as it was, such a combination of documentary and drama has its limitations in that it did not altogether convey the wider clay community.

A more satisfying media construct of the clay-mining region was Tom Clarke's 1975 play for television, *Stocker's Copper*. The text was a fictionalisation of the extremely bitter and violent 'White Country Dispute', the Cornish Clay Strike of 1913, when the clay workers took industrial action over pay and conditions. The events of the dispute are already well-preserved in the ballad 'The Cornish Clay Strike', purporting to have been written by an unskilled labourer:

Perhaps its interesting and I guess that you would like
to hear an account of the CORNISH CLAY STRIKE.
Well, the men at CARNE STENTS were first to down tools,
And for taking that action were counted as fools...
...But as you see their policy proved a blessing in disguise,
and has proved to the world that they really were wise,
VIRGINIA men were next, and they HAD THE NERVE
and around the FAL VALLEY they all did serve. (Restormel Arts 1993, 43)

Its sixty-four stanzas reveal how the strikers were brought to order by a police contingent from South Wales. The breaking up of the clay-workers' picket was particularly brutal and resulted in the near death of some of the strikers:

The Glamorgan police were all watching their tricks,
And demanded like pickets to give up their sticks,
When they caught a small number down in a by-lane,
They acted like demons or men gone insane.

Poor Vincent, our leader, was the first they attacked,
Was truncheoned and batoned and his poor head they cracked;
I suppose they then left him by the roadside for dead
But they couldn't kill his spirit though they opened his head...(*ibid.* 45).

The BBC production managed to convey the specialness and difference of the region with a number of signifiers. The Welsh policeman, Griffiths, notices the hills are white ('Snow in August boys!' he shouts to his colleagues on the train) and in an instant realises the contrast between the tempting 'Cornish Riviera' of the Great Western Railway Posters and the cold, stark landscape he is now entering. He realises though how much he has in common with the striker Manuel Stocker, when he sees the Cornishmen hard at work mining, going to chapel and singing, for they are Welsh attributes as well as Cornish ones. Eventually their Celtic commonality is to unite them.

What strikes the viewer most about this romanticisation of a serious event in clay area history, is the stark visual contrast of the black uniforms of the police with the dazzling whiteness of the landscape when the strikers and policemen line up for a game of rugby. In another sequence, Stocker and his wife escape the pressure of the strike by taking a walk on the moors, but even this does not prevent the industry intruding upon them. Even in this isolated place the distant triangle of the tip frames the picture.

Thus, throughout the twentieth century, Cornwall has increasingly capitalised on its dramatic landscapes and romantic aura. The china clay mining region will provide a new brightness for that aura. It is a geographically manageable place, ideally suited to demonstrate stark and simple contrasts, say between rich clay mine owners and poor clayworkers. Historical romance works by valuing the landscape in which it is set and by projecting characters' emotions on to it. What stranger and more evocative landscape is there than this one?

Resisting romance

The special quality of the region has continued to be expressed in emerging fictions. Inadvertantly, my own 1991 novel *Clay*, in which a dialogue takes place between Cornwall's past and present, has actively contributed to this romanticisation, a process I still consider myself to be working through as a novelist. My intention in using the device of a fictional journal to counterpoint the reality of the clay region before the mining began, was to offer a more realistic vision of the impact of the industry upon the landscape and people:

This was the clay land. Somewhere else. This was no Cornwall. Cornwall
was golden sand, azure seas and picture postcard harbours. Cornwall was a
world away. A world away where things were done differently: prettier than
this. (3)

Perhaps like other literary centres of Cornwall (Fowey, St. Ives and Boscastle), I have unknowingly imposed on this part of Cornwall another mental construct and folkloric past for the consumption of indigenous and tourist populations alike. It might even have been an act of unconscious collusion on my part.

The clay region has been interpreted more recently in the field of poetry. Bill Headdon's anthology *Cornish Links/Kevrennow Kernewek* details a poetic journey through the landscape in work by Julie Burville and Pamela Johnson (1993, 6 and 9). Meantime, Pol Hodge's exploration of the clay landscape in Cornish concentrates on the crucial connection between place and language:

Henwyn mas y'n taves Kernewek,
Ha kemmysk a frynkek has sowsnek,
Henbarrow, Roche ha Rosdowrek.

Kekeffrys, Steneklys, Togarrek,
Karledan, Nansbyglan ha Hornek.
Kann mes poes, pub le loes, morethek.

Good names in the Cornish tongue,
and a mixture of French and English,
Hensbarrow, Roche and Restowrack.

Also, Stenalees, Tolgarrick,
Carludden, Nanpean and Hornick,
-- bright but heavy, -- every place grey, broody. (1995, 98-99)

In 1995, I began to write a sequence of poems titled *The Hensbarrow Homilies*. These poems reflect further on the landscape which has borne much of my work. 'The Refiner at Blackpool' exemplifies my current response to the clay landscape; the vision is one of a community undergoing massive spiritual change:

And when at last shared work's vibrations cease
Sharing itself will fade (as in the clay villages nearby)
with Cookworthy's dream, with Wesley's long since ghosts
down history's pit. Difference and indifference will untie
taut bonds of work that cramp yet mined here a community;
then old Cornwall will have to start a New. (Unpublished)

Despite my reservations about romanticisation, it seems that other industrial centres in the British Isles have found it is a natural part of our culture for us to integrate and reinterpret such a community's significant pasts. They are important because they have held and sustained so many lives in them. Traditional industries carry with them a whole mythology and shared ideology which cannot be denied or ignored.

It is difficult to predict the new texts which may emerge from the clayland. E.V. Thompson may offer a sequel to *Ruddlemoor* and certainly more poets will continue to be inspired by the landscape. Clemo's death in 1994 has meant that his collected body of work will increase in status and the landscape might come to assume the mythic proportions of Thomas Hardy's Wessex. What is clear, however, is that the growth of clayland literature and the romanticisation of the pits and tips of Hensbarrow Downs is no insignificant cultural development. Rather, it comes at a crucial moment of Cornish literary history, and arrives as a result of the recent industrial history and realist fiction of the clayland meeting head on with transplanted historical romance. The future will be one in which these sometimes conflicting, sometimes complementary literary forms vie for an incredible landscape.

BIBLIOGRAPHY

Arthur, Marshel. *The Autobiography of a China Clay Worker 1879-1962*. Federation of Old Cornwall Societies, 1995.
Bell, Ian A. *Peripheral Visions: Images of Nationhood in Contemporary British Fiction*. Cardiff: University of Wales Press, 1995.
Clemo, Jack. *Wilding Graft*. London: Chatto and Windus, 1948.
_____. 'The Clay Dump'. Ed. Denys Val Baker. *Cornish Short Stories*. Harmondsworth: Penguin, 1976.
_____. *The Bouncing Hills*. Redruth: Dyllansow Truran, c.1979.
_____. *The Shadowed Bed*. Tring: Lion Publishing, 1986.
_____. *Selected Poems*. Newcastle upon Tyne: Bloodaxe Books, 1988.
Godden, Rumer. *China Court*. London: Macmillan, 1961.
Haining, Peter. *Doctor Who: A Celebration*. London: W.H. Allen, 1983.
Halliday, F. E. *Richard Carew of Antony: the Survey of Cornwall*. London: Andrew Melrose, 1953.
Hardie, Melissa. Ed. *A Mere Interlude: some literary visitors in Lyonesse*. Newmill: The Patten Press, 1992.
Headdon, Bill. Ed. *Cornish Links/Kevrennow Kernewek*. Tunbridge Wells: Kernow Poets Press, 1993.
Hillier, David. *Trevanion*. London: Warner Books, 1994.
Hocking, Joseph. *What Shall it Profit a Man?* London: Hodder and Stoughton, 1924.
Hodge, Pol, Alan M. Kent and Bert Biscoe. *Berdh Amowydh Kernewek / Modern Cornish Poets*. St. Austell: Lyonesse Press, 1995.
Holmes, A.W. *Out of this Fury*. London: Hutchinson, 1944.
Lee, A. Robert. *Other Britain, Other British: Contemporary Multicultural Fiction*. London: Plato Press, 1995.
Kent, Alan M. *Clay*. Launceston: Amigo, 1991.
_____. *Out of the Ordinalia*. St. Austell: Lyonesse Press, 1995.
_____. 'Smashing the sandcastles: realism in contemporary Cornish fiction.' Ed. Ian A. Bell. *Peripheral Visions* [qv].
_____. *The Hensbarrow Homilies and Other Poems*. St. Austell: Lyonesse Press, forthcoming.
Lowerson, John. 'Celtic Tourism -- Some Recent Magnets.' *Cornish Studies* 2 (1994): 128-137.
Ludwig, Hans-Werner and Lothar Fietz. *Poetry in the British Isles: Non-Metropolitan Perspectives*. Cardiff: University of Wales Press, 1995.
Murdoch, Brian. *Cornish Literature*. Cambridge: D.S. Brewer, 1993.

Orme, Nicholas. *Nicholas Roscarrock's Lives of the Saints: Cornwall and Devon.* Exeter: Devon and Cornwall Record Society, 1992.

Reddicliffe, Sheila. *The Cornish Mistress.* Callington: Lightbody Publications, 1992.

Restormel Arts Clay Stories Project. *Tales from the White Mountains.* St. Austell: Restormel Arts/ Verbal Arts Cornwall, 1993.

Rowse, A.L. *A Cornish Childhood.* London: Jonathan Cape, 1942.

Summers, Rowena. *Killigrew Clay.* London: Severn House Publishers, 1986.

_____. *Clay Country.* London: Severn House Publishers, 1987.

Summertime Specials. A Programme of Green Tourism Events 1996. St. Austell: Borough of Restormel, 1996.

Thompson, E.V. *Chase the Wind.* London: Macmillan, 1977.

_____. *Ruddlemoor.* London: Headline, 1995.

Thurlow, Charles. *White Gold from Cornwall and Devon: an illustrated account of the modern China Clay Industry.* St. Austell: Hillside, 1992.

Val Baker, Denys. *A View from Land's End: writers against a Cornish background.* London: William Kimber, 1982.

Westland, Ella. 'The passionate periphery: Cornwall and romantic fiction.' Ed. Ian A. Bell. *Peripheral Visions* [qv].

Wheal Martyn China Clay Heritage Centre. Promotional Leaflet, 1996.

'A Silent, Desolate Country': images of Cornwall in Daphne du Maurier's *Jamaica Inn*

Helen Hughes

In the following chapter I have linked the dual nature of Cornwall, as presented in Daphne du Maurier's Jamaica Inn, with ideas of 'Englishness' to be found in Robert Colls and Philip Dodds' Englishness: Politics and Culture 1880 - 1920 (1986). Here Philip Dodds argues that the idea of Englishness as constituted at this time had a marginalising effect on such minorities as the Celtic races of Britain, and Alun Howkins similarly contends that 'Englishness' was a concept particularly associated with the South East.

My study of The Historical Romance (1993) shows that this genre in particular was used in the late nineteenth and early twentieth centuries to create a myth of Englishness and accomplish the complementary marginalisation of many British regions. When historical romance became more particularly a female-oriented genre in the hands of Georgette Heyer and her followers, the same features can be seen in their work but less emphasised, foregrounding instead the element of gender relations. Connotations which had helped to build an image of a region now helped to construct gender roles, as described in the work of such critics of popular romance as Janice Radway and Tania Modleski.

In Jamaica Inn du Maurier merged images of Cornwall with those of the men who lived there in such a way as to make the landscape a setting for relationships typical of Gothic romance. This chapter gives an account of the semiotics of the portrayal of landscape to show how such merging is accomplished.

Jamaica Inn (1936), Daphne du Maurier's fourth novel, is a historical novel with a real setting: the village of Altarnun on the verge of Bodmin Moor and Jamaica Inn itself are genuine places, despite the disclaimer with which du Maurier prefaced the book. The legend of the smuggling which took place at the inn is still mentioned in guides and coffee table books.

The social setting, unusually for a romantic novel, is one of farmers and inn-keepers rather than gentry; there is a magistrate and a vicar, but the main concern is with a lower order of society, which adds to the impression of realism. The story itself, however, has strong elements of fantasy which are appropriate for romance: the plot concerns an orphan, Mary Yellan, who takes refuge with her uncle, the landlord of Jamaica Inn. Here she witnesses a number of melodramatic incidents: a hanging, the distribution of smuggled goods, and finally the decoying of a ship onto the coastal rocks and the murder and robbery of the crew. The adventure centres round her efforts to bring the gang to justice, which she eventually does, aided by her uncle's brother, Jem Merlyn, and there is a further element of melodrama when the uncle is shot and Mary is kidnapped by the murderer -- to be rescued by Jem.

There is a strong atmosphere of evil and horror surrounding the action. Although the plot of the book has similarities with earlier romances which dealt with smugglers or outlaw gangs, such as R. D. Blackmore's *Lorna Doone*, it is differentiated by its compression, dramatic intensity and strong atmosphere. It is akin to the earlier romances, however, in being a regional novel and constructing a strong image of the region in which it is set. One of the interesting aspects of such constructions is the varying uses to which they can be put by the writers in different periods.

Historical novels of the nineteenth and early twentieth centuries painted regions such as the West Country or Yorkshire as exotic, wild and marginal. By doing so they emphasised the differences between the rural community and what might be called 'metropolitan' England, which might be viewed as the English 'norm'. *Jamaica Inn* builds an idea of Cornwall as an ancient, wild and marginal land, but uses the image for different purposes: to provide the setting for melodrama and romance, with an erotic undercurrent. The earlier romances created a picture of a picturesque community whose attraction sprang from nostalgia and which had the effect of confirming a concept of 'Englishness' which privileged the South East.

Alun Howkins has claimed that between 1870 and 1900, at a time when the financial operations of the City of London were becoming more important than northern manufacturing industry, an image of essential Englishness began to be developed which was specifically rural and drawn from the south of England. In part, it may be seen as a counterbalance to the growing sense of London's centrality at a time when its slums, vice and criminality were giving increased cause for concern. For Howkins, 'Englishness' is a political concept; the rural population of England was seen as an essentially cohesive community such as that described by George Sturt in *The Wheelwright's Shop*. 'Purity, decency, goodness, honesty... are closely identified with the rural South' (Howkins 63), offering a model to those concerned about the growth of London.

In *Jamaica Inn*, set in the immediately pre-industrial period of the early nineteenth century when such a society might have been supposed to exist, this kind of image is associated with the south of Cornwall, and in particular with the area round Helston and Helford where Mary Yellan, the heroine, was brought up. This district and its community provide a kind of benchmark of human behaviour against which that of the dwellers on Bodmin Moor can be measured. Visions of her life there continually flash into Mary's mind and throw the terrible reality of life on the moor into relief. Thus, at Christmas,

in Helford people would be decorating with holly and evergreen and mistletoe. There would be a great baking of pastry and cakes, and a fattening of turkeys and geese. The little parson, wearing a festive air, would beam upon his world, and upon Christmas Eve he would ride up after tea to drink sloe gin at Trelowarren. Did Francis Davey decorate his church with holly and call down a blessing upon the people? One thing was certain: there would be little gaiety at Jamaica Inn. (Ch. 8, 131)

Helford at Christmas sounds like something from a Christmas card, a stereotype of seasonal cheer, but the effect is to emphasise the strangeness of Francis Davey, vicar of Altarnun, and the miseries of Jamaica Inn. Though Helford 'Englishness' runs through the text, and perhaps accounts for Mary Yellan's particular characteristics of bravery, frankness and decency, the dominant image is much harsher, belonging to the image of the countryside provided by Sir Walter Scott and his followers.

In *The Historical Novel* Georg Lukacs has suggested that Scott's fiction portrays the essential form of a society at a time of change, the real interest of his novels deriving from his portrait of a dying generic or clan-based society giving place to the rising bourgeoisie. One such portrait is painted in *Guy Mannering*, where the account of Liddesdale sports and farmhouse life gives an impression of a rural community whose way of life was about to sink into the past, and which is being given a needful memorial in the hero's account of it. In drawing a picture of a traditional and in some ways primitive society at a time of change, Scott provided a pattern for future historical novels, including *Jamaica Inn*. Books by writers such as R. D. Blackmore (*Lorna Doone*) or J. Meade Falkner (*Moonfleet*) are set in communities very much like those described by Scott.

In Blackmore's *Lorna Doone*, for example, the narrator John Ridd memorialises the farming and fighting feats of his Exmoor community in the seventeenth century, comparing it continually with London and the future. In comparison with London, Exmoor fits the Howkins model well, though Blackmore's work was produced earlier in the century than the period Howkins discusses, and from the South West rather than the South East. The character of the country is very like that described by Howkins in some ways: in comparison with the Londoners whom John Ridd meets, the people of the moor are less worldly wise but infinitely more wholesome.

As far as the future is concerned, Exmoor seems destined for improvement. John Ridd frequently refers to what he has done for the region after the end of his story. Once settled as a wealthy farmer and the leader of the local community, he is able, for instance, to build roads which make the moor accessible to the outside world. By doing so he brings the people of Exmoor into the 'modern' world of the seventeenth century and closer to London. In Meade Falkner's *Moonfleet*, too, John Trenchard makes improvements to his village once he gains his fortune, making it a thriving place to live, and provides a beacon to shipping. All these changes are portrayed as progress, emphasising the backwardness which accompanied the charm of their earlier state. On the other hand, there is a doubtful quality about a progress which destroys so much that is good. The people of Moonfleet and Exmoor are portrayed as unique individuals, far from perfect but with an agreeable combination of simplicity and cunning, and a mutual supportiveness which makes their communities seem very attractive.

The community which gathers at Jamaica Inn is very different. The people of Bodmin Moor who come so furtively to the inn are 'the dregs of the country ... dirty for the most part, ragged, ill-kept, with matted hair and broken nails' and, as the reader is to learn, murderers as well (289). Whereas John Trenchard, narrating the story of Moonfleet, emphatically denies that the villagers would actively harm a ship, and in fact they frequently risk their lives to save wrecked sailors, the gang at Jamaica Inn are wreckers who lure ships on to the rocks of North Cornwall by placing false lights to mislead them.

There is no nostalgic regret, therefore, for this community: but, like those in the other books, it is a society caught at a moment of change, just before it disappears forever. Progress -- undoubted, in this case -- is spreading, and the world of Bodmin Moor will soon be part of a law-abiding England. As they drive back from Launceston on Christmas Eve Francis Davey informs Mary Yellan:

> The false lights have flickered for the last time, and there will be no more wrecks ... [We] were informed at last that His Majesty's government was prepared ... to patrol the coasts... there will be a chain across England, Mary, that will be very hard to break. (Ch. 10, 200-1)

The benefits of law are thus associated with the future, and 'Cornishness' recedes into the past.

Even though, far from needing a memorial, it seems that the ways of the Cornish wreckers are best forgotten, their story does provide the region with a wild, exciting past which adds to its attractions. It is the darker side of the image of Cornwall which the region shares with places in other romances. Exmoor has its Doones and Scott's Liddesdale its robbers. Even in Moonfleet, despite John Trenchard's disclaimer, members of the community have been responsible for the deaths of those who have tried to stop the smuggling, or even simply found out about it.

Rural English idyll and a wilder, more dangerous image therefore co-exist in other books but in the Cornwall of *Jamaica Inn* the two halves of the picture are cut cleanly in half, with the wilder image predominant. The dichotomy is complete: there is either crime or farming, with nothing in between. (There is no reference to mining or fishing, for instance.) Once the wreckers have been defeated, farming would take over: Mary thought that 'Here, on this stretch of moor, farmers would till their plot of soil' (202), and Bodmin Moor, no doubt, will become like Helford. The split runs through the whole story. Aunt Patience could have married a farmer near Helford, but chooses Joss Merlyn, an 'up-country' man from the moor. Mary herself, at the end of the book, is faced with the choice between returning to Helford and going off with a horse-thief from the moors, Jem Merlyn. The choices the women make are significant: in both cases, though they pine for Helford, they opt for the moor-men.

Du Maurier evokes a picture of Helford which is attractive in its soft beauty: where even the rain is gentle and the soil is grateful for it. Helford, however, has no part in the actual story, which is set in bleak surroundings indeed. Bodmin Moor sounds like a tourist department's nightmare. But just as Exmoor is for twentieth century visitors the land of the Doones, not of John Ridd and his neighbours, so it is the bleakness of Cornwall which gives it its romantic character and draws people as the moor-men draw the women in the book. Du Maurier revels in the details of gloomily impending tors and stunted trees.

The first description of the place provides the pattern, the details of which are to be repeated over and over again. As Mary travels towards the inn the coach traverses a desolate, rainy landscape:

> [the rain] spat against the windows with...venom...No
> trees, no lanes, no cluster of cottages or hamlet, but
> mile after mile of bleak moorland, dark and untraversed,
> rolling like a desert land to some unseen horizon. (21)

This is 'a dark and silent land' under 'a black sky' (21) and the tors are 'sinister and austere': when Mary later sees Kilmar Tor, in the shadow of which the Merlyns had been born, she finds its slopes a 'venomous grey' descending to 'deep and treacherous marsh' (51). Throughout the book the details -- dark colours, austere stone, the wind eternally blowing and a sense of malice and treachery in the very hills and marshes -- are insistently repeated.

If the picture seems unpleasant on the surface, it has its attractive qualities. Even though Mary finds the place 'grim and hateful', she nevertheless notices a 'challenge in the air' which is 'more quenching and sweeter than a draught of cider'(42). The effect is bracing: in this description of Mary's first morning at the inn, there is even some rare colour and a sense of vivid movement as the clouds provide a varied, perpetual shifting of light and shadow, and the wind brings a sparkle to Mary's eyes. The abundance of detail suggests close observation, and an author with a deep affection for the Cornish landscape she is describing. Avril Horner and Sue Zlosnik feel that the moor represents for Mary a place where she can 'express a self that is masculine in relation to cultural definitions of gender' (5) -- exploring a 'desire to be differently female' that Alison Light has seen as 'central to du Maurier's best-known novels' (166). Bodmin Moor promises adventure, and space for self-discovery.

A further dimension is added by comments which stress the age of the landscape and the impression it gives of being haunted and in some ways alien to humanity. Here again du Maurier is using a technique employed in earlier romances set in isolated regions. Blackmore's Exmoor, for instance, is also portrayed as a wild, fearful place with its dark heath and marshes, cliffs and secret valleys, made more fearful by traditional tales of the devil and witchcraft. Meade Falkner filled *Moonfleet* with traditional rhymes and stories of ghosts, especially the 'Mandrive', supposed to haunt the caves where John Trenchard hid.

The effects in *Jamaica Inn* are even more startling and awe-inspiring. The past is omni-present in the hills -- a past so ancient that it predates humanity itself. Despite the 'strange winds [which] blew from nowhere' and moan in the crevices of the rocks, there is 'a silence on the tors that belonged to another age...when man did not exist and pagan footsteps trod the hill.'(50) And if the reader should ask who the pagans were who existed before mankind, the answer is clear by the end of the book: these are the old gods themselves, still haunting the moors. In the icy peace of the night when Mary escapes from Jamaica Inn, they 'sleep undisturbed', but later they move through her dreams as she sleeps uneasily on Roughtor. The rocks seem to become like gods, with faces 'inhuman, older than time, carved and rugged like granite'.(334) They move towards her, their stone eyes blind, as though to crush her. The passage is a genuinely frightening one, and there is a sense that the dream has hit on a sort of truth. The tors of Bodmin Moor may not be haunted, but they seem instinct with a consciousness of a kind, and a frightening power.

The inhabitants of the moor are aware of themselves as insubstantial and impermanent by the side of such presences: Mary is 'a leaf in the wind' and senses a spirit which has moved into the inn after her uncle's death and cares nothing for 'the poor dead body lying there' (289). For Francis Davey, the church of Altarnun seems a recent, almost ephemeral structure; the bones of the ancient people which lie beneath its pavement are more enduring and more real. The Merlyns know the moor and the marsh can kill, as the bog swallowed up their brother. Nevertheless, the moor people are shaped by their landscape as well as made afraid by it. When they first meet, Mary surmises that Joss Merlyn has

> grown athwart like the stunted broom, with the bloom blown out of him by the north wind...no human being could live in this wasted country and remain like other people; the very children would be born twisted, like the blackened shrubs of broom...Their minds would be twisted, too, their thoughts evil, dwelling as they must between marshland and granite, harsh heather and crumbling stone. (21)

The close relationship between landscape and people, and the idea of the shaping spirit of nature (however malevolent) is a romantic concept which is used to reinforce the special quality of this landscape and community. The Cornish are presented as a unique race, appropriate to their landscape, and the reference to pagans and the old gods who speak a language Mary 'could not understand' (334) is a reminder that Cornwall is one of the remaining Celtic strongholds, with a Celtic language of its own. The image is obviously one which adds to the attractiveness of the region but it has its dangers. Philip Dodd has argued that, in the last decades of the nineteenth century and the beginning of the twentieth, an image of the Celtic nation not dissimilar to du Maurier's was constituted in opposition to an idea of 'Englishness' which was sited in institutions such as the public schools and the older universities. Dodd contends that

> there is certainly evidence to support the thesis that
> Englishness and the national culture was reconstituted
> in order to incorporate and neuter ... various groups
> ... who threatened the dominant social order. (2)

One such group was the Irish, and they and the Celtic nations of the British Isles in general were presented in a way which to some extent excluded them from 'the dominant social order'. They were presented as belonging to the past and therefore more 'primitive': closer to the ways of our ancestors than were the people of 'metropolitan England'. In many ways the stereotype which defined them was flattering, but it was also marginalising, suggesting that the Celtic peoples did not belong in the seats of power.

Du Maurier's picture of the Cornish can be considered, therefore, one which suggests their inferiority and subordination as well as their unique, special qualities. Perhaps this is how du Maurier herself, for all her love of Cornwall, saw it: as sealed off from the 'main' part of England, with all its sources of power. Certainly the heroines of her two best-known books leave it behind them -- the heroine of *Rebecca* to wander Europe with Maxim, and Mary Yellan to go with Jem, setting her face towards the Tamar and the country beyond: 'the midlands where the people are rich and ahead of everyone'. (23) Cornwall, meanwhile, is left to its cordon of customs officers, who will keep its people safe but also extend the English hegemony to the region, perhaps destroying all but the last vestiges of those qualities which make it, as a place, so intriguing.

This is not to denigrate what du Maurier was attempting in her novel, the first of her books to make a significant impact on the public. *Jamaica Inn* is transitional: du Maurier's work can be divided into tales of smuggling and pirates, and modern Gothic romances, and *Jamaica Inn* has elements of both. The Gothic elements necessitate an impressive landscape; even though as an image of place du Maurier's presentation of Cornwall may be marginalising, the image forms a highly appropriate background for a story of terror and imagination. To create a Gothic atmosphere, the grimmer side of the Cornish picture was necessary.

The power of the Gothic romance derives from the relationships in the novel and in particular those between the heroine and the chief male characters. To achieve its specific blend of disturbing and attractive qualities, the men need to be capable of being both protecting and frightening, and for such a characterisation it helps if they have a kinship with a harsh countryside. Both the Merlyn brothers have this, as the first description of Joss makes clear, and these two divide the function of hero between them. This function, according to Tania Modleski, is to create in the heroine a potent mixture of love and fear: potent because the fear adds an extra, troubling power to the love.

Jem, the true hero of the novel, has something of this quality: Mary is attracted to him, but he has a dangerous, reckless nature. Mary fears he may be allied with his brother as a wrecker, and, even near the end of the novel, she distrusts him, fearing he murdered Joss. As a character, however, he is shadowy by comparison with Joss, the wolf-like landlord of *Jamaica Inn*. Mary has every reason to hate Joss: she is in his power, she knows only too well the villainy of which he is capable, and she finds him personally disgusting: 'the thought of kissing him revolted her'. (25) Du Maurier makes clear enough, however, that there is a strong erotic element in her feelings of revulsion. She constantly notices his slim and graceful hands, and even after he has told her of his wrecking activities she notices that in his drunken sleep 'his long dark lashes swept his cheek like a fringe'. (157) She looks at Jem as she drives beside him to Launceston and thinks she may be seeing Joss as he was 'ten, twenty years ago'. (166) She dare not face her feelings towards Joss: the thought of his likeness to Jem she 'shutters' at the back of her mind. She has a similar reaction when, after Joss's brutal handling of her at the wreck which he forces her to watch, he tells her: 'If I'd been a younger man I'd have courted you, Mary --

74

aye, and won you, too' (247) and lays a finger on her lips. Once she is in bed she puts her own fingers to the place he had touched, and cries. Once again she pushes her feelings to the back of her mind, together with 'those dreams never acknowledged to the sturdy day'. (247)

The figure of Joss gains power from his likeness to the landscape, and the landscape itself gains a kind of erotic charge through its association with him. Germaine Greer has accused women who enjoy romances which feature brutal heroes of 'cherishing the chains of their bondage' (180), and it may be that because there is a sense of something forbidden, and perhaps slightly shameful, about such enjoyment, it runs deeper.

The image of Cornwall in *Jamaica Inn* is thus infused with a power which adds a deep attractiveness to its bleakness and harshness. But the image has an independence of the book in which it was developed, just as the similar image of harsh power created by Emily Bronte in her descriptions of landscape remains associated with the Yorkshire moors even for people who have not read *Wuthering Heights*. Part of the attraction of Cornwall will no doubt continue to be the paradoxical one of its bleak moorland spine. Many visitors who come to the region because of its English Riviera qualities go to the moors, as though by looking they can experience for themselves the highly charged emotional excitement of such novels as *Jamaica Inn*.

BIBLIOGRAPHY

Blackmore, R.D. *Lorna Doone*. 1869; London: Pan Books, 1967.

Colls, Robert and Philip Dodd. Eds. *Englishness: Politics and Culture 1880-1920*. London: Croom Helm, 1986.

Dodd, Philip. 'Englishness and the National Culture.' Eds. Colls and Dodd, *ibid.*

Du Maurier, Daphne. *Jamaica Inn*. London: Gollancz, 1936.

Falkner, J. Meade. *Moonfleet*. 1898; Oxford University Press [World's Classics Edition], 1993.

Greer, Germaine. *The Female Eunuch*. 1970; St Albans: Paladin, 1971.

Horner, Avril and Sue Zlosnik. *'I for this and this for me': Daphne du Maurier and 'regional' writing*. University of Salford: European Studies Research Institute. Working papers in Literary and Cultural Studies No.13. Salford, 1994.

Howkins, Alun. 'The Discovery of Rural England'. Eds. Colls and Dodd, *ibid.*

Hughes, Helen. *The Historical Romance*. London: Routledge, 1993.

Light, Alison. *Forever England: Femininity, Literature and Conservatism between the Wars*. London: Routledge, 1991.

Lukacs, Georg. *The Historical Novel*. 1937; [translated 1962] Harmondsworth: Penguin, 1969.

Modleski, Tania. *Loving With a Vengeance: mass-produced fantasies for women*. Hamden: Archon Books, 1982.

Radway, Janice A. *Reading the Romance*. Chapel Hill: University of North Carolina Press, 1984.

Places Only Dreamers Know: the significance of North Cornwall in the lives of Thomas, Emma and Florence Hardy

Simon David Trezise

The rich tradition of criticism about the life and work of Thomas Hardy includes three tendencies undergoing gradual revision. The first tendency is to present Hardy as mainly a novelist whose literary version of Wessex is mostly derived from Dorset. I join the increasing movement presenting him as not only a novelist but a poet-dramatist whose personal life, prose and verse owe much to his short though intense experience of Cornwall. The second tendency explores Hardy and place in ways that often contribute more to topographical writing and local history than to what is attempted in the following chapter: a literary and cultural perspective tracing a little of the complex inter-action between imagination, ideology and place. The third tendency consists of a biographical version of Hardy's Cornwall which owes much to his own self-portrait and to the views of his second wife Florence, a woman with an understandably partial picture of her predecessor, Emma. Work by Robert Gittings and most recently, Michael Millgate, has helped us to penetrate beneath Hardy's self-image and to treat Florence with a degree of sympathy; Emma has still only partly emerged from gossip and scholarship as a human figure with a valid viewpoint. The incomplete historical record, partly resulting from the destruction of Emma's writings, can only be corrected with informed speculation. However, that does not justify ignoring those surviving parts of Emma's published and unpublished work which help to close the gaps in our knowledge. Emma's attempts to write verse do not qualify her for a major role in the recent critical re-evaluation of Victorian women poets. Her diary and unpublished story inspired by Cornwall certainly deserve more attention from both a literary and biographical viewpoint. The following argument, within the limits of a short chapter, contributes to the continuing process of revising the relationship in Hardy-studies between novelist and poet, Dorset and Cornwall, topography and ideological views of place, his story and her story of Lyonesse.

It is easy to find the Cornwall on the map that is both reflected and imaginatively transformed in Hardy's prose and verse, including the novel *A Pair of Blue Eyes* published in 1873, the well-known elegies of 1912-13 and the drama entitled *The Famous Tragedy of the Queen of Cornwall* which was conceived in 1870, begun in 1916 and finally completed in 1923. Familiarity with these texts and the relevant landscapes will enable you to appreciate the relationship between the fiction and the fact, between 'West Endelstow' and St. Juliot church, 'Castle Boterel' and Boscastle, 'Dundagil' and Tintagel, 'Condol's Crown' and Condolden Barrow. It is less easy to find your way through the tangle of conflicting testimony as to what this territory signified in the minds of the three Hardys who lived there, visited there and re-created it in words. Thomas Hardy's Cornwall is the product not only of his own invention but also of the vision of his first wife, Emma Lavinia Gifford, and his second wife Florence Emily Dugdale. However, their contribution to Cornwall was made with little acknowledgement from Thomas and often under his careful control. Thomas does not draw attention to Emma's role in copying out the manuscript of *A Pair of Blue Eyes* or the way in which her Cornish diary is assimilated by his verse and edited when included in his life story. Florence's name was put on *The Life of Thomas Hardy*, which helps to form the public perception of the Hardys' Cornwall, but as we now know with the benefit of hindsight, Florence's words were mostly dictated to her by Thomas. A more complex image of Thomas's literary and romantic Cornwall emerges when Florence and Emma are allowed, as far as the evidence allows, to speak for themselves. Using a polyphony of male and female voices to structure the following argument reveals how much a sense of place can owe to personal emotions and to gender. Very different Cornwalls appear in the following sequence as Thomas and Emma speak together, Florence speaks, Thomas speaks, and Emma is given the last word.

Emma and Thomas speak
    Emma the diarist frequently decided that Cornwall deserved the accolade of the words 'romance' or 'romantic'. These words are prominent when she describes her first meeting with Thomas at St. Juliot and their subsequent courtship conducted on the airy cliff-paths around Tintagel, Boscastle and Trebarwith Strand, paths so high that sea-birds are often glimpsed beneath rather than above the viewer. Emma re-creates this distinctive coastline with a skill that her poet-husband might have envied. Consult her original words to appreciate her verbal painting of white gulls, black choughs, grey puffins, and red sunsets (*Recollections* 17, 29-31). In the context of the Lyme Regis under-cliff, John Fowles has argued that coastal regions, because they defy cultivation, are one of the few places where the inhabitants of a crowded island can encounter a remnant of the wild, Nature least influenced by human control (Fowles 9). In North Cornwall, Emma found an external wilderness which she could use to express her internal landscape of feeling. Her words show fidelity to distinctive Cornish features and atmosphere but also link the wild sea birds to the wild as an escape from mediocrity into intensity.
    Thomas too romanticises his meeting with Emma and its inextricably connected Cornish setting. In the account of his life supposedly written by Florence but actually largely dictated to her by Thomas, he made his long-suffering amanuensis explain his reaction to the death of Emma's brother-in-law in the language of romance and fairy-tale. Thomas and Emma, we are told, realised that they had lost a living contact in picturesque Lyonesse, the land

that formed the appropriate backdrop for the most romantic episode of their lives (Florence Hardy, *Life* 155). This is a region of paradox: it is a real place where people die but it is also a magic land where love lasts for ever. In a letter of 1914 Thomas claimed that in spite of starting a new life with Florence after the death of Emma, the romance of Saint Juliot would stay with him, even if he lived to be a hundred (*Letters*, Volume 5, 15).

This romantic place that Emma and Thomas share exists on the edge, between the land and the sea in reality, and in the mind between the physical and the spiritual, the material and the atmospheric, life and death, the conscious and the unconscious. Emma's erotic yet spiritualised evocation of Tintagel, as poetic as her husband's better known verse, mixes a sensual world of masculine rocks and rising foam with a metaphysical world where birds indulging in acrobatic revelry are compared to black and white souls (*Recollections* 26). In Thomas's well-known 1895 preface to his Cornish novel, the particular qualities of coastal sounds and light-effects lead us into a vision compounded of the ghostly, the deathly, the sensuous, the passionate, the dream-like and the mysterious. This is a place where the conscious mind discovers it is not master in its own house, that apparently conscious decisions may be pre-ordained by half understood processes. Emma's description of her first meeting with Thomas in the porch of St. Juliot Rectory presents her as falling under a spell, or experiencing a dream of the strange but familiar, the surprising that turns out to be pre-determined (*Recollections* 33). The words of Thomas and Emma perhaps hint that the sense of death is present here in diverse and powerful ways: including death as an end to conscious control and the death of desire in the very moment of its fulfilment. Also consider how much the trickster called 'memory' contributed to the creation of this strange, romantic land. Emma first met Thomas in 1870; her diary and many of his famous Cornish elegies were created in 1911-13.

Florence speaks

After Emma's death in 1912, Thomas claimed that Florence wanted to visit the cliff scenery where he had courted his first wife. In fact, Florence's letters reveal that she initially viewed Thomas's 1913 visit to St Juliot and the accompanying outpouring of elegiac verse as a symptom of psychological disturbance, a doomed attempt to re-create an idealised Emma and an idealised Cornwall. Florence bitterly and sceptically observed how Emma's niece only had to mention the melodic place-name 'Saint Juliot' to send Thomas on a mental voyage to romance-land. However, Florence did agree to accompany Thomas on his second, 1916 pilgrimage to the territory he called love's domain. Her writing suggests that she was susceptible to the enchanting beauty and legendary associations of the Cornish coast, even while she was aware of walking in Emma's footsteps, of entering the territory of a rival's romance. In 1929, long after Emma's death and shortly after Thomas's, Florence chose to make her own pilgrimage to Cornwall and was able to appreciate the beauty and distinctive character of St Juliot and Tintagel in spite of their connections with the first Mrs Hardy (Millgate 81-2, 87, 119, 301). Prior to this period, and especially during the times when Emma's ghost seemed to pose a threat to Florence's relationship with Thomas, the second Mrs Hardy was critical of Cornwall as a landscape of memory and romance. It is possible to briefly represent her counter-myth about Emma's and Thomas's Lyonesse by using some of the conventions of fiction to synthesise and condense her views. Arthur Quiller-Couch thought Hardy had turned his courtship of Emma into a fairy-tale: let this be the cue for an interpretation of Florence's words.

Once upon a time, far, far away in the land of Lyonesse, lived two Ugly Sisters: Helen Catherine and Emma Lavinia Gifford. These sisters hated each other but they did share a common goal: the attainment of perpetual married bliss with a member of the opposite sex. Helen could do no better than marry a gout-ridden clergyman 35 years older than herself called Caddell Holder. She and her sister went to live with him in the remote parish of St. Juliot in North Cornwall. There was even more difficulty in finding the ageing Emma a partner. Since they lived in such a remote, rural area, the choice of Handsome Princes was rather limited. They nearly succeeded in ensnaring an innocent local farmer but this plot was not successful and all hope seemed lost until a Handsome Pauper, called Thomas Hardy, arrived from a distant country to assist in the restoration of the local church. Thomas then fell under the spell of Emma, not knowing the dark secrets about her family's past. The fact was that her uncles were rascals and her father, John Attersoll Gifford, was a bankrupt and a drunkard. Her father's problems did not prevent him from dismissing Thomas as a churl unfit to marry the noble Emma. Despite the disapproval of the wicked father, Emma and Thomas took the fatal decision to marry. However, Thomas did not know the darkest secret of all in the background of his partner: there was a trait of inherited madness in her family. Yes, his bride was doomed to become insane. Instead of living happily ever after, he and Emma ended their days living in separate parts of Max Gate, a large, lonely castle, purpose-built by Prince Thomas. While Thomas was writing in his study he knew that Emma was the mad woman in his attic. Then a strange and marvellous event occurred: ugly Emma died but her ghost was transformed into a beautiful Princess. Thomas loved her ghost more than he had ever loved her when she was alive.

Allowing for an element of exaggeration, this account is substantially a picture of Cornwall and its aftermath as viewed from Florence's perspective (Meynell 296; Millgate 88, 193; Kay-Robinson 78; Gittings *Young Thomas Hardy* 185-6, 192; *The Older Hardy* 233). Benefiting from hindsight, the modern reader finds more truth in some elements of this fairy-tale than in the one created by Thomas and Emma. Florence's account of the Gifford family snobbery is not entirely the product of vested interests. Emma's Cornish diary and novella suggest that her class prejudice did not make Cornwall a romance to her as far as its people were concerned. Thomas's exploration of the Smith family in his novel and the condemnation of snobbery in 'I Rose and Went to Rou'tor Town' take him closer to the male working class figures in the Cornish landscape than Emma could reach. Also, Florence's exaggerations of the truth about the worst side of the Giffords are understandable from her point of view. She perceived that the powerful ghost of Thomas's romance with his previous wife was a threat to her own hope of romance, and consequently created a fiction to counter the fiction of an idealised past that obsessed her husband.

Nevertheless, the least accurate parts of Florence's account over-influenced the biographical exploration of Thomas Hardy's early life and started the process by which Emma was transformed into a monster. Florence's story partly qualifies as an anti- romance. The heroine is not living in a state of perpetual youth, the hero is the victim of deception. The place is not wild and remote in a way that suggests new possibilities for adventure but is only a prison that limits choices in love. Neither the protagonists nor the supporting cast in this melodramatic fairy tale are romantic in the sense of their appearance, their health or their treatment of others.

However, if 'romance', that portmanteau-word stuffed with many meanings, implies going beyond the limits of the normal, we can see Florence's account as a romantic anti-romance. Romance is a coin minted in a world of extremes: on one side is the dream of wish-fulfilment; on the other side, different but linked, is the wish that goes wrong, the nightmare. Florence's nightmare world is not pleasant but it is not dull. All of Florence's characters go beyond the normal limits. The men are not just flawed but villainous, the father-figure is not just in financial difficulties but legally bankrupt, and the heroine is not a little odd but clinically insane. While taking revenge on the ghost of Emma, she makes her at least as interesting as that other fictional stereotype in a nightmare-romance: Charlotte Bronte's Bertha Mason. Florence's anti-romance is based on the same principle as one kind of conventional romance: the secret of happiness is heterosexual love with one partner for all of your life. Failure to achieve this ambitious goal has devastating consequences.

Thomas speaks

Although Thomas cryptically suggested that Emma was an agnostic during her time in Cornwall, her writings do not suggest a bleak, godless universe. Her diary ends invoking Providence. The spiritual other-world that hovers in the background of Emma's Cornwall is not available to Thomas in the same form. Emma's is mystical with a Christian character. Thomas's is mystical with pagan connotations. He has to create a romance in a place ruled by an impersonal fate rather than Providence. In the most famous episode of his Cornish novel, Henry Knight is trapped on the perilous ledge of a Cornish cliff and confronts the visionless eyes of a fossil. Hardy places a trilobite in the Cornish cliff- scape so that he can explore Nature post Darwin's work on evolution and Lyell's on geology. Knight is rescued from the cliff not by divine intervention but by a rope made from the useful underwear of Elfride, the Emma-figure in the story (*A Pair of Blue Eyes*, Chs. 21-2, 206-7, 209-15). This is a Victorian cliff-hanger with a difference: the female rescues the male; the saviour is human not divine. This outlook is echoed in the well-known poem located nearby the cliff and entitled 'At Castle Boterel'. Here the ancient rocks on the road to Boscastle inspire Thomas to insist that their record of non-human and intimidating aeons of time mean nothing by comparison with their witness to his romance with Emma. Again, it is the human rather than the divine that offers hope.

Thomas's romance also differs from that of Emma in that her story, in her diary at least, has a conventional happy ending. Thomas' romantic territory merges with that of tragedy. In the preface to his Cornish novel, Tom refers to the tragic character of the Cornish coast and initially doubts whether this setting could be well used in writing of the Romantic mock-medieval kind. Emma wrote an unpublished novella called 'The Maid on the Shore' set in her contemporary Cornwall although with touches of an Arthurian past. Her fictional equivalent in Thomas's Cornish novel, Elfride, writes a romance that clearly belongs to an idealised past entitled 'The Court of King Arthur's Castle. A Romance of Lyonesse.' Henry Knight does not live up to his chivalric name in his smug review of Elfride's work. He had hoped to find romance renewed; instead he finds tired cliches about tournaments, towers, and unlikely adventures. However, Knight's fictional review also suggests that the Romance as a literary form need not degenerate into the incredible and the cliched. He wants to escape from the lack of Romantic tradition in modern writing, from monotonous details about the social scene and dull character analysis. He wants to find a writer who combines being an antiquarian with the imaginative, inventive powers necessary to explore the passionate, interior life (*A Pair of Blue Eyes*, Ch. 15, 144-5).

Although the review implies that the romancer with this ability is an extinct species who belongs, like his subject matter, in the past, Thomas attempted to resuscitate the Romance form in his re-telling of the legend of Tristram and Isolt in *The Famous Tragedy of the Queen of Cornwall*. The *Life* of Hardy suggests his awareness of Cornwall's existence as a poetic tradition as well as a geographic entity. Legendary and literary Lyonesse were firmly attached by tradition to the Tintagel that so impressed Thomas and Emma. Hardy described his first encounter with Tintagel as if it was a visit to King Arthur's Castle. The vivid memory of this visit lay smouldering in his poetic mind until he constructed his verse drama derived from the Tintagel legends (*Life* 78-9). His familiarity with the actual place is combined with a world of feeling, a world that undoubtedly owes much to Emma but also owes much to the Arthurian Cornwall invented by Malory, Gottfried von Strassburg and Tennyson. Cadell Holder's neighbour and contemporary, Parson Hawker of Morwenstow, also contributed to the creation of Arthurian Cornwall by his own poetry and by, he claimed, his inspiration of Tennyson. Hardy was aware of the medieval and Victorian, the national and local precedents for poeticising Tintagel. In this literary place, Thomas turns Emma's happy romance into Florence's world of Cornish madness.

Thomas's letters and several of his poems support Florence's caricature of Emma as mentally unstable. The figure of Emma the carriage driver is placed next to a figure of madness in the poem 'The Interloper'. The horse-drawn carriage, in which we imagine Emma, her sister and her brother in law, the green track descending to the puffins' lair: this is in keeping with North Cornwall as a wild garden of Eden. However, the poet adds a fourth figure, unseen at the time, but later to become visible as Hardy's marriage to Emma disintegrated: a mysterious, hollow voiced, mirthless creature, a presence which corrodes the best lives. Taken in isolation from the poem, this figure could refer to any of the many causes for the degeneration of a romance, including the changing of character with the passing of time or a failure to communicate. However, Hardy's obscure discussion with Vere Collins about the meaning of this poem could be interpreted to suggest that the spectre here is mainly intended to represent Emma's madness (25). In the wider context of the Hardys' Cornwall, there is a need to explore of whose madness we speak and what kind of madness it is.   It is easy to see why Malory's and Gottfried von Strassburg's Tristram would have appealed to Hardy. Tram Triste, or 'so sad', was like Hardy in almost succumbing to death at birth, before he had experienced life. Tristram's sadness was justified by his experiences but did not prevent him being a singer of beautiful songs. Like Hardy the regional writer sceptical of London society, Tristram is a knight who makes the snobs of Camelot regret their prejudices against the Cornish. Most significantly in this context, Tristram had his period of madness and it is madness brought on by love.

If he saw himself in Tristram, Thomas clearly saw Isolt in Emma. In a letter he specifically links Isolt with Tintagel and his visit there with his first wife. In a poem of 1921, 'Meditations on a Holiday', written during the long gestation of his Cornish play, he links past and present, legend and fact together. The narrator of the poem rejects the project of another visit to Cornwall on the grounds that Tristram and Isolt can no longer be found there. The young Hardy cannot be resurrected; the memory of Isolt-Emma is blurred by the marks of progress on the landscape. However, in Thomas's drama, the physical features and atmosphere of Emma's favoured Tintagel are still appropriate for evoking the landscape of the madness of love. Sea, wind, thunder and spurting spray accompany jealous King Mark's murder of Tristram, Isolt's self-murder and murder of the King. Isolt of the White Hands, Tristram's legal wife but not his true love, hears mad voices in the sound of the wind and waves (*The Famous Tragedy of the Queen of Cornwall* 69-71, 75).

However, it is in Malory's world that Hardy finds the perfect symbol for the madness that led to the tragedy of his own marriage and of many others. In both the Tristram legend and Hardy's modernised version of it, a love potion determines much of the action. Malory's Tristram makes a dangerous journey to Ireland in order to arrange a marriage between King Mark and Isolt. The bride's mother, knowing that this is no love match, sends a potion to ensure that Mark and Isolt will not only be married legally but also be true lovers. Unfortunately, it is Tristram and Isolt who by accident drink this potion. This subtle symbol concentrates in a single object the following notions: passion will not arise according to plan, those tied to each other by convention may not be tied by true feelings, once the potion is drunk its consequences cannot be avoided or undone, those inextricably linked by the potion are subject to arbitrary chance, their lack of control cannot be blamed on them. All the power of feelings to make humanity destroy what is socially sanctioned at the same time as denying responsibility for their actions is focussed in this one symbol.

Thomas also perceived another madness linked to the madness of love: the madness of society in thinking that human passion can be satisfactorily controlled by institutions and rules. Without undermining the genuine nature of his romance with Emma, Thomas the poet acknowledges in poems such as 'At the Word Farewell' that it might so easily have been different: she and he might have partaken of the potion of love with other partners. It is the force of the collision between social convention and true desire which leads to the deaths and tragedy of his play. The moments of sanity in the play occur when the two Isolts almost succeed in sinking their jealousy. They fail, but come closer to success than the jealous Mark. In this play and other poems Hardy shows admiration for those with the courage to behave unconventionally towards their rivals in love. Nevertheless, Hardy is aware of how the heady potion of love cannot be controlled and can lead to death and madness. The frequent quotations from the story of Hamlet and Ophelia in the Cornish novel make this point by allusion. The madness which corrodes love is easier to explore in the context of the play than in relation to 'The Interloper', although both fictions explore similar territory. This madness is not a medical condition, it applies to Thomas as well as Emma, to many men and many women. Elfride shares the potion with more than one suitor; Emma's diary may hint that she did likewise. Like Tristram, Hardy had at least two Isolts, as the references to his two wives in the dedication to his play makes clear. This doubling of the loved one suggests the promiscuous, obsessive, repetitive nature of human desire: Tristram is always faithful to Isolt -- wherever he finds her!

Emma speaks

In Emma's words, fate revealed to her by a fortune-telling gypsy of Cornwall or by a family servant in Plymouth, pre-ordains that she will marry Thomas. All roads lead to the institution of marriage. In Thomas's words, by implication, romance with one partner is not sufficient, but equally romance with more than one partner is shown as leading to death and suffering. Love, the dependency on a particular kind of relationship with others for happiness, is not escaped. However, there is a part of Emma's diary which suggests a world with a different principle.

While class divided Emma from her Cornish neighbours, gender brought her closer to them. Emma the diarist seems particularly interested in collecting the stories that preserve a woman's eye view of the world. She is excited to hear the views of a woman farmer (did this play a part in Thomas's creation of Bathsheba Everdene?). She enjoys conversing with an old woman spinning flax at a remote and ancient cottage near Tintagel. She is happy to recall her meeting with a lively, amusing woman, who told her stories about her youth and her experience of the hardships of domestic service (*Recollections* 26, 31-32). There were clearly limits to Emma's snobbery in these particular contexts. Her sisterly feeling for these people, her fascination and respect for their experience and independence may be linked to the romantic construction of her self as an independent individual free of the shackles of society.

It was on horseback or as the driver of a horse-drawn carriage that Emma tasted something of the freedom allowed to the Victorian male. The diary reveals that Emma suffered from lameness since childhood. Frustrated by this disability, and by Victorian expectations as to the proper role of the female, it is feasible to imagine that the driving and riding of horses were romantic to her in the sense of liberating her from physical and ideological constrictions. In Thomas's Cornish novel, the fact that Elfride can ride and Stephen cannot is a badge of class difference. However, the image of an Emma figure above the walking male also suggests the potential of reversed gender roles. Emma was taught to ride by her father but her treasured mare Fanny, her means of liberation, was a gift from the very woman who in Florence's anti-romance is one of the forces imprisoning the Gifford sisters. I refer to Helen Gifford's elderly companion, a woman of the Tintagel area rich enough to break some of the rules for female behaviour. Contrast Thomas's view of Emma the horsewoman with Emma's view of herself. The poet recalls the power of Emma the horse rider with her hair flowing in the breeze, but he also stresses her loyal love for him. In her diary Emma salutes her romance with the male and describes her hair similarly. However, she also describes riding as a unique experience in which she is free of male influence and protection, facing the elements and the dangerous terrain alone. The independent horsewoman who appealed to Hardy and won the respect of local men, was at one time prepared to reject the automatic option of marriage. When officious people suggested it was time for her to marry, Emma would respond by saying that she preferred the company of her mare to that of any possible husband! (23-4, 31)

In Emma's unpublished Cornish novella, Rosabelle is a partial self-portrait. She is a sensitive, cultured Christian woman who suffers rejection at the hands of Claude Carlenthen. When he proves to be a cad and a fraud by rejecting his social equal Rosabelle and eloping with the lower class Boadicea Darville, Rosabelle learns that the less exciting but more trustworthy Albert During is more worthy as a suitor. Here we have romance of an artificial kind. However, it is significant that the title of her story, 'The Maid on the Shore', could focus our attention either on pure Rosabelle or on Boadicea, the local working class woman who works on the shore. Boadicea can also be seen as a partial self-portrait. She wavers between loyalty to her humble Cornish origins and the instinct for social climbing; eventually the latter wins. The novella ends with her callously disregarding the death of her first husband and rapidly arranging a new marriage with a Lord. The reader is left with this limited choice between a manipulator of the male-dominated class system and a woman willing to pin all her hope on the love of the perfect male partner. The third option, of a woman living alone and in sisterly affection with other women is shown, not in Emma's fiction but in her diary. It is there that she constructs a romantic image of herself as independent from the limits placed upon her by Thomas's romance.

Emma's romance, less influential than Florence's story in the biography of the Hardy family, and far less influential than Thomas's words in the world of literature, includes side by side with the orthodox, a romantic/revolutionary idea of freedom and happiness. Yet independence is denied her within the literary record of Thomas's life and work: she is spoken about in biography and made to speak by Thomas in verse. What would Emma have said of herself and those criticising her? We will never know what she confided in the writings discovered by her husband after her death. If we can trust Florence Emily's evidence, Emma's words were so critical of her husband that he destroyed them. Emma's personal views of the post-romantic phase of her marriage would have been a valuable balance to the evidence of her critics. In life, these documents gave Emma the last word, since Thomas could not reply to her in person about her criticism. In art he took back the right of the last word, engaging both in self-criticism and criticisms of Emma under rules of his own making.

A conclusive verdict on the biographical aspect of the Hardys' Lyonesse is impossible due to the tampering with the evidence and our dependence on Florence for a view of Emma. When Thomas's words are balanced by the surviving words of his female partners, three distinctive, romantic Cornwalls appear, each one valid from the viewpoint of its inventor. Florence's romantic anti-romance, Thomas's romantic tragedy and Emma's romance of liberation are all creative and powerful in their own ways. Despite being obscured by rival inventions, Emma's invention is the one that offers the most interesting example of the potential of romance for the modern reader.

THE CORNISH CONNECTION: A CHRONOLOGY

1840 Birth of Thomas Hardy at Higher Bockhampton Dorset; Birth of Emma Lavinia Gifford in Plymouth, Devon.

1860 Financial difficulties cause the Gifford family to move from Plymouth to Kirland near Bodmin in Cornwall.

1869 Emma's sister Helen marries Caddell Holder, Rector of St Juliot Church near Boscastle in North Cornwall. Emma lives with them at St Juliot rectory.

1870 (March and August) Thomas, working as an assistant to a Dorset architect, sent to restore St Juliot Church.

1871 (May) Thomas visits Cornwall.

1872 (August) Thomas visits Cornwall.

1873 (at the close of the year) Thomas visits Cornwall. Publication of his Cornish novel *A Pair of Blue Eyes*.

1874 Thomas married to Emma in London by Emma's uncle, Canon Edwin Gifford.

1875 Emma writes her unpublished Cornish novella 'The Maid on the Shore', set at Trebarwith Strand and Tintagel.

1876 Thomas and Emma live at Sturminster Newton in Dorset: 'The Sturminster Idyll'.

1885 Thomas and Emma live at Max Gate near Dorchester.

1895 *Jude the Obscure* published, much to Emma's disapproval.

1904-5 Florence Emily Dugdale meets Thomas Hardy. Florence later works as Thomas's secretary and becomes companion to Emma.

1907 Emma travels alone to London to march with the suffragettes.

1908 Emma takes part in another march with the suffragettes.

1908 Thomas writes to Emma explaining that he would rather take her to Cornwall than London.

1911 Emma completes her Cornish diary, published posthumously as *Some Recollections*.

1912 27 November Emma Lavinia's death. December: Florence stays at Max Gate to restore order. Thomas discovers Emma's voluminous diaries kept from about 1891 onwards. One entitled 'What I Think of my Husband' is (apparently) destroyed. The Cornish recollections are preserved.

1913 Thomas Hardy re-visits Emma's haunts in Plymouth and Cornwall with his brother Henry.

1914 Thomas publishes *Satires of Circumstance* including 'Veteris Vestigia Flammae', a sequence of elegies indebted to Emma's surviving diary and his memories of her at St Juliot, The Valency Valley, Boscastle, and Beeny Cliff.

1914 Thomas marries Florence Emily. He was nearly 74; she was 35.

1916 Thomas Hardy re-visits Cornwall with his second wife. Long gestation of *The Famous Tragedy of the Queen of Cornwall* begun at a visit to Tintagel.

1921 'Meditations on a Holiday': a poem in which Hardy considers then rejects returning to North Cornwall.

1923 Thomas publishes *Famous Tragedy*, including his own illustration of Tintagel. In the programme for the Hardy Players' production of the play, Hardy includes both his drawing and a water-colour drawing of Tintagel by Emma.

1924 Thomas writes of wishing to return to Cornwall.

1927 Thomas writes of wishing to return to Cornwall.

1928 Thomas Hardy's death. His last words possibly about Emma. *The Early Life of Thomas Hardy* published under the name of Florence Emily and containing extracts of Emma's Cornish recollections.

1929 Florence visits Cornwall.

1930 The Later Years of Thomas Hardy published under the name of Florence Emily.

1937 Florence Emily's death.

BIBLIOGRAPHY

Collins, Vere H. *Talks with Thomas Hardy at Max Gate 1920- 1922*. London: Duckworth, 1978.

Fowles, John. Foreword to *The Undercliff: A Sketchbook of the Axmouth-Lyme Regis Nature Reserve* by Elaine Franks. London: J.M. Dent and Sons, 1989.

Gittings, Robert and Jo Manton. *The Second Mrs Hardy*. London: Heinemann, 1979.

Gittings, Robert. *Young Thomas Hardy*. Harmondsworth: Penguin, 1986.

_____. *The Older Hardy*. Harmondsworth: Penguin, 1980.

Hardy, Emma Lavinia. *Some Recollections*. Ed. Evelyn Hardy and Robert Gittings. Oxford: Oxford University Press, 1979.

Hardy, Florence Emily. *The Life of Thomas Hardy 1840-1928*. London: Macmillan, 1962 reprinted 1986.

Hardy, Thomas. *The Famous Tragedy of the Queen of Cornwall at Tintagel in Lyonesse*. London: Macmillan, 1923.

_____. *A Pair of Blue Eyes*. Ed. Alan Manford. Oxford University Press, 1987.

_____. *The Collected Letters of Thomas Hardy*. Eds. Richard L. Purdy and Michael Millgate. 7 vols. Oxford: Clarendon Press, 1978-1988.

Kay-Robinson, Denys. *The First Mrs Thomas Hardy*. London: Macmillan, 1979.

Malory, Thomas. *Malory Works*. Ed. Eugene Vinavar. Oxford University Press, 1966.

Millgate, Michael. Ed. *Letters of Emma and Florence Hardy*. Oxford: Clarendon Press, 1996.

Meynell, Violet. Ed. *Friends of a Lifetime: Letters to Sydney Carlyle Cockerell*. London: Jonathan Cape, 1940.

Phelps, Kenneth. *The Wormwood Cup: Thomas Hardy in Cornwall. A Study in Temperament, Topography and Timing*. Padstow: Lodenek Press, 1975.

Strassburg, Gottfried von. *Tristan*. Translated by A.T. Hatto. Harmondsworth: Penguin, 1976.

Reading Virginia Woolf and St Ives

Su Reid

People like to visit the place where a famous novel or poem is set, or where an author lived and wrote. In this essay I discuss some of the ways in which visiting such a place might create meanings in a literary text, drawing on my own experience of reading and rereading Virginia Woolf's 'A Sketch of the Past' and To the Lighthouse and of visiting and revisiting St Ives in Cornwall. My attempt to make sense of my own experience uses two kinds of literary criticism. One of these is feminist criticism which over the last fifteen years or so has rescued Virginia Woolf from the opprobrium of being 'poetic'. Feminist critics have shown that her novels and essays can be read as realist narratives about women's lives, even as histories and autobiographies; and that they dramatise ideas and arguments about the lives of women that are still current and still contested. My reading sees To the Lighthouse as an account of an argument between a husband and wife -- the Ramsays -- and of the significance of that argument within the deeper structure of their marriage. Feminist critics have also argued, using ideas derived from psychoanalytic theory, that Woolf's writing can be seen to reveal a disruptive feminine consciousness within patriarchal society. I argue that To the Lighthouse offers such a possibility through its topography -- through the construction of its land-and-seascape in relation to its characters -- and that it confers this possibility on the 'real' St Ives.

The other literary criticism I draw on is specifically the work of the American deconstructive critic J. Hillis Miller. He reads texts as creating meanings, rejecting the commonsense assumption that they reproduce or represent things that existed before them. In Fiction and Repetition (1982) and 'Mr Carmichael and Lily Briscoe: The Rhythm of Creativity in To the Lighthouse' (1983) he showed how three of Woolf's novels, Mrs. Dalloway, Between the Acts and To the Lighthouse, exploit the traditional linguistic forms of realist past-tense narration so as to expose and re-enact the processes of memory and narration themselves. More recently his Topographies (1995) is a collection of essays reading a variety of texts, none of them by Woolf, in order to consider the function of place, of landscapes, in narratives; and to ask whether, in any given text, the landscape has a function beyond that of setting or of 'metaphorical adornment' for the actions which purport 'really' to have happened there. The word 'topography', Miller says, which combines in its form the Greek words for 'place' and for 'writing', once meant the description of a place in words -- implying that the place was thought of as existing before it was described. But now 'topography' means either the mapping of a place by graphic signs and proper names or, more likely, the place itself when it has been mapped. This third, modern, usage -- which I have just employed when discussing To the Lighthouse -- shows that the identity of a place is inseparable from the signs and names and stories defining it.

I have spent eleven consecutive Easter holidays in St Ives, with my husband and children, and sometimes with other members of my family, and sometimes with friends too, in a rented house. Not always the same house, and not for eight weeks in the summer, and I must reject parallels between Mrs. Ramsay and me or Julia Stephen and me; but for my family in the 1980s and 1990s, as for Virginia Woolf's family a century ago, the time in St Ives is crucial to each year.

We first came to St Ives because of Virginia Woolf. We wanted a spring holiday in Cornwall and I insisted on St Ives because I wanted to find Talland House. I was curious. I wasn't sure why. A combination of images perhaps: the large doomed Victorian family; Quentin Bell's account (I 31) of their annual train journey from Paddington (we came by car); the beach in *The Waves*; an expectation of jackmanii, or at least of flowers; the gaunt and cerebral novelist. I had read biographies of Virginia Woolf which all made St Ives significant. Quentin Bell's, full of details drawn from family knowledge and family papers -- he is Virginia Woolf's nephew -- evokes the delight of the whole family in their summer holidays in St Ives, and the longing with which they remembered, and occasionally revisited, the place in their later lives. Leslie Stephen, Virginia's father, had 'discovered' St Ives in 1881; in 1882, the year of Virginia's birth, he took a lease on Talland House, high above the station and Porthminster beach and looking out over St Ives Bay to Godrevy lighthouse. The family, with servants and friends, spent long periods there every summer until 1895 when Julia Stephen, Virginia's mother, died. Almost immediately the house was given up by the grief-obsessed widower. In Bell's narrative, and in that of all subsequent biographies, the remembered St Ives summers are inseparable from the lost and beautiful mother. Later biographies, making use of *Moments of Being* which was only published in 1976, tell, with varying degrees of excitement, another tale too. Towards the end of her life, in the essay 'A Sketch of the Past', Virginia had described how she was 'explored' on the hall table at Talland House by her step-brother Gerald Duckworth when she was six (*Moments of Being* 78-80).

The novels, I think, contributed much less to my images of St Ives. Certainly *Jacob's Room* relates explicitly to the region of Penwith and is a clear precursor of *To the Lighthouse*. The opening scene, presenting a mother and children, is set on a Cornish beach facing a lighthouse (3-9). The lighthouse 'wobbles' as the mother's eyes -- she is a widow -- fill momentarily with tears. Little Jacob finds a skull among the debris further up the beach and picks up its jaw, leaving behind the rest which, although 'a more unpolluted piece of bone existed nowhere on the coast of Cornwall', his mother will not let him take into their lodgings. At bedtime his brother has to be talked gently to sleep by their mother, murmuring of fairies and of birds' nests. There is a 'hurricane out at sea'. Later in this novel St Ives Bay and Gurnard's Head are specifically named, as Jacob, now a taciturn young man, sails in a small open boat from Falmouth round past Scilly and is then the guest of his sailing companion's mother (IV 38-52). She, having visited a poor woman in a 'white Cornish cottage' presides over a dinner party in a house with a view of the sea. But the geographical locations are not specific or crucial enough in the narration to make one want urgently to visit their real-life originals. *To the Lighthouse*, set in a house overlooking a bay with a lighthouse, reworks all these images in its representation of a family before and after the death of the children's mother. Biographers and critics, and Woolf herself (*Diary* 14 May 1925), have made connections between *To the Lighthouse* and St Ives; but the narration, in spite of the jackmanii in the garden, names the setting as Scottish, as Skye. And in *The Waves* the beach scenes have no explicit naming at all, so I certainly did not expect to locate them in a particular real place. I came to St Ives with no expectation of 'finding' any Woolf novel there.

Anyway, for years I had been teaching undergraduates, in an ancient Scottish university and in a northern English polytechnic, to read and to write about *To the Lighthouse* as an example of high modernism. I wasn't interested in reading it as a realist narrative about recognisable people in a recognisable place. I didn't think you could. Since coming to St Ives, however, I've written one short book and edited another arguing that that is exactly what *To the Lighthouse* is.

On our first day, in 1985, I was entranced by the view of Godrevy Lighthouse from both St Ives and Carbis Bay, where I sat on the beach and painted; and by the experience of going, later the same day, to the lighthouse -- not in a boat but in our car, to Godrevy Point. Like James, I fantastically thought, I saw the lighthouse both as 'a silvery misty-looking tower' across the bay and as 'the tower, stark and straight', close to (202). I was convinced at once that, never mind its named Hebridian setting, this is where *To the Lighthouse* actually happens -- even though Godrevy Lighthouse is not, like James's, 'barred with black and white'.

St Ives does not market itself in terms of Virginia Woolf. One house in Downalong bears a plaque saying Daphne du Maurier used to stay there. Nothing,in 1985 and still in 1995, marks Talland House as Virginia Woolf's. It was recently For Sale. Its old owner was very discouraging, allowing in one party of Americans each year. The keepers of the bookshop in Fore Street say they stock Woolf sometimes, if people ask. The curator of the St Ives Tate Gallery did not reply to a letter in which I mentioned the St Ives connection with Virginia Woolf and her sister, the artist Vanessa Bell. Some of this must result from the prejudice against, or fear of, middle-class English intellectuals that characterised much of the local resistance to the plan to build the Tate. But some of it might be to do with the way Woolf writes about St Ives and with the ways in which her writing constructs the place.

In this essay I want to compare two different kinds of literary tourism. The first kind is visiting a place so as to act out something one has read, to give a story a physical 'fix' -- like tracking Bloomsday in Dublin, or *Mrs Dalloway* in London. The second is living a known place in its absence -- much as Wordsworth lived the Wye Valley in his 'lonely rooms, and 'mid the din/Of towns and cities' -- by reading words about it. In this second case the place does not explain the text, as it appears to in the first. On the contrary, the text creates the place -- and might remake what we see when we go back there.

Wordsworth is, of course, a poet of both kinds of tourism. He describes his visits to the geographical sites of other people's stories -- stories such as Michael's; he also constructs and then rereads landscapes-in-words that stand for and re-create absent places, such as the lakes and rivers of his childhood. The Lake District National Park is now a place where we are all literary tourists of my first kind -- watching the Wordsworths pretending to be poor in Dove Cottage, climbing Coniston ourselves as the Swallows and Amazons' Kanchenjunga, staring at Peter Rabbit's garden gate ....

I went to St Ives in the first place with a similar kind of intention perhaps; and my startled first conviction that this was where *To the Lighthouse* really happened was indeed an experience of that kind. This first kind of literary tourism is a defining, limiting experience -- a comfortable and reassuring one. Visiting the places named in a novel or poem and finding them recognisable defines the fiction. It merges very quickly into an experience that confirms the reality of the author: so people visit Bronte country or Hardy country or Lawrence country or Catherine Cookson country or, more defining still, Shakespeare country. This makes the writing safe. It might even mean you don't actually have to bother reading it at all. The reader/tourist can control what the words mean or might mean by fixing them to specific, usually visual, data. As Foucault (translated) said,

the author...is a certain functional principle by which, in our culture, one limits, excludes, and chooses; in short, by which one impedes the free circulation, the free manipulation, the free composition, decomposition, and recomposition of fiction.

And, 'the author is ... the ideological figure by which one marks the manner in which we fear the proliferation of meaning.' (Rabinow 119) In this spirit, perhaps, tourists visit the Woolfs' house at Rodmell in Sussex, owned by the National Trust, and Vanessa Bell's nearby Charleston Farmhouse, run by the Charleston Farmhouse Trust. Visiting the places enables them to 'understand' -- that is, to rewrite and limit and control -- not only the writer and the artists but also their works, which threaten to change every time we read or look at them.

The second kind of literary tourism is as common, or even perhaps more so -- we all 'daydream' about remembered absent places, and many of us do it when reading about them. But this experience cannot be guaranteed and so it cannot be marketed in the same way. Even 'travel books' do not guarantee it. Indeed it cannot be articulated at all except as a memory in its own absence; I can only write that I 'live' St Ives in Middlesbrough when I am not actually doing that but am remembering that I do it most days.

The difference between these two experiences is paralleled by ways in which Woolf writes about places. I want now to examine the difference more closely by considering some of her writings 'about' St Ives specifically, 'A Sketch of the Past' and *To the Lighthouse*. 'A Sketch of the Past' opens with two memories named within the text as being connected with St Ives: the red and purple flowers of Julia Stephen's dress, and 'the most important of all my memories' -- waking up and hearing the waves and the movement of the blind-cord, and seeing the St Ives light. Woolf writes:

If life has a base that it stands upon, if it is a bowl that one fills and fills and fills - then my bowl without a doubt stands upon this memory. It is of lying half asleep, half awake, in bed in the nursery at St Ives. It is of hearing the waves breaking, one, two, one, two, and sending a splash of water over the beach; and then breaking, one, two, one, two, behind a yellow blind. It is of hearing the blind draw its little acorn across the floor as the wind blew the blind out. It is of lying and hearing this splash and seeing this light, and feeling, it is almost impossible that I should be here; of feeling the purest ecstasy I can conceive. I could spend hours trying to write that as it should be written, in order to give the feeling which is even at this moment very strong in me. But I should fail (unless I had some wonderful luck); I dare say I should only succeed in having the luck if I had begun by describing Virginia herself. (*Moments of Being* 75)

Woolf's authorial voice in the second of these paragraphs is claiming actually to be reliving the absent experience and place. But she says she can only 'write' this, represent it, by defining someone else, a third-person 'Virginia herself' who becomes the owner of the original experience within the narrative. In other words, the writer does not relive the experience as she writes; it becomes instead the property of someone else, of the child 'Virginia', a character constructed within the story. And that is explicitly what happens next:

...there was one external reason for the intensity of this first impression: the impression of the waves and the acorn on the blind; the feeling, as I describe it sometimes to myself, of lying in a grape and seeing through a film of semi-transparent yellow -- it was due to the many months we spent in London. The change of nursery was a great change. And there was the long train journey; and the excitement. (76)

At once this is so distanced: the 'feeling' is entirely absent from the text and from the authorial narration, and is substituted, in its absence, by the metaphor of the grape. At the same time it is defined as the result of the long-ago London months, and so denied as an experience repeatable in the present.

Woolf's narrative voice goes on to do the same thing again:

At times I can go back to St Ives more completely than I can this morning. I can reach a state where I seem to be watching things happen as if I were there. That is, I suppose, that my memory supplies what I had forgotten, so that it seems as if it were happening independently, though I am really making it happen. In certain favourable moods, memories -- what one has forgotten -- come to the top. Now if this is so, is it not possible -- I often wonder -- that things we have felt with great intensity have an existence independent of our minds; are in fact still in existence? And if so, will it not be possible, in time, that some device will be invented by which we can tap them? ...There...are the garden and the nursery. Instead of remembering here a scene and there a sound, I shall fit a plug into the wall;

and listen in to the past. I shall turn up August 1890. I feel that strong emotion must leave its trace; and it is only a question of discovering how we can get ourselves again attached to it, so that we shall be able to live our lives through from the start. (77-8)

The idea of a past experience and a past 'self' still really existing somewhere is presented here as a fanciful one, but it is not, of course, really so strange an idea either to Woolf or to her readers who know anything of psychoanalytic theory. In this passage the authorial voice describes in reasoned terms her desire to 'go back' and exist in past experiences without the intervention of the directing and representing consciousness which alienates her from them. In doing so she constructs that very consciousness whose thinking about the original experiences replaces and so represses them. And this happens repeatedly. She goes on to describe herself as trying to 'tap' a particular memory which contains strong emotion:

There was a small looking-glass in the hall at Talland House. It had, I remember, a ledge with a brush on it. By standing on tiptoe I could see my face in the glass. When I was six or seven perhaps, I got into the habit of looking at my face in the glass. But I only did this if I was sure that I was alone. I was ashamed of it. A strong feeling of guilt seemed naturally attached to it. (78)

She does not actually recreate or 'tap' the feeling, but defines and explains it in distancing rational terms first by saying she and Vanessa were tomboys and admiring oneself in a mirror was against their code; and secondly by making the admission to which biographers relate so much importance and describing the fondling of her genitals by Gerald Duckworth in that same hall.

The scenes described in 'A Sketch of the Past' are objects within the narration. This kind of writing easily allows the first kind of 'literary tourism': we can join in with, and confirm, the narration by standing in front of Talland House and thinking that 'it' really happened 'there'. To the Lighthouse reads differently. The narration is itself famously shifting. An attentive reader can easily spell out a set of chronologically and sometimes causally linked events, but the voice defining them seems caught up in the shifts in the characters' attention, and in its own shifts from one narrative discourse to another as it moves through the novel's three parts. Therefore the things we make ourselves 'see' and 'hear' as we read -- the people, their words, the places -- are much less defined and distanced than in 'A Sketch of the Past'.

Is this novel, really, set in St Ives at all? Woolf herself related her inspiration to start writing the novel to

father's character ...; and mothers; and St Ives; and childhood; and all the usual things I try to put in -- life, death etc. But the centre is father's character, sitting in a boat, reciting We perished, each alone, while he crushes a dying mackerel. (Diary, 14 May 1925)

93

On the other hand, after it was published she wrote to a friend: 'I'm so glad that you like some of *The Lighthouse*. People in The Hebrides are very angry. Is it Cornwall? I'm not as sure as you are.' (Letter to Violet Dickinson, 5 June 1927)

Of course the narration of the novel itself says it's set in the Hebrides, in spite of the rooks and very unScottish vegetation. (In a letter to Vanessa Bell, her sister, on 22 May 1927, Woolf wrote 'Lord Olivier writes that my horticulture and natural history is in every sense wrong: there are no rooks, elms, or dahlias in the Hebrides ...')

Jane Goldman has developed a reading of the novel's Scottish names and references which sees them as a manifestation of interest in the 1745 Jacobite rebellion, and so as a sign of Woolf's anti-establishment and anti-patriarchal politics. Nevertheless, *To the Lighthouse* does recall St Ives, not because its author spent her childhood summer holidays there (I spent some of mine in the Hebrides), but because some visual details of St Ives are unmistakeable in the novel. Here are some examples:

... but here, the houses falling away on both sides, they came out on the quay, and the whole bay spread before them and Mrs Ramsay could not help exclaiming, 'Oh, how beautiful!' For the great plateful of blue water was before her; the hoary Lighthouse, distant, austere, in the midst; and on the right, as far as the eye could see, fading and falling, in soft low pleats, the green sand dunes with the wild flowing grasses on them .... (17)

The really crucial phrase is 'on the right'. As anyone who knows St Ives will have to agree, the visible sand dunes, those of Hayle, are only 'on the right' as one looks from the harbour across St Ives Bay. 'They should have gone already -- they had to catch the tide or something' (159) is perhaps not quite so crucial: other Cornish harbours, like St Ives, are dry at low tide, stranding boats. But this next passage is decisive:

It was like that then, the island, thought Cam ... It lay like that on the sea, did it, with a dent in the middle and two sharp crags, and the sea swept in there, and spread away for miles and miles on either side of the island. It was very small; shaped something like a leaf stood on end. (204)

From Carbis Bay especially, but also from Porthminster Beach in St Ives, the island on which Godrevy Lighthouse stands is quite unmistakeably 'like a leaf stood on end.' Organisationally things are not quite the same, for this passage describes the island the Ramsays are staying on, not the island with the lighthouse. But this detail is insignificant beside the visual brilliance of the description of the real place, and its power to evoke that place when one is away from it.

Thus awakened, one might go to St Ives to 'fix' *To the Lighthouse*. Just so, seeing the ways in which the men's college and 'Fernham' in *A Room of One's Own* resemble King's and Newnham Colleges in Cambridge can help one 'fix' that book, not only in terms of Woolf's family relations with Cambridge as Jane Marcus has done, but also in terms of the idiosyncrasy of constructing a single-sex college as the universal sign of women's education. But instead, and in contrast to that urge, reading *To the Lighthouse* makes me remember St Ives when I am away from it. Or, *To the Lighthouse* creates St Ives for me when I am not there; and that creation of St Ives gives shape and significance to the place itself as I revisit it annually. Further: St Ives carries a shifting chain of experience for me, not a single defined significance. In what follows I want to explain how it is that the novel constructs the place as the site of a constantly re-enacted struggle between self and other; and how it dramatises that struggle in terms of the confrontation of femininity and masculinity.

It is easy to say that the lighthouse is a phallic signifier longed for by James, initially denied him by his father, and finally owned by James as he steps ashore in companionship with that father at the end of the novel, watched by Cam and, in effect, by Lily. But the lighthouse is claimed by other characters too, and then lost by them.

When Mrs Ramsay is left alone for a brief peaceful moment, after James is taken away to bed, she retreats into a secret state in which she identifies her own consciousness as the third stroke of the light:

Losing personality, one lost the fret, the hurry, the stir; ... and pausing there she looked out to meet that stroke of the Lighthouse, the long steady stroke, the last of the three, which was her stroke, for watching them in this mood at this hour one could not help attaching oneself to one thing especially of the things one saw; and this thing, the long steady stroke, was her stroke. ... (70)

But at the end of the passage she abandons this private identity, turns away from the lighthouse, and gets up and assumes the social role of dependent wife:

And again he would have passed her without a word had she not, at that very moment, given him of her own free will what she knew he would never ask, and called to him and taken the green shawl off the picture frame, and gone to him. For he wished, she knew, to protect her. (72)

This, surely, prefigures and is echoed in the closing moment of Part I of the novel, 'The Window', when finally Mrs Ramsay resolves the irritation between herself and her husband by giving him the role of thinker for both of them. Just as here she gives him 'of her own free will what she knew he would never ask', the role of protector, so there she will leave to him the power of 'knowing':

...as she looked at him she began to smile, for though she had not said a word, he knew, of course he knew, that she loved him. He could not deny it. And smiling she looked out of the window and said (thinking to herself, Nothing on earth can equal this happiness) --
'Yes, you were right. It's going to be wet tomorrow.' (133)

He can not deny it because she has made no statement to be denied. The trouble between them was caused at the start of the novel because she made a statement: her soothing words to James, 'Yes, of course, if it's fine tomorrow ...', did, as words do, carry with them a statement -- about the probable weather. Statements invite opposition, and that one certainly provoked it. But here, in the last scene of the novel in which the husband and wife appear together, she speaks only to recant even that accidental statement -- 'Yes, you were right. It's going to be wet tomorrow' -- and he now has undisputed power to 'know'. This passage at the conclusion of 'The Window', famously, ends with: 'And she looked at him smiling. For she had triumphed again.' She has triumphed by using words only as a gesture, by refusing to deploy them as initiators of meaning.

If she has 'triumphed' because she has now given her husband the right to be the one who 'knows', who creates meaning, the power in the relationship could still be hers. He has not achieved his own right to 'know'; she has constructed it and granted it to him -- and can, therefore, either destroy it or guard it. But in exercising this power she has sacrificed not only her own right of speech, and not only poor James's trip, but also the very identification of the lighthouse's beam as 'her stroke'. As she grants her husband the right to 'know', Mrs Ramsay looks 'out of the window'-- presumably towards the lighthouse because we were told a few lines earlier that 'she did not mind looking now, with him watching, at the Lighthouse'. Her lighthouse with its 'long steady stroke' has been replaced by this token over which they have argued and she has made him win.

The lighthouse, then, was claimed by Mrs Ramsay as a sign of self, of that which words are not. But in functioning as a signifier within her commerce with her husband it replaces forever its own original presence as something felt. This process is repeated by other characters through the third part of the novel. Lily, who wanted 'to get hold of' 'that very jar on the nerves, the thing itself before it has been made anything' in her picture of Mrs Ramsay wanting to take James to the lighthouse (209), has to settle for her single line which the narration of the end of the novel links inextricably with Mr Ramsay's taking possession of the lighthouse (226). Cam is roused by her father out of her dreamlike state in the boat, and made to replace her own image of 'the island' -- which the reader who knows St Ives recognises as the 'leaf stood on end', the misplaced lighthouse rock -- with the lighthouse he wants her to visit (221). And James too is distanced during the voyage from his own unarticulated memory of his mother and of his desire for the lighthouse (201-3). Mr Ramsay turns the voyage for both Cam and James into the first kind of tourist experience: an expedition you go on to banish a proliferation of meanings.

In other words, the novel constructs the lighthouse not as a stable object within its own narration but as a process. Repeatedly the women and the children in the novel represent 'self' to themselves in terms involving the lighthouse. Repeatedly, the lighthouse then becomes, for each of them in turn, merely a signifier in a contest with Mr Ramsay, and 'self' becomes unreachable. For each of them the experience is parallel to that acted out in the narration of 'A Sketch of the Past': they represent 'self' to themselves but can only do so by means of a sign which is not 'self' but a substitute for it, and presently that sign itself is hijacked and defined by the discourse initiated by the dominant man. In contrast, Mr Ramsay is associated, by other characters as well as by himself, with the sand-dunes rather than the lighthouse; and the sand-dunes are made to signify solitude accompanied by the effort towards abstraction, when 'abstraction' means structure without human referents -- a total repression of images of self:

...on the right, as far as the eye could see, fading and falling, in soft low pleats, the green sand dunes with the wild flowing grasses on them, which always seemed to be running away into some moon country, uninhabited of men. That was the view, she said, stopping, growing greyer-eyed, that her husband loved. (17)

and

Looking at the far sandhills, William Bankes thought of Ramsay: thought of a road in Westmorland, thought of Ramsay striding along a road by himself hung round with that solitude which seemed to be his natural air. ... (25)

and

That was the country he liked best, over there, those sandhills dwindling away into darkness. One could walk all day without meeting a soul. ... One could worry things out alone. (76)

To the Lighthouse, then, has the lighthouse on its rock across the bay, and the sandhills 'on the right', as its clearest topography, its delineation of a space within which readers will work out their understandings of its complex narration. Taken together the sandhills and the lighthouse construct a repeated confrontation between desire for 'self' and the unavoidability of structure; between an image of private individuality and the inevitable hijacking of that image by public, or shared, discourse; and between the women and children on the one hand and, on the other, the man to whom his wife has given the power of 'knowing'.

Mrs Ramsay and Lily and the children might have lost the real presence of the lighthouse but the novel does not. The lighthouse is triumphantly there at the end, still not quite reached even by Mr Ramsay as he steps ashore onto its rock. So in St Ives, the lighthouse continuously teases the gaze as the light changes. Whenever I revisit St Ives, whether in person or in imagination as I reread the novel, I re-enact the violent confrontation between the enjoyment of private sensations -- light, sound, colour, shape, texture -- and the awareness of perceived general structures of time, of geology, of economic history, of the ways in which I have been taught to admire 'landscape'.

As the new St Ives Tate Gallery demonstrates, both in the building itself and in the way the exhibits are labelled and displayed, St Ives art derives from and leads back to the Penwith landscape. St Ives 'abstract' art confronts contiguous colour or shape in paint or carving on the one hand with the recognition of structure in the cliffs and moors and the sea on the other. The tension between still life or landscape on the one hand and abstraction -- structure or contrast without specific reference -- on the other is central to the work of Ben Nicholson and Barbara Hepworth and Wilhelmina Barns-Graham and, often, Peter Lanyon. It is what is so extraordinary in the work of Alfred Wallis, especially in his rows of square houses and his repeated boats. *To the Lighthouse* also, as I read it, constructs St Ives Bay as a place where that confrontation continues without any final resolution -- and so as a place where resistance is forever possible.

BIBLIOGRAPHY

Bell, Quentin. *Virginia Woolf, A Biography* . Two volumes, London and New York: The Hogarth Press 1972; Paladin, 1976.
Goldman, Jane. Metaphor and Place in *To the Lighthouse*: Some Hebridean Connections. Ed. Caroline Gonda. *Tea and Leg-Irons, New Feminist Readings from Scotland.* London: Open Letters,1992.
Marcus, Jane. *Virginia Woolf and the Languages of Patriarchy.* Bloomington and Indianapolis: Indiana University Press, 1987.
Miller, J Hillis. *Fiction and Repetition, Seven English Novels.* Oxford: Blackwell, 1982.
_____. Mr Carmichael and Lily Briscoe: The Rhythm of Creativity in To the Lighthouse'. Eds. Robert Kiely and John Hildebidle. *Modernism Reconsidered.* Cambridge, Mass.: Harvard University Press, 1983.
_____. *Topographies.* California: Stanford University Press, 1995.
Rabinow, Paul. Ed. *The Foucault Reader.* London: Penguin, 1984.
Reid, Su. Ed. *To the Lighthouse.* London: Macmillan, The Critics Debate Series, 1991.
_____. Ed. Mrs Dalloway *and* To the Lighthouse. London: Macmillan, New Casebooks Series, 1993.

CITED WORKS BY VIRGINIA WOOLF
Jacob's Room. 1922; Penguin, 1992.
Moments of Being, Unpublished Autobiographical Writings. Ed. Jeanne Schulkind. London: Chatto and Windus, 1976; Triad Granada,1978.
Mrs Dalloway. 1925; Penguin, 1992.
A Room of One's Own. 1929; Penguin, 1992.
'A Sketch of the Past', written 1939-40, published in *Moments of Being.*
To the Lighthouse. 1927; Penguin, 1992.
The Waves. 1931; Penguin, 1992.
The Diary of Virginia Woolf, Volume III, 1925-30. Eds. Anne Olivier Bell with Andrew McNeillie. London and New York: The Hogarth Press, 1980; Penguin, 1982.
A Change of Perspective, The Letters of Virginia Woolf 1923-28. Eds. Nigel Nicolson with Joanne Trautmann. London and New York: The Hogarth Press, 1977.

Women, Symbolism and the Coast of Cornwall

Judith Hubback

This chapter offers readers a new angle on the general terms 'the shore', 'the beach' and 'the cliffs', new meanings, and a psychological comment on them, combined with references to well- known novels and poems. I have a particular loved place in Cornwall, and have always enjoyed a variety of literary works touching on the coast, poetry as well as novels. I bring them together through the experience of half a lifetime as a Jungian analytical psychologist. They are also the mainspring of my own novel set in Cornwall, The Sea Has Many Voices (1990). I want to convey how the personal, the literary and the academic can be combined to produce something familiar and general, yet also new. Many writers have based their work on thoughts and feelings about the sea that surrounds the islands of Great Britain. Cornwall of course is not quite an island, and its active men have been paramount in countless ways, on land, in inshore waters and further away. But, to my mind, the unspoilt stretches of its coast mirror, with the interaction of sea and land, the receptivity and the potentialities of women's psyches. Far from being passive, women both conscious-ly and unconsciously interpret what shore, beach and cliff offer as symbols of the human struggle with nature. For many of us, the struggle brings its joyful rewards.

The parts of my title are organically linked through my interest in women's views, experiences and inner lives, and my enjoyment of coastal places, most particularly two small areas, one on the south and the other on the north coast of Cornwall. Both those places are, of course, completely conditioned by the sea. I know their shores well, their moods, their cliffs, fields, birds, plants and villages. So I cannot be mainly objective, as perhaps an academic might be, such as a marine biologist or a geographer. I am subjective as well, since my feeling roots are there rather than in the towns where I have had to spend so much of my working life.

It was much the same, I think, for Virginia Woolf when she wrote the novels which are set by the sea, *To the Lighthouse* and *The Waves*, both prefigured to some extent in *The Voyage Out*. Moreover the way in which all her writing flows reminds the perceptive reader (perhaps at an unconscious body-level) of her woman's attunement to the flux and fall of the sea's tides. Another aspect of the sea is represented in Daphne du Maurier's novels, with their strong emphasis on the story and the action: in Woolf the is-ness of the sea is paramount, what it does is reflected in the eventfulness of du Maurier's plots and people. Yet another aspect of the sea's nature is indicated in Mary Wesley's *Jumping the*

Queue and *The Camomile Lawn*: her characters are either ruthless or at the mercy of other more powerful people or impersonal forces. In *The Sea Has Many Voices* I use a house, its garden above the cliffs, and the beach, as the backcloth and the stage for the lives of a mother and a father, their family of five daughters and their friends. The cliffs are rocky, and perhaps they stand for traditional firm male decisiveness? The beach is curved like the new moon, which has often been associated with femaleness. Those material facts are the bases for the emotions of the people of three generations, with their differing perceptions of themselves and of their personal interactions. Their feet are on dry land, but their lives, though full of practical concerns and relationships, are inherently influenced by the coast and its symbolism.

The symbol, as I use that term here, re-presents to the mind in a creatively new form what the original suggests. In this chapter the coast carries the meaning of the mother/land that bore us and that we grow up from, for work, or pleasure or adventure, and the haven is the mother/refuge that we come back to. In my novel the mother who is pregnant in the first chapter dies in the last. Both the going out from the haven and the coast, and the returning, carry a wealth of female meanings. There are two directions of the tides at each stage of the book with different gains and losses, which illustrate the flux and flow of how the sea shows its power on the beach. In one incident it is when swimming that a man historian conceives of an idea for a new book: he and the sea are its 'parents'. It is down the rock-strewn cliffs and into the sea that one of the women might have committed suicide. And on the beach that a boy was resuscitated.

In the village I know best it used to be said that the small open boats, many with girls' names but manned (of course) by the men, were registered in the names of their wives who 'employed' them. So they could draw unemployment benefits in the winter when fishing was impossible and poverty was dire: there was no powered winch and the boats had been dragged up the sand most arduously, into the safe pound (metaphorically the mother's or the wife's lap). The ruthless easterly gales could not break the boats or drown the men. That arrangement was in effect a good partnership at a time when most of life there was in other ways dominated by a clear division of labour on male-female lines. In the village, the marriage partners put into practical form the symbolic cooperation of the two contrasted sexes. People who were unmarried built up various forms of socially valuable work partnerships. In my novel, as well as in the actual village, while the years unfold and the younger generations push the older people towards the past, the man-woman patterns change greatly. Writers such as myself work in close partnership with our material, the human and the non-human interacting to create something new. Moreover each of us writers has a duality between two inner gender poles, even if one pulls more strongly than the other. Winds and storms contribute, and the sun affects the tides up and down the shores as well as does the moon, whose influence is perhaps better known generally. The sea gives and the sea kills. The first chapter in *The Sea has Many Voices* is about a physically and mentally energetic man going to swim before breakfast, his wife, pregnant with their first child, and his puzzled stepdaughter, sadly disappointed when she discovers the friendly young man

100

guest already has a girl friend. The last chapter shows the tide of life ebbing in the now old woman, while her grandchildren sketch in their various futures. There is point and counterpoint between the men and the women: however strong each of them is, they have to work out their different destinies without falling into the hands of blind fate.

To describe and comment on the symbolic relations between women and the coast of Cornwall it will be convenient to distinguish between the lower shore, the beach and the cliffs. Each has characteristics, attributes and functions that differ in important ways from those of the others. Various readers may have particular places brought to mind in what follows, which do not fit exactly with what is here, but I hope there is enough in common to make it acceptable.

By the lower shore is meant the area, often rocky and sea- weedy, which is revealed when the tide is out, and covered when the tide has risen again, twice in every twenty four hours: it is essentially an area of change. Change, of course, is a feature which women are particularly and obviously aware of in the course of their lives, both their biological and their emotional lives. For some girls, even today, major upheavals, like great waves coming from the ocean, accompany the onset of menstruation and the loss of childhood. If that major change is not fully met, they may try to speed up the natural tide and rush at once into adult sex. In the lives of others their emotions are postponed, as happens to many anorexic girls. Then, some women find the menopausal time, which used to be called 'The Change', difficult to cope with, even when the skill of scientific medication helps them with the physical side of it. But gradual though it usually is, the menopause marks the end of the previous stage of life, the reproductive or the potentially reproductive one. There is a definiteness and an undisputable quality to it which has much in common with the tide. One of the discoveries of young children is that there is no arguing with the tide. They learn about a mysterious force which is stronger than their mothers and fathers. For many women there is a mourning for the loss of the possibility of any more child-bearing, and that sadness is at work in them during the months or years of 'the change'. The sea sometimes looks heavily mournful, almost as though it is empathising with the loss of brighter and younger times. When colour has gone in the dusk, when the gulls' cries sound disconsolate and the damp sand is messy, there is a similarity with the woman's mourning, even if it is indefinable and unmentioned. Yet the sea's mourning heralds potentially the next phase. The tide will turn, the shore will reveal its rock pools and be offered renewal: the anemones, and all the other shore creatures will partake in the changes. In a similar, symbolic way, the woman has the chance of entering the next stage of life if she manages to welcome the major adjustment even though it is not as smooth as the movement of the tides. Then there can be a new phase, a new kind of creativity: but that needs faith in her potential and perhaps experimentation.

The shore is revealed in a gradual way during the flux of the tide, opening to light and air the many beautiful creatures and plants which both prosper and are at risk from natural predators such as wading birds (the goodies) and

101

unnatural enemies, such as oil pollution and the detritus of plastics (the baddies). The natural factors can be considered as analogies to the changes in a woman's life when it moves, like the tide, not too fast for her. The unnatural ones are akin to events which are at enmity with organic development, such as unexpected disablement or sudden death. There is something in the usually crude-coloured plastic containers, thrown out when they are empty and have no future, which feels totally alien to the character of the shore, where colours mostly harmonise well: sea weeds wilt, shrivel and die, perhaps torn from the rocks under water, and then the tide brings them up the beach, but they never look as absolutely discrepant as plastic cans do. It is part of nature for sea weed to have a limited life anyway, and it can be used most successfully as fertiliser, thereby activating and facilitating transformation, which a woman can also enjoy if she goes along with the symbolism there is in first the tolerance then the acceptance of gradual change.

The last similarity I would like to develop is how, as the tide does on the shore, some or perhaps many women periodically reveal and conceal their feelings, according to what they either intentionally or unconsciously consider appropriate and possible. I am thinking, on the one hand, of how some women respond when someone expresses love to them: they uncover emotionally, they undress and they are ready to experience, in the writer Lesley Blanch's pictorial phrase, 'the wilder shores of love'; and on the other hand, in contrasted situations, but not necessarily overt sexual ones, they hide their reactions, or fears, or potentially damaging states of mind. Concealing feelings may be entirely appropriate if, for example, they think telling a white lie will be a considerate thing to do. Or refraining from telling a very young child everything that is going on in a painful partnership, while waiting for a time when it can be more openly explained -- that may be right for the child just then. Recognising the child's vulnerability is a valuable trait which excessive rationality should not be allowed to damage. Molluscs whose shells have been battered on the sharp edges of rocks are not granted a second chance of life during a wild sou'westerly gale, but most women feel such harsh life conditions are bad for too-young humans. It would of course be ridiculous to convey that such adult sensitivity is not there in men, but if the small child has asked its mother questions before turning to the father, it is she who will have to be the one to judge when its skin or protective 'shell' is strong enough to cope with the stormy and puzzled feelings evoked by the parents' difficulties. Like a hermit crab living in the shell of a large sea-snail it will need for a while to use someone else's developed thick-enough skin. In reverse, children can be powerfully protective towards the grown-ups, concealing in the privacy of their personal prawn-shells the violence of the fantasies and emotions which they believe it would be devastating for the parents to discover. I once knew a small girl who said it felt right for the tide to be high in the evening when the picnic was over: though the sand was washed clean of castles and other great engineering works, she hoped her inner thoughts (unacceptable to the grown-ups) would also disappear into the helpful sea.

The beach is the next area to be considered. As compared with the lower shore being, for women, symbolically the place of change, the beach is where people sit, or walk, or play, where small boats can be drawn up, beached temporarily until the rising tide will refloat them for the return trip, or taken up for safety from winter storms. The beach can be part of a haven village, where there is a harbour with its protective walls and space for all the fishing gear. It is less a place of change than one for being: resting, eating, talking, sun-bathing -- but also in essence a place for activity. I think that women who are comfortable with themselves understand both being and doing, but there may be tension between the two. Often stress, or a particular stage of life, demands more activity and doing of all sorts than we can easily tolerate. Then the idea of a beach in winter is more congenial than the summer one, with the deep refreshment of a strenuous walk along a windy mile. Some women, perhaps very many, need to get away from the demands that relationships with other people make on them in their ordinary lives, and the winter beach can give them that short break to freedom. Others who are especially creative, such as the painter Lily Briscoe in Woolf's *To the Lighthouse*, have to have some way of escaping from impingements. Cliffs, dunes and beaches offer that: they have no need of humans, so the creative woman can be in harmony with them and receive from them. The only cost she has to pay is getting her perhaps intolerant family, if she has one, to understand the value to her of her temporary retreat.

The beach furthermore demands acceptance of natural fact when we people are turned off it by high tide. Most mothers, and perhaps especially single mothers, know that children have to accept material reality, as well as enjoying old stories. So I like the one of King Canute sitting on a chair, near the edge of the oncoming waves. His courtiers were trying to flatter him, saying he was all-powerful, but he easily demonstrated that the on-coming tide was far more powerful than he. His apparent obstinacy and arrogance have been highlighted in the most commonly presented versions of the legend, whereas it really shows his wisdom in understanding that natural forces have to be respected.

The beach is also symbolic of the dual life of women, especially those still living as women throughout most of history have had to do. I refer to the fact that the beach, as well as having its own intrinsic nature, has things done to it: the tide moves up and down it, storms alter the amount or the angle of the sand or the shingle, they uncover new rocks, tear up sea weed and leave it around until they clear it up perhaps many weeks later, and they beat up against protective cliffs and dunes. The beach might appear to be passive, in the hands of the sea's assertiveness. Similarly some women, in spite of all the changes brought about by over a hundred years of feminism, still see themselves as passive. But another view of the beach is that it is receptive and that it participates in its own way, as women also can, with a shift of attitude. The duality of the essential nature of the beach includes, on the one hand, the aspect of it as being a place of activity, and on the other as being the setting for the interactivity of people and wildness. Also there is the way in which various birds make use of what is on offer: for example rock pipits and pied wagtails peck for insects on the banks of brown sea weed, wading birds find just the food to delight them. And when sand hoppers are pullulating they seem to behave as though they owned the beach. Such an observation verges on anthropomorphism, and that is a risk when one is trying to demonstrate or illustrate symbolism.

The beach is where overlap takes place, between the sea which is as it were raw or wild nature, and the land which is, at least relatively, tamed and civilised. And one of the tasks which still fall primarily to women, over most of the world, is to enable babies and children to accept having their raw instincts tamed. It is something which happens in the course of upbringing and education. Yet we need not, and indeed cannot, leave all aspects of childhood behind when we grow up; we might lose their vitality and creativity. I find that the wild waves hurling themselves against high Cornish cliffs appeal to me at a deep level because they revive the rages of childhood. There was a time, in certain parts of the country, when a child in a tantrum used to be said to be 'creating' -- certainly doing that in a vital way. In some families rages are meant to be quickly controlled, they must not get out of hand, being unwelcome to the grown-ups who have presumably forgotten the times when they were gripped by stormy emotions. But the sea cannot be stopped from raging, when the wind has become all-powerful. The fascination of watching a gale, from the safety of land, keeps us in touch with the child inside, the symbolic child, and that means the capacity to grow, develop and change.

Where the appeal of fiction overlaps with the enjoyment and stimulation of places we find romantic, it has the effect of refreshing the human spirit which can all too easily get bogged down under prosaic daily life. A list of such novels set in Cornwall would be very long indeed, many being historical, and they carry an enduring appeal to most ages of reader. They are not necessarily escapist, rather are they important in that they keep moderns in touch with the roots of the present. One of the earliest story tellers, who came before novelists, was Homer, who was probably not a woman, although that was proposed by Samuel Butler in *The Authoress of the Odyssey*, in 1897. The stories he told have certainly lasted: Odysseus' ten-year voyage home with his companions after the Trojan War, their struggles with the sea's many difficult moods and with the over-powerful demi- goddess Circe, Odysseus' seduction by Calypso, his idyllic meeting by the water's edge with the young princess Nausicaa, the intellectual and protective Athena, and his amazingly patient wife Penelope. The Odyssey is a romance. Many characteristics of the sea can be read into those various female figures.

Then there is the old nurse, who had of course seen many tides rise and fall on the island of Ithaka, and who (with the dog) was the first to recognise Odysseus. There is also the legend of him setting out again to sail westwards, towards the setting sun, leaving the presumably ageing Penelope behind. That was the place for the future, although it also implied death. Before getting there he was going to seek and strive, in the mood of Tennyson's Ulysses, as much as he could. He had dealt with men in the war years, depicted in *The Iliad*, and with women in *The Odyssey*. After that, I think, he had to face himself. The West for him symbolised being fully stretched, expressed in outward form. Walking meditatively along western beaches and watching the sea from the cliffs offers moderns the chance of an inner journey, a search into themselves.

Finally, the cliffs and dunes call for attention, being the places of approach to the sea and return from it. They are pre- eminently the areas of linkage between land and water. Linking as concept and fact, including connecting via analogies, and relating, as between people, are women's specialisms. That well-known dictum of E.M.Forster's in *Howards End*, 'Only connect! That was the whole of her sermon. Only connect the prose and the passion, and both will be exalted, and human love will be seen at its highest' (ch.22), is from the pen of a male writer, but one who was all his life irretrievably connected with his mother. Some readers find his women characters more believable, and even more congenial, than the men. When someone he had created had to die, for example Rickie in *The Longest Journey*, or the baby in *A Room with a View*, he finished that person off with sudden death. It is as though the cliff's edge had been reached, and he had to go over it. Just because cliffs represent symbolically linkage, connectedness and relationship, so they can switch into their opposite, rupture and the ultimate cut-off of death. Thomas Hardy's poem 'Beeny Cliff' is one of the most poignant evocations of lost love linked to a particular Cornish place. He connects and contrasts past happiness, 'As we laughed light-heartedly aloft on that clear-sunned March day', he and 'The woman whom I loved so, and who loyally loved me', with his pain many years later, when he returned to Beeny, since 'The woman now is elsewhere whom the ambling pony bore,/ And nor knows nor cares for Beeny, and will laugh there nevermore.' The links between the past and the present, between the man and the woman, the place and the emotions, are pictured on that Cornish cliff, with the gulls and the waves unaware of human tragedy. It has something in common with Bruegel's painting of the death of Icarus, where the earth-bound ploughman takes no notice of the young man falling into the sea.

Actuality and symbolism, seascape and landscape, inner and outer meet on the cliffs, and on the dunes, where small children have sometimes been tragically engulfed by sand falls. In a more positive way, cliffs and land have the down-to-earth quality of ordinary life (the shopping and the cooking have to be done), as compared with something almost transcendent that the sea calls up: the life of the imagination in all its potential richness. It may contain over-painful or bizarre features to particularly sensitive novelists and to their readers, especially those who easily identify with the people in the stories. The changeable and unreliable sea is difficult to portray or paint satisfactorily. Those characteristics seem to have been the same for writers of all past ages who have shown up the subtle combination of similarities and differences, which also are demonstrated in the ambivalent portrayals of women. Apart of course from the erosions that cliffs are subject to, they are the unmoving land when they are contrasted with the beach, the shore and the sea. In the same way, women are (or are seen to be, in the collective view) the ones who stay, who can be left and returned to. The sea flows away from the cliff while the tide drops, but the symbolic woman/cliff waits for its return, in the still-primitive general assumptions about nature and people, even in our developed world. Although those ancient patterns are changing quite considerably at the end of this century, they still persist in many ways. Examples can be found in both everyday life and contemporary literature, of the rootedness of attitudes as well as the changes in them.

The duality implicit or very obvious in many novels set in Cornwall is illustrated both by the women in them, created by the authors, and by the symbolism of the coast which is non-human. Since it is in novels, it is of course also in the ordinary world. The coast, which comprises outer shore, beach, cliffs and dunes, is a reflection of the natural phenomena studied by scientists, and also a representation of the composite nature of women, who are difficult to study with the same scientific methods. The sea beckons people towards each other to meet on the active 'beach' of relationships, and beckons them to look outwards in the direction of the fascinating and unreachable horizon. It also calls them inwards in the direction of self- understanding. The dualities I have attempted to characterise sometimes symbolise relatedness and partnership. At other times they convey a Janus-like looking in both directions, contrasts, struggles and storms.

BIBLIOGRAPHY

Blanch, Lesley. *The Wilder Shores of Love*. London: John Murray; 1954. Penguin,1994.

Butler, Samuel. *The Authoress of the Odyssey*. London: Longmans. 1897.

Forster, E.M. *The Longest Journey*. London: Arnold, 1907; Penguin, 1996.

_____. *A Room with a View*. London: Arnold, 1908; Penguin, 1996.

_____. *Howards End*. London: Arnold, 1910; Penguin. 1996.

Hardy, Thomas. *Poems of 1912-1913*. London: Macmillan, 1914. *Complete Poems of Thomas Hardy*. London: Macmillan, 1988.

Homer, *The Odyssey*. Oxford: World's Classics, 1980.

Hubback, Judith. *The Sea has Many Voices*. Henley-on-Thames: Aidan Ellis, 1990.

Wesley, Mary. *Jumping the Queue*. London: Bantam, 1984.

_____. *The Camomile Lawn*. London: Bantam, 1985.

Woolf, Virginia. *The Voyage Out*. 1915; Penguin, 1996.

_____. *To the Lighthouse*. 1927; Penguin, 1996.

_____. *The Waves*. 1931; Penguin, 1996.

Yonge, C.M. *The Sea Shore*. London: Collins, 1949 and 1961.

See Your Own Country First: the geography of a railway landscape

Chris Thomas

One of my main concerns as a cultural geographer is with the easily overlooked significance of the everyday: the importance of everyday life, culture, landscape. In Cornwall I have found the everyday elided with the extraordinary, the poetic with the political and the personal, a subtle but diverting realisation. In my research, and in this chapter, you will find a continued engagement with everyday geography -- and evidence of a belief in Raymond Williams' assertion that culture is ordinary (Williams 1958).

This chapter might best be understood in terms of what has become known as 'new' cultural geography, an offshoot of human geography. Such a cultural geography, which has grown rapidly since the 1970s, drew (and continues to draw) much nourishment from the humanities, rather than directly from the social science and natural science traditions more readily associated with geography. My own critical sensibilities -- as will become apparent -- have much in common with authors who offer post- colonial and feminist theories of possession, representation, otherness and cultural imperialism.

This chapter considers some of the texts -- the stories -- of Cornwall and their (re)telling. The Great Western Railway's invention and promotion of the Cornish Riviera may be understood as predominantly an outsider view of place. Yet the insider / outsider relationship is not an easy dichotomy. Whilst insider landscapes may be far more experientially derived than outsider landscapes, they are both partial; their co-existence blurs the distinctions between outside and inside, the imagined and the real. I return regularly to Cornwall, although not always materially. For me, it is the metaphor and the material that make Cornwall important; I do not seek any (presumed) hidden truth beneath metaphors, but accept the diversity and vibrancy of Cornwall that such wordplay offers. As another writer has recently suggested:

> *Metaphor is real, and the real is metaphor; and living by the sea -- so prevalent as a metaphor for writing the body -- has brought this 'home' to me. There is no deep real (or engine-room) below the surface; there is no extra-textual ground for social analysis to cling on to. We, like writers of 'fiction', are at sea. (Game 1991, xii)*

In this chapter I want to consider one of the most enduring imagined geographies of Cornwall: the Cornish Riviera. My title is taken from a railway advertising poster which was first seen around 1907 [fig 1]. This shows a tinplate version of a printed-paper poster by the artist Arthur Gunn. The poster illustration consists of two maps, two fruit trees and two women; a collection and comparison of images, which under the exhortation to 'see your own country first', suggest that Cornwall has (at least) an equivalence to Italy as a holiday destination. The popular and enduring manifestation of the Cornish Riviera was -- at least in the beginning -- the invention of the Great Western Railway. In many ways, it was not the technological innovations associated with the expansion of the railways that were to have the greatest social and cultural impacts. Despite their direct influence (employment, travel), railways, as well as improving communications, were themselves communicators. Railway advertising and promotional materials were an integral part of this communication.

Courtesy of the National Railway Museum & the National Science Museum

The arguments of this chapter, therefore, are built mainly around the publicity 'texts' of various guide-books and posters issued by the Great Western Railway between 1904 and the 1930s, set in the context of a wider range of publicity materials and operating practices developed by the railway companies throughout this period. (Although, given the immense volume of material produced by the GWR alone [1] -- see Wilson 1987 -- such consideration is necessarily selective.) Not only did the railways provide the physical link between Cornwall and an industrialising Britain (see Simmons 1994, 1995; Woodfin 1972), the railway companies subsequently provided a symbolic span -- of at least equal importance to Brunel's Royal Albert bridge at Saltash -- that (re)constructed Cornwall as a land of romance and residual values in a changing, modernising world. In the processes of production and reproduction of railway services and the places they served we can identify practices and discourses [2] that attempted both material and metaphorical colonisation of an other place and people -- in this case Cornwall and the Cornish. At the same time it is my contention that we must question the effective hegemony [3] of such processes, given the caprice of the travelling public and the uncertain mutability of consumption [4].

Geography, fiction and advertising

It is important to stress at the outset that an imagined geography of Cornwall deals with places and landscapes that are no less 'real' than more immediately concrete topographies that we might believe to be the 'real' geography of Cornwall. Even this geography is a fiction (in the sense of something made), no matter how 'factual' the content of the representation (Game 1991). My concern within the following chapter is to argue for a more conscious consideration of the fictions that make places important for us -- and to suggest that it is the frictions in our fictions that help us make sense of the social world (see, *inter alia*, Duncan and Duncan 1988; Game 1991; Quoniam 1988). To this end I will examine the specific texts of railway publicity, as I do not wish to rehearse a long theoretical argument here about the importance and variability of (lay and academic) geographical representations; the interested reader can find such issues more than adequately discussed elsewhere (see, *inter alia*, Duncan and Duncan 1988; Barnes and Duncan 1992; Duncan and Ley 1993, Lunt 1994).

As I have stated, the focus of this chapter is on the place promotion -- the advertising of Cornwall and the Cornish Riviera -- carried on by the GWR in the first half of this century. Gold (1994) suggests that three emphases can be located in the study of promotional messages. In short, these may be seen firstly as part of production (i.e. messages designed with an intent to communicate certain information), secondly by concentrating on the message (i.e. as meanings in the encoded and communicated material), and thirdly through the confused lens of consumption (i.e. how the material is received and re-written by the consumer). It is useful to bear these differing emphases in mind when reviewing the railway construction of Cornwall, although it will become apparent that the relationship between them is frequently complex and sometimes confused.

Other theorists have suggested that there is no natural relationship between the words we use and the 'objects' to which our words adhere (Barthes 1975, 1977; Derrida 1978) and that the language we use constitutes, rather than merely reflects, or reports, the experienced world. My consideration of GWR publicity rests on the understanding that the material outcomes of descriptions and depictions of the world [5] (e.g. posters, guide books) do not merely reflect an external reality, but are re- presentations of it. Such re-presentations are inevitably selective and partial. The framework for the critical review of GWR publicity which follows is built upon the notion that such representations of

Cornwall may be understood as texts and, as such, they may therefore be 'read'. This reading is possible as texts are always social and cultural constructions -- that is, they are situate in and contingent upon social and cultural values and practices. Reading is not, however, a passive practice. In reading (or 'mis'-reading) the opportunity arises for re-writing the text. Where there is a discursive dimension to the social world there exists the potential for non-understanding when users of an ostensibly shared language talk past each other -- indeed such misunderstanding may be basic to the constitution of everyday social reality [6]. Moreover, the co-existence of different but competing discourses allows the exercise of power in social relations (Foucault 1970, 1972; Hoy 1986; Shotter 1993). Frequently, for example, 'academic', 'expert' or 'scientific' expression is given greater weight than lay opinion or 'anecdotal' evidence. This evidences a power relationship where one form of knowledge is 'known' to be 'better' than another. Although this chapter is primarily concerned with the various and variable discourses of railway publicity, it should be realised that such power relationships exist in all use of language, not just advertising.

Crucially, when we 'read' advertisements we also re-write them. For example, we do not believe everything an advertisement tells us (see Myers 1994) and yet we are intended to recognise the product. We may 'mis'-understand the intention of the advertisement. We may even like the advertisement but dislike the product it is advertising (or *vice versa*). In advertising a 'product' (soap powder, railway transport) the advertisement itself becomes a product which we consume. People are frequently able to refer to favourite advertisements as they might refer to the thing being sold to them by that ad. We can remember the advertisement without knowing what was advertised. Increasingly we may purchase items that have advertising functions, for example, 'heritage' tins for storing tea-bags, bread or some other product. It is in recognising the multiplicity and the openness of texts such as advertising, that the possibilities, not only for understanding but for resisting the power of the text emerge (see Game 1991).

Railways, advertising and place promotion

The Great Western Railway was pre-eminent in its field in *selling* its guide books, posters and jigsaws. A product themselves, they were also selling railway travel and more particularly the GWR as the means of that travel (Wilson 1987). This was, and is, an undeniably powerful technique for raising the profile of the advertised (product). It also raises the profile of the advertisement *and* the practice of advertising. Because the advertisement becomes desirable in and of itself, there is even greater potential for the consumer to re-write the publicity intentions of the advertisement. Many GWR posters were undoubtedly popular with the public *not* because the public had an intrinsic interest in railway transport and travel (although they would certainly have used the railways more for everyday purposes and holidays than is the case today), but because the poster art was aesthetically pleasing, and had resonances with other areas of the lives and lifestyles of the travelling public.

If we are to believe some authors, it is difficult to overstate the significance of railways on the social construction of our world. Nicholas Faith asserts that '[t]he modern world began with the coming of the railways... They made a

110

greater and more immediate impact than any other mechanical or industrial innovation before or since'. (1990, 1) This is quite a bold claim given the other contenders for 'explosive' social impacts such as the advent of moveable type, the internal combustion engine and electronics. That all of these have an impact on 'improved' communications in common should not surprise us, given the arguments about the discursive content of the constitution of social reality. Faith's claim for the railways can, in many ways, be substantiated. The literature on railways is vast. It may, in numerical terms, be dominated by a plethora of repetitive photographic albums and near hagiographic writings, but even amongst such 'hobby' literature there is work of much scholarship which should not be overlooked. In itself, such a vast literature hints at the impact of railway transport not merely on our travel practices, but on our conception of the social world. Much 'academic' writing on the railways has concentrated on their economic impact, rather than considering such broader issues as redefinition of concepts of time and space, or the social and cultural impacts of the new forms of labour and leisure that the railways made possible. Yet even casual reference to various academic considerations -- although some of this material perhaps overemphasises the significance of the technology of industrialisation -- offers plenty of evidence for the wider world the railways made. (Alderman 1973; Burton 1994; Davis and Wilburn 1991; Faith 1990; Jordan and Jordan 1991; Kerr 1995; Revell 1994; Robbins 1965; Schivelbusch 1986; Simmons 1994, 1995; Smith 1988; Turnock 1990) We should resist the more uncritical acceptance of any technocentric argument as there is a more complex relationship between technology and society than the culture of technology might at first admit. There was, however, perhaps something special about railways and the new imaginations of territory which they allowed -- the linkage of moving things (people, troops and goods) and moving ideas with similar rapidity.

Railways, in particular, were associated with territorial transgression and possession. As Robinson suggests in the context of other nineteenth-century industrial innovation,

... only the locomotive carried such widespread imperial territorial implications. Even before the tracks were laid, it was the fantastic effects of imagined lines on the political and strategic thinking of Europeans and non-Europeans alike that made railways intrinsically imperialistic. (1991, 195)

Whilst we can accept this as the case in more distant imperial possessions, it is also true in some degree closer to the bases of imperial power. Reece argues that railways were more than complicit in the internal colonisation of Brittany within a united France; '...Breton railroads do not facilitate the expansion of local commerce but instead operate to the advantage of the larger economic system'. (1979, 285) This may be have been true of the national rail system in Brittany, but there were many kilometres of metre gauge light railways which did serve local communities. [7] It is possible to draw parallels from Brittany with the working of the railways in Cornwall (and Wales and Scotland) regarding the behaviour of centrally administered railways, but the picture in Britain is equally complex, as several schemes for the promotion of railway lines

-- especially following the 1896 Light Railways Act (see Davies 1964) -- were initiated or strongly supported by local interests. [8]

Regardless of how they were conceived, railways had an immense influence on the world of leisure and, particularly with the increase in paid holidays between the world wars, made leisure destinations available to the working classes. (Walvin 1978) One of the most popular areas for such leisure were the coasts and countrysides of South West England. (Shaw and Williams 1991) But it is worthwhile pausing to consider the implications of this specific development of leisure spaces; the dominant representation of coastal and rural leisure has been -- and even today in academia remains -- an urban one. As Patmore observes: 'funnelled by the railway, the movement to the seaside was urban in origin and urban in expression'. (1983, 43) A point of interest here is that whilst the move to countryside and seaside was from urban centres of industrial type (Walvin 1978), Cornwall was *both* a seaside / rural destination *and* a locale itself associated with the extractive and fishing industries.

The more rapid and reliable distribution system railways offered, not only took people to the seaside, but created a space for the growth of national advertising. Railways encouraged the growth of national publications through which advertisers could hope to reach much larger audiences than before. Billboard and poster sites at stations and alongside railway lines provided further opportunities for reaching a wider section of the public. In the realm of leisure travel to which the railways were central there was the potential for considerable sales of domestic tourist guide books. Black's and Ward Lock's Red Guides not only 'advertised' the region concerned to visitors, but also contained advertisements for various sundry products (including, with warming candour, in the 1946 Red Guide to North Wales, raincoats and travel sickness pills). The railway companies themselves were not slow to judge the advantages of such publicity material aimed at visitors to the area of the country they served, including companies with lesser grand plans than the Great Western (e.g. Cambrian Railways 1904; Corris Railway 1908; North Staffordshire Railway 1908. [9] Railway advertising became far more important in the last few years of the nineteenth century, and particularly significant in the first half of the twentieth century. One reason for this growth is quite simple; increasing competition meant that for railway companies to maintain (or increase) their market share (and thus profits) they needed to encourage people to use one company over another. This period of growth in advertising is also often recognised as the 'golden age' of Britain's railway companies. The significance of advertising and publicity in this period should not be overlooked; as Wilson points out, the 'virtual monopoly which [the railway companies] held in the transport of passengers and goods' (1987, 15) in the late nineteenth century was eroded both by increasing railway company competition but also, as the twentieth century grew older, by improvements in road transport. The regional nature of the pre-nationalised railway companies dictated the style of advertising, where one area would be promoted as the best to visit and/or in which to live. This practice has left some memorable images of advertising. The Southern Railway's 'Sunny South Sam' and 'Summer comes soonest in the South', or 'Skegness is so bracing' from the Great Northern Railway (later re-used by the London and North Eastern Railway), are examples of railway place promotion that persist in popular perceptions of places, and to a lesser degree, of the railways that made them. (Gold and Ward 1994; Cole and Durack 1992)

Making Cornwall possible

It is my contention that the railways -- and particularly the Great Western Railway -- made Cornwall possible for much of the British population:

> Cornwall, the last [county] in England to be connected to the main railway system... was more strongly individual, one might almost say separate, than any of the other 39, and when the last link was forged, by the bridging of the Tamar at Saltash, that produced some consequences, for Cornwall and for England, attributable... to railways alone. (Simmons 1994,7)

Yet it is not only the physical bridging of the Tamar that mattered. Since 1859 [10] the fabrications of the railways have shaped hundreds of thousands of experiences of Cornwall. After the introduction of the Cornish Riviera train and advertising in 1904, the impact on tourist numbers visiting Cornwall was notable. However, whilst there was an overall increase, the impacts were localised within Cornwall. For example, between 1903 and 1913, the passenger traffic receipts at Newquay (one of the resorts promoted strongly in Riviera literature, posters and film) increased by 69%. Receipts at Penzance dropped, however. (Simmons 1994) Increasing numbers brought increased profits, both to the railway company and local traders, but had attendant difficulties in the larger tourist population giving a heavy ironic gloss to the claims of Cornwall as a place of solitude and repose.

Of all the railway companies the GWR has been noted for its attention to advertising and publicity matters from early in its history (Cole and Durack 1992; Thomas, D. 1996; Wilson 1987):

> Few British organisations have conducted their publicity so successfully, and made so much money even out of the direct sales of publicity material to the public, as the Great Western Railway... The GWR had been publicity conscious from the start. (Whitehouse and Thomas, D. 1984, 145)

The Great Western Railway's invention of the Cornish Riviera was incredibly successful. It informed, and was informed by, new ways of seeing [11] Cornwall (see Payton and Thornton 1995; Bennett 1992a, 1992b, 1995). A GWR map, published between the first and second world wars showing Great Western territory, identified places with experiences and values before commonplace use of such terms as heritage landscapes (Russell 1978). On this map we may locate not only the Cornish Riviera, but also Devon 'Shire of the Sea Kings', Wonderful Wessex, Shakespeare's Country, North Wales 'the British Tyrol' and South Wales 'the Country of Castles'. We also find 'rural' London. Rather more prosaically, the map also shows Southern Ireland and the Severn and Wye valleys; located for us in the railways terms, but not yet re-named for place promotion. Russell, a former Great Western employee, gives a personal comment on this map which expresses something of the power of the cartography:

It was beautifully coloured in the same colours as the OS maps of the day, namely the sea blue, sands and foreshore yellow, lowlands green, and as the altitude rose, so the colour deepened from light brown to dark purple brown of the mountain ranges of Snowdonia. To my simple mind, these maps spoke volumes, I could see quite clearly how the Great Western marched over the Midlands, Wales and far West. (Russell 1978, 6)

It is not difficult to see the attraction of such cartographic reproductions. The same must be said for the guide books, whose text was obviously written to be read as narrative, although it was of course possible to sample from them. But in such narratives (linguistic or pictorial), the ideology is already becoming evident: 'I could see quite clearly how the Great Western *marched over* the Midlands, Wales and far West' (my emphasis). The inferred connection with Ordnance Survey map colours adds further (spurious) authenticity to what is, essentially, a commercial propaganda map. [12]

I have suggested that it is possible for the advertisement to gain product status, in that it may become an object of consumption in its own right. Equally, in guide books, posters etc. advertising the basic commodity (i.e. railway travel) which the railway companies provide and from which they intend to profit, we may also identify the creation of the end destination, and the landscapes passed through en route (GWR 1924), as commodities. They become objects to be possessed (if only momentarily) from the window of a train. The passenger not only buys the ticket and the guide book (a copy of the poster, a postcard, a jigsaw), but is, through these acts of consumption, also purchasing the place. The GWR's possessions are marked for us on the map, in the book, through the window. In buying travel we are buying part of that possession, something of the place and an associated lifestyle. In many ways the GWR affected an entire economic, social and cultural existence:

The railway... was just the starting point. The GWR had extensive shipping, bus and lorry, and even air services. It ran docks, restaurants and hotels, designed its own linen and laundered it, published a magazine and had its own bands. In the restaurant car you read Great Western literature, drank Great Western whisky and ate Great Western biscuits with your cheese. (Whitehouse and Thomas 1984, 9)

Edwardian enterprise and the Cornish Riviera
The actual *title* Cornish Riviera is not used in the poster that gives this chapter its title, although the *concept* is certainly informing the images. The Cornish Riviera name dates from 1904 and the concept has shaped our understanding of Cornwall, both as a place to visit and as a landscape in mind ever since. The Cornish Riviera name appears to originate in a competition held by The Railway Magazine in 1904 to name a new express train service to Plymouth and Penzance (Adams 1993). Two men shared the three guinea prize for suggesting the 'Cornish Riviera Ltd', although eight valid entries included Riviera in their suggestions. The general manager of the GWR chose 'The Riviera Express', but when adopted officially, the name had become 'The Cornish Riviera' and was variously known as Express or Limited throughout its life. The same year -- 1904 -- the first ever GWR regional holiday guide book *The Cornish Riviera*

114

(Wilson 1987) was issued, beginning a successful forty plus years of advertising and publicity publishing. The first five editions were written by A. M. Broadley (1904;1905;1908;1914;1924/6), although he was never credited on the cover, nor on the title page. An entirely new book, with the same title, but this time written by S.P.B. Mais was published in 1928. This ran to three editions (1928;1929/32;1934). An entire county (*the Duchy* as the traditionalist [13] GWR liked to call it) was carefully made for visitors' consumption. [14]

The creation of the Cornish Riviera needs to be seen in the context of the Great Western Railway's changing practices in the early years of the twentieth century. The years from the close of the nineteenth century to the beginning of the first world war are generally recognised as a 'golden age' for the railway companies of Britain (Booker 1985; Faith 1990). Whilst we might find in such a recognition evidence of the mythology of all golden ages (see Williams 1973), it is fair to state that this was a period when social, cultural and economic conditions appeared most favourable to the railways. The impetus for the Great Western's 'Edwardian enterprise' (Norris *et al.* 1987), has been variously argued, but a growing commercial sensibility in the face of competition and a sense of pragmatism following the final removal of the broad gauge tracks in 1892 [15] are likely contributory factors. Bryan (1991) notes another *fin-de-siecle* event as a 'milestone' heralding this golden age: the first non-stop London to Bristol train, with no refreshment stop at Swindon. The significance of this train was that it marked a break with restrictive practices that had been in place since the railway company had been incorporated in 1835. This train, appropriately enough, was the *Cornishman.* The event represented the final resolution of the 'Swindon question' and 'the beginning of a vibrant period of rebirth for the company, which one commentator called the "Great Awakening"'. (Bryan 1991) Despite the inevitable oversimplification that picking out 'milestones' involves, it is important to recognise the spirit of enterprise and near-imperial fervour that marked the turn of the century, [16] which found a metaphorical and material focus in the Great Western Railway's renewed vigour regarding its speed to the west, thereby re-inventing Brunel's vision of sixty years earlier.

Shape, climate, beauty

Although the poster art of the GWR was not to reach outstanding heights of graphic design and innovative artwork until the 1920s and '30s (Cole and Durack 1992; Wilson 1987), early posters advertising Cornwall are worthy of attention for their written messages and the visual metaphors they contained. *See Your Own Country First* is a classic of its kind. The poster offers interesting and favourable comparisons between Cornwall and Italy. [17] It suggests to the viewer/reader that rather than Italy, he (or she) [18] should visit Cornwall, as the similarities, in Shape, Climate and Natural Beauties make 'your own country' preferable to continental travel.

Most importantly, and informing the comparisons we are expected to make, the poster, being a visual medium, reflects (and relies upon) the visuality of holiday experience that is the tourist gaze. The poster (and much in the guidebooks) considers Cornwall as seen, despite attempts by both Broadley and Mais to elaborate on the place relations that sight-seeing offers. There continues to be an emphasis on visuality in what have become everyday discourses -- including those of visiting places. This visuality is highly partial, and not only in terms of being a rather limited and brief encounter with place. Vision becomes voyeurism. Vision as a discourse and presumed practice has both class and gender dimensions; it is also highly ethnocentric. (Cosgrove 1984; Daniels 1993; Trinh Minh-ha 1989; Pollock 1988; Rose 1993) So you 'See your own country first'. We must see it. And only first; not exclusively. Europe still awaits the more adventurous and more wealthy travellers of the tourist trail. Seeing was, of course, believing. (See *inter alia* Benjamin 1992; Crary 1993) Seeing is the basis of the dominant discourses of empiricist science, the modernist world and the then increasingly available medium of photographic reproduction which illustrated the guidebooks and gave an activity focus to leisure experience. This construction of vision and modernity was closely bound up with photography, which was to become, perhaps, the paradigmatic tourist practice. (Beloff 1985; Bourdieu 1990; Burgin 1982; Sontag 1977) In this poster of Cornwall, we find the tourist gaze, [19] early and colourful (and, as yet, not photographically reproduced). The primacy of vision as sensory perception sits above the implied full sensual experience of a favourable climate -- and perhaps, too, the natural beauties. The authors of the posters and guidebooks do, however, demonstrate the ambivalence inherent in the experience of place rather than in the selective gaze encouraged by the poster view or the photographs that illustrate the books. The notion of climate is inevitably one that requires more than seeing to appreciate (although the 'quality of light' is an oft repeated justification of the attractiveness of Cornwall for artists of every type). Vision tends to be discriminatory. Mais warns against this tendency:

> The visitor who opens his eyes to the wooded loveliness of the Fowey Valley, and closes them to the deserted broken down chimneys of old tin mines and the mountainous white pyramids of china clay refuse that litter the hillsides, has no chance of getting to know the real Cornwall (1928a, 3).

In other words, authentic 'seeing' seems to require something other than the exclusive gaze. This was further acknowledged by a publication *The Homeland Handbook*, which seemed concerned that the 'real identity and character of Cornwall' (Bennett 1992a, 55) were being obscured by a predominantly tourist glaze. Speaking of railway induced visitors, it asks:

> how many of these people know the real uniqueness of Cornwall? Very few. For this land of primeval solitudes and prehistoric monuments is not to be discovered in a few weeks of sight seeing. Its true spirit does not reveal itself on the sea fronts of its watering places, or in the show spots of the guide books. (Quoted in Bennett 1992a, 55)

Sight seeing is a discriminatory practice, and it has distinct origins. (Adler 1989) The guide books suggest that it may not be enough for the visitor in search of a real Cornwall, however. But the poster invites us to see.

116

Yet where is this great similarity that we are meant to see? The peninsula shape is similar -- but then again so is Llyn in north Wales. Similarly the comparison of climate seems specious, given the equation of the far South Western trip of the British mainland with the climate regimes of an entire Mediterranean country. Natural beauties? There are Alps in Cornwall too, but the Cornish Alps are waste tips from the china clay industry, which although romanticised by language are ultimately only waste tips; quartz sand and mica in the main, they cannot offer alternatives or similarities to Mont Rosa. The green-reflecting pools of water from the clayworks and tinworks pumping houses are not Lake Como. These then are not the Natural Beauties of the poster. The reference seems to be to the beauties of landscape, vegetation and cultivation -- with the orange tree counterposed to the apple tree. The beauty also seems to embrace peasant women. A bare-foot Cornish woman in (clean) peasant clothing, is presented in opposition to her Italian counterpart. Here we have the elision of Cornwall and the female. Is the female so easily encompassed in the tourist gaze -- reduced and promoted at the same time to being a *natural* beauty, when in fact we are being openly confronted by social and cultural values?

These constituent elements of the poster require further consideration. The emphasis on shape is a cartographic sleight- of-hand, presuming the shape the poster is referring to is the coastline, and not the women. The sharp-eyed geographically- minded viewer might also notice that Sicily has been excised. The function of these simplified maps is, however, immediate. The comparison made between two very different places by the juxtaposition of easily recognised geographic shorthand is instantly apprehended. Such is the power of carto-graphic representation (Wood 1992); map making being yet another hege-monic, visually dependent, practice (and one tied, almost umbilicus-like, to geography). Beyond this immediate (and less than candid) visual echo, the similarity in shape is difficult to sustain. However, much more is said in the publication(s) *The Cornish Riviera* about climate.

The first edition of *The Cornish Riviera* was subtitled 'our national health and pleasure resort'. The emphasis on health came through not only the sustained vogue for sea air as being beneficial for mind and body, but through constant reference to the benefits of the temperate climatic regime the visitor would encounter in Cornwall. The climate and health issue had been present in the promotion of Cornwall as a resort since the beginning. As Shaw and Williams point out, 'the first guide book on Cornwall was published on Pen-zance and district in 1815 [and]... gave great emphasis to the benefits of the climate, comparing it to Mediterranean resorts'. (1991, 17) The GWR was, therefore, only following tradition, although reinventing it to its own ends. The entire second chapter of *The Cornish Riviera* (1914 edition) goes into some depth about the advantages bestowed by climate on Cornwall, and by reflection on those who visit Cornwall. There is a even an appendix containing 'statistical tables of the climatology of the Cornish Riviera'. (Broadley 1914, 13) The popular understanding of the Riviera as a climatic holiday haven is entrenched by such material. As the idea of the Cornish Riviera was established and as the popularity of railway encouraged holidays spread across the social spectrum, it was felt unnecessary to offer such statistical and expert proof of the suitability of the temperate nature of Cornwall for health. In the opening sentence of the 1928 edition of *The Cornish Riviera*, this time written by S.P.B. Mais, we are told that:

Cornwall is recognised as an area where visitors may be reasonably assured that they will escape the rigours of winter. With regard to climate it is quite time we had some plain speaking. Statistics may be seen and compared by any one... The simple truth is that in Falmouth it is as warm in January as it is in Madrid, and as cool in July as it is in Petrograd. There is an incontestable fact for you, and gives the main reason for visiting Cornwall at any time of year before anywhere else. (1928a, 1)

Along with climate, cost was also a major consideration, of course, and was even before the Great War. Thus given the favourable climate which can be accessed with less financial and time costs and less fatigue than continental travel, it becomes evident why the Cornish Riviera is such a desired leisure locus. It is evident also that this access would be provided by the Great Western Railway. In this way

a maximum of amusement at a minimum of expense is provided for those who elect, either for pleasure or health, to judge by actual experience of the advantages of the Cornish Riviera as compared with its foreign rivals on the shores of the Mediterranean, or amidst the waves of the Atlantic'. (Broadley 1914, 12)

This suggests which class of visitors we may expect; despite the opening statement that '[i]t is becoming more and more apparent to all classes of English men and English women that ... the necessity of costly and fatiguing foreign travel exists no longer', this publicity is very clearly aimed at the affluent middle class (i.e. those that might have afforded to engage in such costly and fatiguing foreign travel, not to mention that would buy a guide book costing 3d). The working classes were to benefit later from the railways' expansion of holiday making and had yet to venture much abroad -- before, that is, the First World War sent them in great numbers to France and the Low Countries of Europe.

Broadley's book is constructed to be read as narrative and as an accompanying volume to a tour of the county, like an Edwardian travelogue -- though of course it is possible to abstract parts of the tour and the book. Although well written, it is generally free of the greater uses of rhetoric in its depiction of Cornwall. The same cannot be said of Mais's 1928 version. In his edition of *The Cornish Riviera*, S.P.B. Mais writes of Cornwall both as an 'it' but equally as 'her'. There is nothing particularly unusual in this. But it is perhaps *because* of the ubiquity of the constructions of land and landscape as feminine, and the visitor/the expert/the user as masculine, that the unthinking generic needs to be pointed out. (See *inter alia* Monk 1984; Pollock 1988; Porteous 1986; Wolff 1990.)

In Cornwall's case, (natural) beauty and hidden knowledge are emphasised much as in the poster from 20 years before. And with that emphasis goes an underwriting of these as 'already recognised' (i.e. 'natural') female qualities.

These social qualities are naturalised and removed from the spheres of cultural and social production, thus limiting the possibilities of their contestation. The narrative is offering us the yet-to-be-encountered in terms of the familiar; as Barnes and Duncan suggest, the narrative's power resides in the evocation of the familiar, and is thus persuasive. So metaphors such as body-landscape (Porteous 1986) 'are implicated in the very fabric of society and social processes; if they are to work they must resonate against an existing set of social and cultural representations' (Barnes and Duncan 1992, 12). It is only in this way that can Cornwall be made for us; whilst it is different (Cornwall, its people and places have been, and still are emphasised as 'other' in various representations), we can only recognise that difference in terms of the same. Indeed, as Barnes and Duncan suggest, in the resonance between new and extant representations 'there is often conflict, intellectual and sometimes physical'. (1992, 12)

Mais offers an example of this -- almost reflexively aware of this conflict whilst nevertheless assisting in the construction of another Cornwall:

Artists and archaeologists, metallurgists and miners, botanists and philologists, historians and antiquarians, bird lovers and church lovers, fishermen and farmers have all had a cut at her and have come away enriched, but there is a richer measure beneath the soil of Cornwall than tin and arsenic, copper and silver, a richer haul to be netted from her deep seas than pilchards or pollock, richer colours on her granite covered hills and in her thickly wooded valleys than any artist will dare reproduce, a richer etymology than the philologist knows, richer eyries than the ornithologist will ever reach, and a rarer storehouse of myth and legend than your scholarly antiquarian ever penetrates. (1928a, 2)

It is Mais's belief and suggestion that 'he who would know Cornwall at all must know the whole of her'. (3) That a degree of intellectual possession is required is evident; but Mais recognises that this act of masculinist occupation is ultimately impossible, suggesting he would rather 'fail in a severe undertaking... than... succeed in an easy one'. He seems to be offering possibilities for irony and for contestation.

If we are seduced by the female land/landscape imagining, then Mais's treatment of Cornwall's geography is worth another look. Because for Mais, Cornwall was not pretty; instead she possessed a rugged beauty. He states that:

The soft prettiness of the Southern shires she neither has nor pretends to have, her beauty is bracing and austere, rugged and fine. (1928a, 7)

Interestingly, a cross current of Mais's geographical observation may be found in Alun Howkins' perceptive review of the discovery of rural England. In this he suggests that the strong ruralist strain in English popular culture is closely tied to a geographical specificity -- the landscape of the 'south country'; ideal-type of rolling hills and a hedged, farmed land. But this South country could (and did) break the bounds of geographical actuality. In Howkins' words, 'Shropshire could be incorporated into the 'South Country' but Cornwall could not, since part of Shropshire conformed to the ideal type whereas practically none of Cornwall did' (1986, 64). Thus whilst Cornwall is a repository of rural values (simultaneously understood as traditional values -- see Bunce 1994; Bennett 1992a; Howkins 1986), it is a rurality elided with a distinct (and potentially contradictory) understanding of female qualities -- attractive yet not pretty, domestic yet not too homely.

Paradoxically, this rurality, this beauty, was being projected at the same time that the same railway company was promoting industrial advance. The GWR was serving and promoting the expanding china clay industry around St Austell, Fowey and Par, and was finding considerable profit in this endeavour (Barton 1966; Vaughan 1987). This parallel development of industry and modernity with leisure and romantic past was implicitly acknowledged in Broadley's edition of *The Cornish Riviera*, as not only does it mention (albeit briefly) 'St Austell as the centre of the commerce in china-clay, now one of the foremost Cornish industries' (1914, 35), it also includes a full-page, illustrated advertisement for machinery associated with Cornwall's extractive industries. Mais's book has lost the advertisement for industrial plant, but still manages to comment on the china-clay industry, making a point that it would be easy to pass such an industrial intrusion into a leisure landscape 'contemptuously' (Mais 1928a, 39), as many later guidebooks have done.

It becomes apparent then, that the writers of those promotional guidebooks were not unaware of the problem of partial and superficial experience. Yet the promotion of Cornwall, for leisure or labour, had an inevitable outcome if it worked: more people in Cornwall. Mais was quite sanguine about this in his publication from the Southern Railway *My Finest Holiday* (1928b). Here he acknowledged the ideal of parts of Cornwall as restorative recreation sites, away from the 'multitudes of fellow visitors' that come to view Land's End or the Lizard, as 'there are always fresh unsuspected beauties to be discovered'. Yet he realises that tourist growth will reduce such discoveries. He may even be acknowledging his own part in the idyll's destruction when he says of the sense of solitude North Cornwall inspires: 'I cannot believe that it will remain so much longer, but one of the chief charms of this incomparably majestic coast-line is that it is as yet unexploited'. (1928b, 12)

Cornwall and the domestic exotic

We must return to the poster to question whether it is 'our own' country that we are seeing here. Howkins' comment about exclusion from the 'south country' suggests that Cornwall would have difficulty finding a place in popular culture as rural England. Mais certainly emphasises this in his two 1928 books. I have already suggested that the comparison with Italy hinted at un-Englishness. Whilst offered up here (and elsewhere) to the gaze as 'our own' country, it is to be understood from other evidence, including that emanating from the same publicity department, that Cornwall was not England. Cornwall was and is 'other'. [20] Here we have the beginnings of a widely available, discursive construction of place that is immediately ambivalent. A trip to Cornwall becomes an encounter with the domestic exotic; 'the other-we-are-comfortable-with' (particularly on holiday). This sense of place/way of seeing I identify as the oxymoronic 'domestic exotic' is built around a highly distinctive admixture of safety (the domestic -- because it was, in some senses, at home) and

120

excitement (the exotic -- because it was distinctly un-English in its Celtic cultural traditions, and because of its steadfast, peripheral rurality). (21)

Mais takes us over the Tamar and into foreign territory:

> The simple truth is that Cornwall is far more different from any other part of the British Isles than most foreign places are. It is the only entirely foreign place you can reach without changing from train to boat after leaving London. (1928b, 24)

and:

> Brunel's Royal Albert Bridge... is the means, and an almost magic means, of transporting travellers from a county, which if richer than others is yet unmistakably an English County, to a Duchy which is in every respect un-English. (1928a, 9)

It is worth noting that Cornwall is not just slightly un-English, but in 'every respect'. Yet we encounter the suggestion that Cornwall is a repository for English values -- whatever we might presume such values to be. There is a mixing of two already ambiguous metaphorical constructions of Cornwall here: Cornwall is not English, but part of Britain (and therefore 'better' than other un-English places) and Cornwall as rural (though not 'South-country-English-rural') where industry is either already heritage by the 1920s (copper and tin's greatest years have gone), or can be offered as community based and solid -- such as the fishing village, a subject which became highly popular with the poster makers in the 1920s and '30s. For leisure consumption, china clay extraction and processing, one of the two expanding Cornish industries (tourism was, and remains, the other), was rarely featured -- save for a few brief appearances in the guidebooks.

Not only does the past become reified in the Cornish landscape, but the un-Englishness is confusingly turned (as the *See Your Own Country First* poster suggests) to represent a shared, national (and, therefore, English?) heritage despite protestations that 'Cornish people are not English people'. (Mais 1928a, 9) Mais expresses it thus:

> Old England is everywhere crumbling about *our* ears and it is a sorry business trying to find any traces of *her* nowadays in the Home Counties, but in the Duchy mediaevalism still exists, the candle lit by the early saints still burns, the age of chivalry is emphatically not dead, and *our* most remote ancestors still haunt the ancient places. (1928a, 7) [emphases added]

Our most remote ancestors? Remoteness in time and space makes malleable icons of *our* ancestors; makes them safe but powerful. But if Cornish people are not English people, who are the *we* that claim *our* ancestors, and suggest that an old England is to be found in a Duchy that is not England? There is contradiction in Mais's writing, even irony. If there is humour in the confusions of identity, of people and places both, perhaps we might take time to ask who is Mais smiling at, if anyone at all?

Leaving Cornwall, living Cornwall

We are left, after considering only very few samples, with a Cornwall of too many texts, diverse discourses and multiple metaphors. After a measured consideration of such material, it is usual to expect a conclusion to be drawn; however, I offer no such comfort of closure. Rather I want to destabilise any certainty of my entire thesis regarding the impacts of dominant discursive constructions, drawing on the notions of hegemony and resistance outlined by others. (Game 1991; Sassoon 1987) If, as suggested at the beginning of this chapter, we re-write advertisements (and other texts) as we read them, we make space available for resistant, counter-hegemonic discourses. In this case, I want to do this by offering a superficial consideration of the consumption of Great Western Cornwall and by reference to an autobiographic recollection by the Cornish-born historian, A. L. Rowse.

A locally produced Cornish postcard of the 1900s, recently republished in a collection of old postcards (Paston-Williams 1989), shows a Cornish farmer and his wife, Jan and Jane, reading a poster -- which appears to show St Michael's Mount -- advertising the Cornish Riviera on their local station. The verse by A. E. Philp that accompanies the image is telling (it is, of course, the man speaking):

> The Carnish Riv-reera! Well, Jane!!
> I wonder what that there do mane?
> It do seem some queer;
> Let's read this 'ere 'ere
> P'raps the readin' do av ut explain.
>
> It do say 'you mus go by thess line
> Hef you want to find 'ealth and sunshine'
> If the picture be true
> What the artis' 'ave drew,
> We'll go theere wan day when tez fine.
>
> But we can't 'ford the train now-a-days,
> So we'll go in our old donkey chaise.
> Niver knawd theere wor such
> A gran' plaace, wethin touch;
> Tho' we've lived 'ere in Carnwall always.

Our local couple, encountering the Great Western Publicity encounter a landscape with which they are familiar but do not recognise. Not only is the pictorial image subverted by its reading and re-writing, but the intention of the text -- travel by train -- is circumvented by the financial circumstances of the farmer. [22] So the couple say they will go 'theere', even though it is obvious to us, viewing the postcard, that they already inhabit a more prosaic version of this fantastical landscape.

Thus, in a pleasingly circular manner (seeing the representation of Cornish people seeing a representation of Cornwall and not seeing it as Cornwall), the overwhelming message of the card is that the Cornwall of the poster is a fiction. But if humour is present in the card, are we smiling at the failure of the GWR, the transparency of advertising hyperbole, or at the Cornish who 'fail' to understand the advertisement? One of the main readings I have developed from the poster and the guidebooks of the Cornish Riviera is that of the domestic exotic. But even this is not so simply expressed. The postcard offers us a couple to whom this truly is their domestic landscape, yet it is also, through the lens of the representation, exoticised for them. It seems that in the end, regardless of the advertisement, the exotic is what we (re)construct in relation to our own experience. For example, as children, the spaces that may seem quite mundane to adults can seem exotic. The historian, A. L. Rowse, writing of his childhood in china clay country, recollects a trip on the Pentewen Railway [23]:

what violent pleasure it was: we couldn't have been more excited if we were making a journey into darkest Africa. And actually when we left the obviousness of the roadway behind us and the track took us beside the river skirting King's Wood, the river might have been the Limpopo and the wood equatorial forest, it was all so exotic and thrilling. (Rowse 1975, 139)

In this recollection, and in the postcard, the hegemony of Cornwall as exotic for tourists -- as made by the undeniably powerful Great Western Railway -- is challenged. Cornwall is the Cornish Riviera, and many images rooted in this invention seem almost natural today, but Cornwall is, at the same time, much more than the Riviera. Its sense of the exotic is found even in everyday experience. For the tourist, the exoticism of Cornwall is made by its proximity and contrast to their everyday, whilst for the resident that exotic landscape is their everyday. Both are true.

To understand anything of 'Cornwall made', experience has to go beyond seeing our own country first. As Jan and Jane suggest, posters like guide books can represent places and ideas that are not always evident at a glance.

'P'raps the readin' do av ut explain.' P'raps.

NOTES

1 The developing poster art of the GWR (and indeed other railway companies) has been documented elsewhere (see Cole and Durack 1990, 1992; Palin/British Rail 1987). I feel, however, that there remains room for a more critical, thematic examination of the evolution of poster and guide book representations of Cornwall, Ireland, Scotland, Wales and the regions of England.
2 Although, as Game (1991), drawing on the ideas of French social theorists, correctly points out, discourse is a practice, and by extension, it may be understood that certain social practices may be understood discursively.
3 The concept of hegemony is here used in a sense after Gramsci. This suggests that dominant power is exerted over others not merely (and indeed rarely) by economic or military force, but

by a routinisation of ideas and ways of seeing the world which become reified in 'common-sense', and thus do not readily accept challenge.

4 The concept of consumption implied here is metaphorical as well as material, and one that has been gaining widespread use and acceptance within cultural geography, cultural studies and sociology. It depends upon a notion of consumption beyond that of narrow economism, where produce other than food or material goods can be consumed. For a series of papers that focus on the consumption of place see Urry (1995). For a more general introduction to the theoretical and practical debates about the study of consumption see Bocock (1993).

5 This includes academic or scientific writings. Including this one.

6 Some theorists such as Bakhtin and de Certeau suggest this is the case. See de Certeau 1988; Hirschkop and Shepherd 1989; Gardiner 1992.

7 Several metre gauge lines radiated from Carhaix, central Brittany, and served local agricultutre and industry, including the major fisheries at Crozon and Douarnenez in Finistere. (Many thanks to Gordon Gravett for bringing this to my attention.)

8 Although it must be said that despite often vigorous local lobbying and support for a rail connection, hard cash in the form of share subscriptions was notoriously difficult to raise (see e.g. Green 1986; Jenkins 1991). In the final event much of the finance was often supplied through local and central government loans and grants. Equally, under-capitalised railways were frequently operated or even absorbed by larger railway companies like the Great Western, who effectively extended their own rail network with little initial expense and without being involved in early speculative ventures.

9 Interestingly, all these publications referred to their hinterlands as 'picturesque', also an element of advertising Cornwall, but ultimately subservient in the latter case to climate. An investigation of the relationship between the idea of the picturesque and its railway landscape inheritance should prove interesting, given the sometime opposition of, *inter alia*, Ruskin and Wordsworth to the railway's 'transgression' of valued landscapes.

10 The Royal Albert Bridge, Saltash, designed by Isambard Kingdom Brunel was opened on 2nd May 1859. It connected Cornwall's railway network with the rest of Britain.

11 See Berger (1972) in general, and Cosgrove (1984) regarding landscapes and place.

12 For a more detailed discussion of maps and the worlds they make, see Harley 1988, 1992; Pickles 1992.

13 The Great Western was not averse to inventing tradition, of course, as will become apparent in the Cornish context, but see Hobsbawm and Ranger (1983) on tradition generally, or Payton and Thornton (1995), on the GWR and the Cornish-Celtic revival.

14 A Cornish Pastiche, perhaps?

15 It is worth noting that the last broad gauge railway to be authorised was in Cornwall -- the St Ives branch -- in 1873, and that the last tracks to remain broad gauge were also in Cornwall.

16 The Diamond Jubilee of Queen Victoria in 1897, the coincidence of a new century and the Edwardian era, and 'victory' in the Boer war created rich possibilities for national -- and imperial -- myth making.

17 A contemporaneous poster used Mont St Michel in Brittany and St Michael's Mount in Cornwall to similar effect -- although of course that case is more complex given the Celtic ancestry of both places and the fact that both were served by the Great Western Railway -- Italy was not. What was missing from the Brittany poster was the female personification. This may, however, be found in later posters advertising travel to Wales, and to Ireland via the GWR's ferry services. The frequent representation of Ireland as woman has received critical attention elsewhere (Nash 1994).

18 Although it seems fair to presume that the intended audience, both for the poster and the guide-books, was male.

19 After Urry (1990), after Foucault.

20 In the idea of Cornwall as 'other' again we see the significance of the female personifications of Cornwall (Blunt and Rose 1994; Trinh Minh-ha 1989; Spivak 1988).

21 Messages about Cornwall as a safe haven were discernible in publicity aimed at industry in the late 1930s, which contained thinly veiled suggestions that the further away from continental Europe a company might be located, the safer it would be in time of war (Wilson 1987, 37). The effect of the bombs of the Luftwaffe on Swansea and Exeter, for example, demonstrated the fiction of this particular advertising ploy.

22 Local poverty in tourist destinations is ever a concern, whether it is Cornwall then, now or some more distant present day resort.

23 The Pentewen Railway was a mineral line with an interesting history. It ran from St Austell to the harbour at Pentewen, and closed to traffic in 1918. Once a year it washed out its china clay wagons for Sunday School trips to the seaside (Lewis 1981).

BIBLIOGRAPHY

Adams. W. Ed. *Encyclopaedia of the Great Western Railway.* Yeovil: Patrick Stephens, 1993.

Adler, J. 'Origins of Sightseeing'. *Annals of Tourism Research* 16 (1989): 7-29.

Alderman, G. *The Railway Interest.* Leicester: Leicester UP, 1973.

Barnes, T. and J. Duncan. Eds. *Writing Worlds: discourse, text and metaphor in the representation of landscape.* London: Routledge, 1992.

Barthes, R. *The Pleasure of the Text.* New York: Hill & Wang, 1975.

_____. *Image, Music, Text.* Glasgow: Collins-Fontana, 1977.

Barton, R.M. *A History of the Cornish China Clay Industry.* Truro: Bradford Barton, 1966.

Beloff, H. *Camera Culture.* Oxford: Blackwell, 1985.

Benjamin, W. *Illuminations.* London: Fontana, 1992.

Bennett, A. *Southern Holiday Lines in North Cornwall and West Devon.* Cheltenham: Runpast, 1995.

_____. *Images of Cornwall.* Cheltenham: Runpast, 1992a.

_____. *The Great Western Railway in Mid Cornwall.* Cheltenham: Runpast, 1992b.

Berger, J. *Ways of Seeing.* London: BBC & Penguin, 1972.

Blunt, A. and G. Rose. Eds. *Writing Women and Space: colonial and postcolonial geographies.* New York: Guilford Press, 1994.

Bocock, R. *Consumption.* London: Routledge, 1993.

Booker, F. *The GWR: a new history.* Newton Abbot: David & Charles, 1985.

Bourdieu, P. *Photography: a middle brow art.* Cambridge: Polity, 1990.

Broadley, A.M. *The Cornish Riviera.* London: GWR, 1904 *et seq.*

Bryan, T. *The Golden Age of the Great Western Railway.* Yeovil: Patrick Stephens, 1991.

Bunce, M. *The Countryside Ideal: Anglo-American images of landscape.* London: Routledge, 1994.

Burgin, V. Ed. *Thinking Photography.* Basingstoke: Macmillan, 1982.

Burton, A. *The Railway Empire.* London: John Murray, 1994.

Cambrian Railway Company. *Cardigan Bay, Illustrated: gems of picturesque scenery in wild Wales.* Oswestry: Cambrian Railways, 1904.

Cole, B. and R. Durack. *Railway Posters 1923-47*. 1992.

_____. *Happy as a Sand Boy: early railway posters*. York: National Railway Museum, and London: HMSO, 1990.

Corris Railway. *Real Picturesque Wales*. Machynlleth: Corris Railway Company, 1908.

Cosgrove, D. *Social Formation and Symbolic Landscape*. Beckenham: Croom Helm, 1984.

Crary, J. *Techniques of the Observer: on vision and modernity in the nineteenth century*. Cambridge, Mass.: MIT Press, 1993.

Daniels, S. *Fields of Vision*. Cambridge: Polity, 1993.

Davies, W.J.K. *Light Railways*. London: Ian Allen, 1964.

Davis, C.B. and K.E. Wilburn. Eds. *Railway Imperialism*. New York: Greenwood Press, 1991.

de Certeau, M. *The Practice of Everyday Life*. Berkeley: University of California Press, 1988.

Derrida, J. *Writing and Difference*. Chicago: University of Chicago Press, 1978.

Duncan, J. and N. Duncan. '(Re)reading the Landscape'. *Environment and Planning D: Society and Space* 6 (1988): 117- 126.

Duncan, J. and D. Ley. Eds. *place/culture/representation*. London, Routledge, 1993.

Dyer, G. *Advertising as Communication*. London: Routledge, 1982.

Faith, N. *The World the Railways Made*. London: Pimlico-Random House, 1990.

Foucault, M. *The Order of Things*. London: Tavistock, 1970.

Foucault, M. *The Archaeology of Knowledge*. New York: Pantheon, 1972.

Game, A. *Undoing the Social*. Milton Keynes: Open University Press, 1991.

Gardiner, M. *The Dialogics of Critique: M.M. Bakhtin and the theory of ideology*. London: Routledge, 1992.

Gold, J.'Locating the Message: place promotion as image communication'. Eds. Gold and Ward. *Op.cit.*, 1994. 19-37.

Gold, J. and S.V. Ward. Eds. *Place Promotion: the use of publicity and marketing to sell towns and regions*. Chichester: John Wiley, 1994.

Great Western Railway. *Through the Window: the Great Western Railway from Paddington to Penzance*. Ed. J. Burrow & Son, 1924.

Green, C.C. *The Vale of Rheidol Light Railway*. Didcot: Wild Swan, 1986.

Harley, J.B. 'Deconstructing the map'. Eds. Barnes and Duncan. *op. cit.*, 1992. 231-247.

_____. 'Maps, knowledge and power'. Eds. Cosgrove and Daniels. *The Iconography of Landscape*. Cambridge University Press, 1988. 277-312.

Hirschkop, K and D. Shepherd. *Bakhtin and Cultural Theory*. Manchester: Manchester UP, 1989.

Howkins, A. 'The discovery of Rural England'. Eds. R. Colls and P. Dodd. *Englishness: Politics and Culture 1880 - 1920*. London: Croom Helm, 1986.

Hobsbawm E. and T. Ranger. Eds. *The Invention of Tradition*. Cambridge University Press, 1983.

Hoy, D.C. Ed. *Foucault: A Critical Reader*. Oxford: Blackwell, 1986.

Jenkins, S.C. *The Leek and Manifold Light Railway*. Oxford: Oakwood Press, 1991.

Jordan, A. and E. Jordan. *Away for the Day: the railway excursion in Britain, 1830 to the present day*. Kettering: Silver Link, 1991.

Kerr, I. *Building the Railways of the Raj*. Oxford University Press, 1995.

Lewis, M.J.T. *The Pentewen Railway*. Truro: Twelveheads Press, 1981.

Lewis, N. *The Book of Babel: words and the way we see things*. London: Viking-Penguin, 1994.

Lunt, P. 'Rethinking Space and Place: the transformation of cultural geography'. Journal of Environmental Psychology 14 (1994): 315-326.

Mais, S.P.B. *The Cornish Riviera*. London: GWR, 1928a.

_____. *My Finest Holiday*. London: GWR, 1928b.

Monk, J. 'Approaches to the Study of Women and Landscape'. *Environmental Review* 8: 1 (1984), 23-33.

Myers, G. *Words in Ads*. London: Edward Arnold, 1994.

Nash, C. 'Remapping the Body/Land: new cartographies of identity, gender and landscape in Ireland'. Eds. Blunt and Rose, *Op.cit.*, 1994. 227-250.

Norris, J., Beale, G. and J. Lewis. *Edwardian Enterprise*. Didcot: Wild Swan, 1987.

North Staffordshire Railway. *Picturesque Staffordshire: the official illustrated guide to the district adjacent to the North Staffordshire Railway*. Hanley: Wood, Mitchell, 1908.

Palin, M. / British Rail. *Happy Holidays: the golden age of railway posters*. London: Pavilion, 1987.

Paston-Williams, S. *Old Picture Postcards of Cornwall*. Bodmin: Bossiney Books, 1989.

Patmore, J.A. *Recreation and Resources: leisure patterns and leisure places*. Oxford: Blackwell, 1983.

Payton, P. and P. Thornton. 'The Great Western Railway and the Cornish-Celtic Revival.' *Cornish Studies* 3 (1995): 83-103.

Pickles, J. 'Texts, Hermeneutics and Propaganda Maps'. Eds. Barnes and Duncan, *op. cit.*, 1992. 193-230. Pollock, G. *Vision and Difference*. London: Routledge, 1988.

Porteous, J.D. 'Bodyscape: the Body-Landscape Metaphor'. *The Canadian Geographer* 30:1 (1986): 2-12.

Quoniam, S. 'A Painter, Geographer of Arizona'. *Environment and Planning D: Society and Space* 6 (1988): 3-14.

Reece, J.E. 'Internal Colonialism: the case of Brittany'. *Ethnic and Racial Studies* 2: 3 (1979): 275-292.

Revell, G. 'Working the System; journeys through corporate culture in the railway age'. *Environment and Planning D: Society and Space* 12 (1994): 705-725.

Robbins, M. *The Railway Age*. Harmondsworth: Penguin, 1965.

Robinson, R.E. 'Conclusion: Railways and Informal Empire'. Eds. Davis and Wilburn, *Op. cit.*, 1991. 175-196.

Rose, G. *Feminism and Geography*. Cambridge: Polity, 1993.

Rowse, A.L. *A Cornish Childhood*. London: Cardinal, 1975.

Russell, J.H. *Great Western Miscellany*. Oxford: Oxford Publishing Company, 1978.

Sassoon, A.S. *Gramsci's Politics*. London: Hutchinson, 1987.

Schivelbusch, W. *The Railway Journey: the industrialisation of time and space in the nineteenth century*. Leamington Spa: Berg, 1986.

Shaw, G. and A. Williams. 'From Bathing Hut to Theme Park: tourism development in South West England'. *Journal of Regional and Local Studies* 7 (1991): 16-32.

Shotter, J. *Cultural Politics of Everyday Life*. Milton Keynes: Open University Press, 1993.

Simmons, J. 'The Railway in Victorian Cornwall'. *The Express Train and Other Railway Studies*. Nairn: Thomas and Lochar, 1994. 56-78.

_____. *The Victorian Railway*. London: Thames and Hudson, 1995.

Smith, D.N. *The Railway and its Passengers: a social history*. Newton Abbot: David and Charles, 1988.

Sontag, S. *On Photography*. Harmondsworth: Penguin, 1977.

Spivak, G.C. *In Other Worlds*. London: Routledge, 1988.

Thomas, D. St John. 'The Great Western's Second Coming'. *Country Origins* (Spring 1996), 122-127.

Trinh Minh-ha. *Woman, Native, Other*. Bloomington: Indiana UP, 1989.

Turnock, D. *Railways in the British Isles: landscape, land use and society*. Newton Abbot: David and Charles, 1990.

Urry, J. *The Tourist Gaze*. London: Sage, 1990.

_____.. *Consuming Places*. London: Routledge, 1995.

Vaughan, J. *An Illustrated History of West Country China Clay Trains*. Oxford: Oxford Publishing Company, 1987.

Walvin, J. *Beside the Seaside: a social history of the popular seaside holiday*. London: Allen Lane, 1978.

Ward Lock. *Red Guide to North Wales*. 10th ed. London: Ward Lock, 1946.

Whitehouse P. and D. St John Thomas. *The Great Western Railway: 150 glorious years*. Newton Abbot: David and Charles, 1984.

Williams, R. 'Advertising, the magic system'. *Problems on Materialism and Culture*. London: Verso, 1980.

_____. *The Country and the City*. London: Chatto & Windus, 1973.

_____. *Culture and Society: 1780 - 1950*. London: Chatto & Windus, 1958.

Williamson, J. Decoding *Advertisements: ideology and meaning in advertising*. London: Marion Boyers, 1978.

Wilson, R.B. *Go Great Western: a history of GWR publicity*. Newton Abbot: David St John Thomas, 1987.

Wolff, J. *Feminine Sentences: essays on women and culture*. Cambridge: Polity, 1990.

Wood, D. *The Power of Maps*. London: Routledge, 1992.

Woodfin, R.J. *The Cornwall Railway to its Centenary in 1959*. Truro: Bradford Barton, 1972.

Poldark Country and National Culture

Nickianne Moody

Raymond Williams (1958) saw culture as a social response to the acknowledgement of historical change. Cultural studies, which emerged as a designated academic discipline after the second world war, accommodates a broad range of social and political interests, but above all it legitimates the study of everyday life and popular culture at a given historical moment. In the process of examining the ordinary articulations of power, its concern is with a politics of difference rather than the homogeny of experience.

Research in cultural studies examines a wide range of communicative and cultural practices. Amongst the principal concerns of this research are issues of identity, popular culture, discourse and textuality, cultural difference and change. With such a variety of cultural practices and products, the researcher's approach needs to be flexible, drawing from such diverse methodologies as textual analysis, ethnography, semiotics and oral history. It is this absence of disciplinary boundary lines which enables research in cultural studies to understand the connections between individual (or collective) experience and the patterns of social life.

This study of Winston Graham's Poldark novels and their reception therefore encompasses the texts, the media industry and the reader, situating these activities of production and consumption within the cultural climate of the periods in which they took place.

The crucial component in the Poldark construction of Cornwall is not its local geography but its national significance. This is borne out by the nation-wide success of its multi-media forms. Its video release in 1993 came amidst the potential for revenue generated by nostalgia. The satellite channel UK Gold had already screened the period dramas *The Onedin Line* and *The Duchess of Duke Street*. The later quality television productions of *Brideshead Revisited* and *The Raj Quartet* had been offered for video sale. The reception the Poldark videos received was extraordinary: with very little pre-publicity they sold out. Perplexed staff at W.H. Smith's shops in Liverpool, Reading and Exeter recalled that they seemed to disappear as fast as they were put on the shelves. Poldark's Cornwall, like 'Herriot's Yorkshire', 'Ellis Peter's Shropshire', 'Last of the Summer Wine Country' and 'Pop Larkin's Kent' came onto the heritage trail because of a particular set of cultural conditions which amplified their appeal to the popular imagination.

Although the first of the Poldark novels was written fifty years ago, it is not a forgotten best-seller revived by a television drama. The continued popularity of the Poldark series is evident not only in book shops, but also in second hand sales and the current circulation of Winston Graham's novels in public libraries. Consideration of the publishing history for these eleven books does more than confirm their success in both print and televised form. It provides a basis from which to explain the text's relationship with successive audiences and to explore the changing cultural climate in which Poldark has been reproduced.

The books which comprise the Poldark series were written in distinct stages. The first book was planned as a single novel which focused upon a love triangle between mine-owning cousins and the daughter of impoverished landed gentry (Graham 1994, 144). *Ross Poldark: A Novel of Cornwall 1783-1787* was published in 1945, to be followed a year later by *Demelza*. Ross Poldark's marriage to a miner's daughter activates a love triangle and expands the original concept to take further interest in the eighteenth-century landscape and politics of Cornwall. The scope of Graham's knowledge of the period resulted in two further books published in 1950 and 1953. As well as creating a study of sexual and social rivalries, Graham became fascinated with speculative mining ventures and Cornwall's economic climate in the early 1790's.

These four books were given a paperback reprint in 1968. By that time Graham was well known for his contemporary writing, particularly through screen adaptations of his work like Hitchcock's *Marnie* (1964). The sales of the paperback edition of the Poldark series encouraged Associated British Pictures to take out an option on all four books. The company commissioned a writer and producer to prepare the film, and Graham describes their intentions as a four-hour Cornish 'Gone with the Wind' (1994, 162). However, film production was abandoned in the wake of a take-over by EMI. The option was then taken up by London films who eventually collaborated with the BBC on a television version. Negotiations took place in 1973 and during that year Graham published a fifth Poldark novel, *Black Moon*, which he refers to as the first of the 'new' Poldarks. The construction of the novel does not acknowledge the twenty-year break in the writing of the series. Having favoured modern settings during the interim, Graham recounts how he informed his accountant that he was returning to the 'non-profit making activities' of the historical romance (1994, 154).

The Poldark television series was screened as part of the BBC's 1975 Autumn season. Its 7:15 pm Sunday viewing slot was prestigious, but the programming was not unusual. Poldark took over from another costume drama, and for the first part of its run competed with the third series of *Upstairs, Downstairs* shown on ITV. Poldark's cast were all familiar faces. Anghared Rees and Judy Geeson had featured on the cover of *The Radio Times* for their appearance in other costume dramas. Richard Morant had played Flashman in a teatime-viewing production of *Tom Brown's Schooldays*. Robin Ellis, who played Ross Poldark, had appeared in the BBC dramatisation of *Sense and Sensibility*. The drama's success was rooted in its appeal to a family audience through storylines featuring different generations and treating the concerns of both men and women. Viewing figures rose from a respectable five million at the beginning of the series to a remarkable fifteen million at its conclusion. Graham agreed to write further books to provide the basis for a second BBC series. He was also closely involved with the screen writers working with the three later books to be televised, whereas in the first series quite substantial changes had been made to Graham's work without consultation. The last four untelevised books, written at the end of the 1980's, dealt with a second generation of Poldarks. Graham concluded his saga in 1990, launching the eleventh book from Cornwall and attracting two thousand supporters on the day of its publication. From the 1968 paperback edition the Poldark series has only briefly been out of print. Fontana produced an edition to coincide with the television series and have recently relaunched the books in association with the 1993 video collection. The new cover of *Ross Poldark* claims that over five million copies have been sold in the Fontana edition. It has been reprinted twenty-seven times, the mark of a true best-seller.

The cover for the BBC Enterprises video version of the television series gives an address for the Poldark Appreciation Society. This group was launched after the 1987 autumn television repeat of the series. The society's newsletter places an emphasis on 'Poldark Holidays', conventions, pen-pals, charity events and a mail order service. The society has campaigned vigorously for a further television repeat or a video release. Recently they have campaigned for 'Poldark Three' -- the television adaptation of the remaining books. News that HTV had bought the rights to the last four Poldark books prompted national newspapers and morning magazine programmes to consider the potential of 'Poldark: the Second Generation'. HTV announced that it had commissioned a Poldark Christmas Special and appointed a production team which comprises members of the original series (*Daily Mail* 5/1/95). By the summer of 1996 the programme still had not been shown, but a reprint of Graham's books featured cover photographs from the new dramatisation. Part of HTV's motivation for the new productions seems to have been not just the popularity of Poldark, but the national reception of programmes such as the *Wycliffe* detective series, which is also set and filmed in Cornwall (*Western Morning News* 29/1/95).

In Poldark, then, we see the evolution of a national cultural phenomenon from popular print quartet, to television series, to extended saga, and to a life beyond page and screen in the appreciation society organised by Poldark consumers. Its success in both its original postwar publication form and its later television and video versions suggests that Poldark meets the specific criteria of nostalgia required by the market and the popular imagination in two distinct periods: the decade of post- war settlement and the phase of industrial decline in Britain after 1974.

The historian David Cannadine has examined the recycling of nostalgia between these two periods in relation to Winston Graham's contemporary, Evelyn Waugh. To explore the association between tourism and nostalgia, Cannadine considers the touring exhibition, 'The Treasures Houses of Britain: Five Hundred Years of Private Patronage and Collecting', which he sees as an excellent example of nostalgia as a commercial cultural practice in the 1980's. He locates this type of tourism not necessarily in places but in periods, in a distinct cultural climate of nostalgia which has recurred during three economic depressions: the last quarter of the nineteenth century, the inter-war years and the post-1974 period.

These periods of depression have produced intense national interest in nostalgia, which has manifest itself in cultural forms. They have seen several other common characteristics: high unemployment, loss of overseas markets, complaints about the inadequacies of entrepreneurs and workers, renewed awareness of urban deprivation, and the expression of popular and urban unrest. Cannadine suggests that recession breeds reaction in Britain rather than revolution. He describes cultural life at such times as withdrawn, escapist and discontented with contemporary society. It is in this general mood that he locates the appeal of the rural and the cult of the country house.

Brideshead Revisited was published in the same year as Ross Poldark: 1945. Waugh mourns the country house and the world we have lost, just as Agatha Christie is nostalgic for the pre-First World War country house set. Waugh is equally concerned about who will inherit 'our heritage'. The potential barbarism feared by Waugh in his characterisation of postwar attitudes to the past is realised in H.E. Bates' protagonist Pop Larkin, who cheerfully sees the worth of the country house in its scrap value. Bates' The Darling Buds of May was published in 1958, the year when Waugh was invited to revise Brideshead Revisited.

Whereas Waugh's novel is an example of nostalgia squared, recycling the previous periods of economic depression for the later cultural industry, Graham's work is very different. The Poldark narrative is able to reclaim the period when the country house was first being built. Nostalgia for the eighteenth century here relates not to a period of grandeur, but to a period of a particular set of employment conditions which the creation of the country house represents. Ross Poldark is a postwar settlement hero. His greatest love is neither his wife Demelza nor his cousin and former sweetheart Elizabeth, but his business ventures, which will provide jobs for the redundant and prospects to improve health and housing.

Cannadine sees the country house exhibition as celebrating

> people who enjoyed income, not just from agriculture, but from the East Indian Trade, London building estates, coal mines, canals, harbours and railways. They endured damp, draughty, insanitary houses; they could stay for hours in the saddle; they condoned man traps, employed game keepers, and favoured the death penalty for poaching. Above all, they stood for oligarchy, hierarchy, inequality and exclusiveness: all things against which the Americans rebelled in 1776. (266)

At the start of the Poldark saga, Ross Poldark Esquire is a captain in the army returning from the American War of Independence. It is made clear that he is sympathetic to its aims. Graham leads his character to a series of vantage points from which he can observe and respond to native injustices to the Cornish people. In the 1974 television version, Ross says:

> Savages! They think because they are done up in their finery they are almighty civilised people, but they're savages. And worse they treat their animals better than they treat their labourers. One day the knives will be out and then God help them.
> 'And whose side will you be found on Ross?'

'Not on the side of the gentry you can be sure of that. I despair of my own class sometimes.'

The motivating force of Graham's books is not its love story but the the developing feud between the social climbing George Warleggan and the would-be paternal capitalist Ross Poldark. The rivalry between the two, which supplants the sexual rivalry between Ross's wife and cousin, starts at the trial of one of Poldark's tenants for poaching:

'These savage laws,' Ross said, controlling his temper with the greatest difficulty 'these savage laws which you interpret without charity send a man to prison for feeding his children when they're hungry, for finding food where he can when it's denied him to earn it' . (Fontana 1975, 227)

In the third book, *Jeremy Poldark: A Novel of Cornwall 1790-1791*, which opens the second television series, it is Poldark himself who is on trial. He has been charged with inciting riot and is again defending the Cornish people on the grounds of rights for the unemployed. The rest of the original series charts his pas sage to parliament, and the vicissitudes of his marriage are marked by his involvement with the black economy of smuggling, unemployed rioters and popular protest. These are themes which mark less of a connection with Waugh and much more with the television drama of Alan Bleasdale.

Poldark achieved its popular appeal in its recycled 1970's and 1980's form because it satisfied modern nostalgia for a particular aspect of the past: the idealised social contract. As the political and cultural institutions of the post-war democratic settlement were being abandoned by the policymakers of the post-1974 period, their memory persisted in the popular imagination. Poldark's 1974 televisual success took place against an actual backdrop of discontent, strike action and redundancy, most apparent in the contemporary mining industry. The television series featured an earlier mining industry at the cutting edge of technology, an industry with roots and traditions predating the industrial revolution that it could be proud of. It offered a fantasy of fair employment and social progress, gained through a partnership between community and technology. In the fiction, the integrity of private enterprise profits the whole community; a reconciliation between classes seems possible at a time of major and highly visible social change. At the same time the Poldark world also allows for social protest and possibility of political negotiation. (The huge popularity of Catherine Cookson's historical romances over the same post-1974 period has similarly been credited to the readership's longing for a past where people had more of a stake in their society and could take action to promote their interests (Fowler 1990, 95-97).) Poldark achieved its mass appeal because it engaged with the desires and anxieties of both middle-class and working-class sections of the audience in a comparable period of social adjustment.

Cornwall is the setting for Poldark, and a vital part of the myth which Winston Graham created for the national imagination. It is a beautiful, bleak

133

and dangerous terrain, which, in Graham's eighteenth-century fictional mode, embraced oppositions of the wild and the civilised, community and individuality, gentry and peasantry, parliament and province. But Cornwall is also a real place, a holiday location which the Poldark fan can visit. We are not looking here at a tourist board campaign the like of 'Catherine Cookson Country', 'Robin Hood Country', 'Captain Cook Country' or 'Rochester - City of Dickens'. Indeed Poldark Country has recently vanished from the official tourist map because it proved notoriously difficult to market. The old mining area has its own strange landscape, but it is remarkably different from the West Country's other attractions:

> Those [mine] chimneys have tremendous power. They tell their story so strongly just by being there -- the story of Cornwall in fact -- a land of great scenic beauty scarred inevitably by the need of survival. (Ellis 1987, 12)

A Poldark Mine and Heritage Complex does exist. Wheel Roots mine and its surroundings were purchased in 1966 as an industrial archaeological site, but when the mine was reopened to the public in 1971 it failed to draw tourists. Relaunched as The Poldark Mine after the television series, the underground tour was successfully promoted as a tourist attraction. The Poldark Village and Cornish Heritage Collection were added, alongside more typical theme park activities. Ticket admission now offers bumper boats, vintage photographers, prize bingo, quiet garden walks, a restaurant and the Miners Arms. The eighteenth-century tableau, complete with Ross and Demelza's parlour and kitchen, was designed to appeal to all age groups and provide a focus for educational visits.

The Poldark Mine has a schizophrenic relationship with Wheel Roots, whose history it appropriates. Poldark's optimism sits ill with the story of the nineteenth-century decline of Cornish mining and with uncontextualised statements in the guide book such as: 'John & Jane Young were victims of the Industrial Revolution, so it is fitting that they are remembered in an industrial environment.' Some of the staff are ex-coal miners from the north of England. This is not the place for a fan to enjoy an unadulterated Poldark experience.

Another problem with Poldark Country is that it is composite. Its existence as television locations and evocative descriptions in Graham's books can be physically realised only with specialist knowledge and a great deal of travelling. Graham took the names of several characters from local villages (Demelza, Warleggan, Clowance and Cuby), but the villages themselves have no other Poldark connections and many of the placenames in the novels, beyond the centres of St. Austell, Truro and Redruth, are fictitious. Nampara, Ross's home, is actually the name of a district in the centre of Perranporth:

> But the image of Nampara retained by so many viewers is a little more tangible. Two buildings served the purpose as TV locations for the first series, both way down the coast near St. Just in Penwith. One was Pendeen Manor Farm and the other Botallack Manor Farm, neither open to the

public, but both close to some emerging cliff scenery and one of the old copper mines that were used as locations (Clarke 10).

Afficionados can find such locations, but only through dedicated exploration. Holidaymakers are rarely expected to do so, but the Poldark tourist is obliged to leave the beaten track.

Tourists do more than consume when they go on holiday. The contradictions on the Poldark Heritage site, however unacceptable they may be to the Poldark purist, can generate family debate and family memories. Serious fans on the Poldark trail can recreate their reading and viewing experiences in the context of a memorable personal quest. As much as the reader or viewer of Graham's work, the Poldark tourist is engaged in the active creation of meaning. Being a Poldark fan is never as complaisant as it may seem.

BIBLIOGRAPHY

Bates, H.E. *The Darling Buds of May*. London: Michael Joseph, 1958.

Cannadine, David. *The Pleasures of the Past*. Glasgow: William Collins, 1989.

Clarke, David. *Poldark Country*. St Teath: Bossiney Books, 1981.

Ellis, Robin. *The Making of Poldark*. London: Crossaction, 1987.

Fowler, Bridget. *The Alienated Audience*. London: Harvester Wheatsheaf, 1990.

Graham, Winston. *Poldark's Cornwall*. Webb & Bower and Bodley Head, 1994.

Waugh, Evelyn. *Brideshead Revisited*. London: Chapman & Hall, 1945.

Williams, Raymond. *Culture and Society 1780-1950*. London: Chatto & Windus, 1958.

Graham, Winston: THE POLDARK SERIES

Ross Poldark. London: Werner Laurie, 1945.

Demelza. London: Werner Laurie, 1946.

Jeremy Poldark. London: Werner Laurie, 1950.

Warleggan. London: Werner Laurie, 1953.

The Black Moon. London: William Collins, 1973.

The Four Seasons. London: William Collins, 1976.

The Angry Tide. London: William Collins, 1977.

The Stranger from the Sea. London: William Collins, 1980.

The Miller's Dance. London: William Collins, 1982.

The Loving Cup. London: William Collins, 1984.

The Twisted Sword. London: Chapmans, 1990.

POLDARK ON BBC VIDEO

First screened 1975:

Part One 1993:   written by Jade Pulman, directed by Christopher Berry.

Part Two 1993:   written by Paul Wheeler, directed by Paul Annett

Part Three 1993:   written by Peter Draper, directed by Kenneth Ives

Part Four 1993:   written by Jack Russell, directed by Paul Annett

POLDARK 2 ON BBC VIDEO

First screened 1977:

Part One 1994:   written by Alexander Baron, directed by Philip Dudley
Part Two 1994:   written by Martin Worth, directed by Philip Dudley
Part Three 1994:   written by Martin Worth and John Viles, directed by Philip Dudley and Roger Jenkins
Part Four 1994:   written by Alexander Baron and John Viles, directed by Philip Dudley and Roger Jenkins

Jamaica Inn: the creation of meanings on a tourist site

Harold Birks

This consideration of Jamaica Inn as a tourist/leisure site is predicated upon the argument that the site consists of a set of signifiers that have been cultivated for the purpose of forefronting a particular set of meanings. The chapter also considers the argument that people are capable of reading such sites and selecting what they find most valuable, and that they are capable of creating their own relevant spheres of sociality and do not need to have them created for them.

These arguments take as their starting point a group of texts that theorise tourism, including Rojek's Ways of Escape: Modern Transformations in Leisure and Travel *(1993) and the collection* Modernity and Identity *edited by Lash and Friedman (1993). The operation of signifiers in the context of tourism was analysed at length in Urry's seminal study* The Tourist Gaze *(1990).*

The souvenir guide for Jamaica Inn contains, in common with promotional material for other sites and organisations, a wealth of information about how the site is intended to be perceived by its audience. It offers clear evidence of how a set of signifiers has been brought together to construct a set of meanings. By considering the souvenir guide, before turning to the site itself, we can examine the ways in which history and heritage, nostalgia and narrative, the private and the public have become entwined, and assess the central role of Daphne du Maurier's fictionalised 'Jamaica Inn' within this process.

The guide offers its readers a particular set of representations of Jamaica Inn, Bodmin Moor and Cornwall. The inn is extolled as Cornwall's most famous coaching inn, 'Immortalised by Daphne du Maurier's novel of the same name.' Connotations of old world charm are underpinned by a description of Christmas Eve 1853 at Jamaica Inn: 'In the tap room were a lot of boozers, principally old moormen singing songs of sea pirates and highwaymen, with Billy Lee, the gypsy fiddler providing the music. Boswell, the rat catcher was dancing a fine horn pipe.' This description of conviviality and yo-ho-hoery contains references to sea pirates and highwaymen, placed alongside a description of smuggling and an inset illustration of a scene from du Maurier's *Jamaica Inn* (1936), which was set in the nineteenth century. Thus an authentic description of Christmas Eve 1853 is intended to lend authenticity to the meanings that have been attached to the inn.

On the page entitled 'As good an Inn today as ever,' images are offered of a cosy, comfortable, safe hostelry, which all the family can enjoy; we can partake of a drink and good Cornish Fayre in an atmosphere not much different, we are told, from the days of smugglers and the times when Joss Merlyn, the fictitious drunken, murderous leader of the wreckers of the novel, ran 'Jamaica Inn'. Considering that the inn of the novel is a place where the coach does not stop, that no respectable person uses it and that the only people who do are Joss Merlyn's gang of wreckers, whose idea of a night out is drunken debauchery, mayhem and even murder, we might be excused for thinking that perhaps things are not quite what they used to be, or were purported to be. But of course we can enjoy the promise of Gothic horror in safety and comfort, without having to experience the reality. The dominance of du Maurier's 'Jamaica Inn' is further forefronted by the information that the bedrooms are named after characters in the novel: Mary Yellan, Aunt Patience, Joss Merlyn, Harry the Peddler, Francis Davey, Jem Merlyn and Squire Bassett. The guide points out that you can stay the night, 'and imagine what it is like to be Mary Yellan.'

A subtitle in the souvenir guide offers its audience the inset 'Daphne du Maurier Country', laid out alongside a portrait of a youthful Daphne du Maurier, a bedraggled Jane Seymour (a still from the television adaptation) and a landscape (Bodmin Moor). We are asked to consider whether the events recounted in the novel were 'Fact or Fiction', but told that they are 'uncomfortably close to the way things were in smugglers Cornwall' -- despite the fact that the novel is based upon wholly ahistorical tales of wrecking. Further information includes a depiction of the Daphne du Maurier Room, along with a dish of Daphne's favourite sweets, views of romantic and mysterious Bodmin Moor and Cornwall, and last but not least, Mr Potter's Museum of Curiosity, with its collection of curios, stuffed animals and various oddments and oddities, first opened in 1861 and brought to Jamaica Inn in 1988.

The souvenir guide, therefore, promises an experience that could be described as: County House visitor meets Coaching Inn clientele, meets Barbara Cartland and Bill Sykes at the Berni Grand Steakhouse next door to the Old Curiosity Shop in a lovely rural setting.

The site at Jamaica Inn is every bit as eclectic as the guide's representation. In the Potter Museum complex, and spilling out into the inn's front yards, there is an astonishing collection of rural and urban bric-a-brac. It is folk museum, industrial heritage exhibition and rural craft centre rolled into one. The machinery, parts of machinery, anchors (several miles from the sea) and tin plate advertisements, all connote past times and past lives. You knew when you stood when that telephone box was in use, and the man who used that piece of machinery smoked the tobacco advertised by that tin plate on the wall. Were not times less problematic then, lives more contented? The museum offers its audience a display of stuffed animals, the loot of Empire, oddities from nature, and objects from everyday life. Here an audience is offered an experience reminiscent of the antique and junk shop, arousing nostalgia and promising a lucky bargain. It is the kind of experience that makes us want to dash off and watch the *Great Antiques Hunt* and eat Hovis for tea. As Patrick Wright explains:

Alongside the stately museum and the National Trust mansion there now comes the vernacular pleasure of the junk shop. There is an altogether more secular amusement in which worn out and broken rubbish can be appreciated at the very moment of its transformation but something worth saving, a bargain perhaps, but more significantly something resonant of an ordinary and more hand-made yesterday which is just about becoming precious in yet another lost world. (72)

In contrast to Mr Potter's Museum of Curiosity, the du Maurier Room in Jamaica Inn evokes culture and taste. It represents Daphne du Maurier as a famous person of English letters who is part of Cornwall's (and England's) heritage; the room is linked to the Gerald du Maurier bar with its memorabilia of the actor, manager, father. The du Maurier Room is set out in a manner that connotes stately home/museum. What is presented to us is a kind of cultural capital that can be acquired by the majority and spent on a variety of social occasions.

Jamaica Inn could be accused of being inauthentic, staged and commercial, but similar concerns have also been voiced about heritage sites and even stately homes. In 1995 National Trust shops achieved a turnover of £19 million, English Heritage shops took £7 million, and the retail outlet at Chatsworth House 1 million. The boundaries between public and private, what is legitimate culture and what is perceived as not, what should be fun and what should be taken seriously have become blurred. Such blurring does appear to be profitable.

The restaurant named Merlyn -- the family name in the novel of the two brothers, one a drunk, a murderer and a wrecker, the other a horsethief -- is designed to signify respectability, taste and a certain old world charm associated with country houses. These gentrified former stables are fitted out with prints and the kind of bric-a-brac that is associated with middle-class gentility; in the alcoves stand antique bronzes which are part of the proprietor's private collection. The correct selections have been made, investments have been prudently chosen: this is a place of safe judgement in the spheres of taste, culture, social standing and money. If we could take this cultural capital to the Antiques Roadshow we would surely be advised to insure it for a decent sum.

People seek reassurance in matters of taste and culture. We look for identity and worth, especially in a society which in recent years become more fragmented, its cultural certainties less reliable. The most discreet restaurant patronised by a cultural elite is designed to attract a particular clientele, whose self-image is flattered by the food, the wine, the service, the other diners. If we like to eat there, while seeing the punters of tourist sites like Jamaica Inn as gullible, perhaps we should examine our own claim to be authentic diners, and turn our attention to the set of cultural signifiers with which our favourite restaurant underpins that illusion of authenticity.

Jamaica Inn's new carvery extension imitates a type of Tudor style that connotes old Englishness, part of the nostalgia- informed designs which have been produced in Britain in recent years. Influences that have shaped the heritage and nostalgia industries in the 1980s and 1990s have also worked upon Jamaica Inn, making this site as representative of what has occurred in British society and culture as any heritage or commercial site. But, unlike new supermarkets and shopping malls where a variety of past styles and signifiers are put to use to the point of rendering them moribund, Jamaica Inn does possess an historical past, though one that is now almost inextricable from du Maurier's fictional recreation.

There has been a building on the present site on Bodmin Moor since the sixteenth century, though when it became an inn is unknown. A bill for beer dated 23 April 1789 is the earliest recorded evidence of Jamaica Inn; it was advertised to be let in the *Royal Cornwall Gazette* of 2 March 1811. There are several later references to Jamaica Inn: Murray's *Handbook for Travellers in Devon and Cornwall* (1856) reports: 'The Inn is frequented in the winter by sportsmen and affords comfortable though somewhat rude accommodation;' the *West Briton*, 9 March 1871, advertises: 'To let: a lucrative business carried on for many years by John Colwell: in course of complete reconstruction: has 17 rooms including 8 bathrooms: with good shooting, fishing and occasional coarsing.' It is advertised again in the *West Briton*, 30 August 1878, as being 'entirely reconstructed', and according to the *West Briton*, 9 March 1876, William Mason of Jamaica Inn was fined for allowing sheep with scab to stray on the moors. This is hardly the stuff of Gothic horror: Mary Yellan discovered the awful truth about Joss Merlyn, the villainous landlord of Jamaica Inn, he ran sheep with scab on the moors. The hunting and the fishing fit with images of old world coaching inn up to a point; less apt is the reference in the *West Briton* of 15 June 1893: 'To let: Jamaica Inn Bolventor Temperance Hotel.' It was a temperance house when Daphne du Maurier visited it in the 1930s.

Smuggling was indeed carried on in Cornwall, at times on a large scale and by well organised participants (who called themselves free traders rather than smugglers), but there is no evidence of ships being deliberately wrecked, and no connection between wreckers and Jamaica Inn. Wrecking is a misunderstood term, which can be characterised as follows: helping yourself to goods after the ship is wrecked and the passengers and crew have gone, helping to rescue the passengers and crew and helping yourself, helping yourself and then helping the passengers and crew, ignoring anybody and helping yourself, and helping yourself and not letting anyone get in the way. There is some evidence of the latter two instances, but a lot more evidence that the shipwrecked were often rescued with no small acts of heroism before the rescuers helped themselves to what they saw as bounty providentially supplied by the sea. There is no evidence of deliberate wrecking at all.

In this chapter we have considered the way in which the site of Jamaica Inn has been constituted through a set of signifiers, narratives and fictions. These signifiers, narratives and fictions are predicated upon a complex of signifiers flowing from history, heritage, myth, legend and a powerfully influential novel, and they have been constituted in a particular formation in order to attract an audience to the tourist and leisure site that is Jamaica Inn for the legitimate purpose of making a profit. We have noted that the boundaries which formerly defined distinct, differentiated spheres of social, cultural and economic activity have become at Jamaica Inn (as at other tourist, heritage and commercial sites) blurred, indistinct, de-differentiated.

Any audience for the set of signifiers that can be found at Jamaica Inn will bring to it a variety of experiences, and will take from it a variety of experiences which they will use for their own purposes and needs. Chris Rojek argues that even on an organised package tour, tourists are capable of irony, capable of seeing through sets of staged signifiers. (176) Outside the package tour, people do not need to have sites of social, cultural and economic activity produced for them; they can create their own sites of social interaction which '[speak] not of "dead signifiers" but of aesthetically energised forms of sociality' .(Lash and Friedman, 1993, 6)

On Sundays a car boot sale is held at Jamaica Inn, in a field adjacent to the museum. The car boot sale involves work and leisure, pleasure and serious business, free trading and bargaining. It is a space mixed to varying degrees in age, class, gender and race. Though it is not the shopping mall with its allures and advertising, it does offer opportunities for the indulgence of daydreams and fantasies. Here bargains are sought, fragments of desire, daydreams, work and everyday life are sold, and people meet to socialise.

People may be offered 'dead signifiers', they may be offered a variety of spaces, but this does not mean that they will necessarily accept them, or that they will not convert them to their own uses. Nor does it mean that different sections of society will not constitute their own spaces, and create their own 'aesthetically energised forms of sociality,' for they will and do, even at Jamaica Inn.

BIBLIOGRAPHY

Bagguley, P., and J. Mark-Lawson. Eds. *Restructuring: Place, Class and Gender.* London: Sage, 1991.

Bourdieu, P. *Distinction. Social critique of the judgement of taste.* London: Routledge, 1986.

Campbell, C. *The Romantic Ethic and the Spirit of Modern Consumerism.* Oxford: Blackwell, 1989.

Du Maurier, Daphne. *Jamaica Inn.* London: Gollancz, 1936.

Giblett, R. Philosphy (and Sociology) in The Wetlands. The Sublime and the Uncanny. *New Formations* 18. London: Lawrence and Wishart, 1992.

Lash, S. *Sociology of Postmodernism.* London: Routledge, 1992.

Lash, S and I. Friedman. Eds. *Modernity and Identity.* Oxford: Blackwell, 1993.

Lowenthal, D. *The Past is a Foreign Country.* Cambridge University Press, 1990.

Rojek, C. *Ways of Escape. Modern Transformations in Leisure and Travel.* London: Macmillan, 1993.

Roome, N. Fantasy, Reality, Metaphor and Management: the case of Euro Disney. *Journal of Industrial Affairs* 1 (1992).

Tower, J. The Grand Tour: a key phase in the history of tourism. *Journal of Tourism Research* 12 (1985).

Urry, J. *The Tourist Gaze.* London: Sage, 1990.

Wright, P. *On Living In An Old Country.* London: Verso, 1991.

Telling It As It Is: storytelling in the china clay villages

Mike Dunstan

I come to this paper wearing two hats, the first as an academic researcher based at the University of Exeter and the second as a professional arts practitioner working with storytelling. Since 1989 I have been working as a professional storyteller in a variety of community-based venues throughout the country and beyond, but particularly in Devon and Cornwall, and it is in this role that I have primarily approached this paper. Hence, I have deliberately steered clear of overburdening my argument with academic references, but have relied mostly upon my direct experience of involvement in storytelling as practice, although that is inevitably closely informed by my academic background. It is also the reason why I have decided to publish this paper under my professional Equity name, Mike Dunstan, rather than the name that appears on my birth certificate and under which I normally publish papers in academic books and journals, Michael Wilson.

It has always been my belief that a storyteller is not simply a performer; at least half of the job is concerned with listening to stories, encouraging other people to tell stories and, moreover, culturally empowering communities by raising an awareness of existing storytelling cultures and traditions. Since 1991 I have been developing, through a series of residency commissions, a working methodology which is characterised by The Restormel Arts Clay Stories Project and with which this paper concerns itself.

I have attempted to do two things in the following chapter. Firstly, I have given a brief introduction to the theory and methodology which lie behind 'community storytelling' by, in fact, telling a story -- the story of the work I carried out in the china clay villages of Mid-Cornwall in 1993-94. Secondly I have conducted an analysis of the oral storytelling currently happening in these communities to underline the strength of these traditions.

This chapter is inspired by the twin beliefs that we are all culturally active and creative individuals, shaped by our environment and our working and living conditions, expressing our cultural agenda through the poetry of everyday speech, and that professional arts practitioners need to embrace and engage in the academic debates that currently circulate around the notions of popular culture and folklore. I hope this paper makes a serious contribution to that ongoing academic discourse.

A supercomputer is built and all the world's knowledge is programmed into it.
A gathering of top scientists punch in the question: "Will the computer ever re-
place man?"
   Clickity, click, whir, whir, and the computer lights flash on and off.
   Finally a small printout emerges saying, "That reminds me of a story".
   (Quoted Bauman 115)

We are all storytellers. We all tell stories and we all listen to stories; there
are no exceptions to this 'essential component of our humanness'. (Rosen 1985,
24) The 'readiness or predisposition to organise experience into a narrative
form' (Bruner 45) is perhaps the single element that distinguishes us as a species.
In fact, we *must* tell stories, because it is by the recreation of experience and
event into narrative form that we give *meaning* to that experience, to the extent
that the story becomes an essential part of the event.

   Furthermore, it is through our stories that we define ourselves as social beings
and, likewise, it is through the stories told within a community that it defines
and celebrates itself. It was from this thinking that *The Restormel Arts Clay
Stories Project* was born, and it is the purpose of this paper to look at an example
of the application of a method of work coming to be known as 'community
storytelling'. As Richard Bauman reminds us, 'in exploring the social nexus of
oral storytelling we explore one of the most fundamental and potent founda-
tions of our existence as social beings'. (Bauman 114)

The Restormel Arts Clay Stories Project -- the background
   In January 1993 I was approached in my role of professional storyteller by
Phil Webb, Director of Restormel Arts, the arts promotion and development
agency for the borough of Restormel in Mid-Cornwall, and Sally Tonge,
Literature Development Worker for Cornwall (now Verbal Arts Cornwall),
with a view to developing a storytelling residency for the china clay villages
around St. Austell. Sally had become aware of some of the work I had been
doing in communities around Plymouth and when Phil declared an interest in
promoting some community-based developmental work, Sally suggested a
project on similar lines.

   The project brief ran as follows. To liaise with a variety of agencies within
the clay villages (schools, libraries, youth clubs, etc.) and to engage and work
with residents of the clay communities with a view to establishing an archive
of local stories and narratives. We were not aiming to revive storytelling in the
clay villages, but rather to raise an awareness of existing storytelling traditions.

   It was proposed that I would initially work with teenagers, through schools
and youth clubs. I would introduce them to the project and encourage them to
begin telling stories themselves and begin collecting, on cassette tape, those
stories which they already tell. The next phase of the project would be to
encourage those teenagers to become collectors themselves. They would be
encouraged to talk to their families and neighbours to collect a wide range of
stories and I myself would continue liaising with groups and individuals,
encouraging people to share their stories with us. At the same time Sally Tonge

and Jonathan Aberdeen from Restormel Arts were busy talking to people on the mobile libraries and many people, particularly Karen Nash, were fully engaged in transcribing the cassettes as they came in.

Inevitably, much of my time was spent drinking tea and eating cakes in people's living rooms as they told me stories, but let us not forget that storytelling is, first and foremost, the art form of social interaction.

The upshot of all this was that in a relatively short period of time we had filled nigh on thirty cassettes with stories and still felt that we had only scraped the surface of all the narrative material that existed within the clay community. This archive was then used as a basis for an intensive week of work during the November half-term, the end product of which was *Tales from The White Mountains*, a book of stories selected, compiled, edited and illustrated by a formidable group of about a dozen local teenagers. It should be stressed that editorial control throughout the project remained purely in the hands of those local people working on it and the professional artsworkers served only to advise, when requested, and facilitate the whole process.

That first book, which was published in December 1993, sold over one thousand copies within a couple of months and the proceeds from those sales were used to fund a second stage of the project, aiming not only to collect a further batch of stories, to mine deeper into the vein of community narrative, but also to involve the community more centrally in the decision-making processes around the project. The democratisation of such work is central to its philosophy and is an ongoing process from the very outset. The start of the project's second phase offered the opportunity to take a further large step down this road and place power and ownership in the hands of all those who had become involved.

By December 1994 another book had been published, a series of short pieces for radio, featuring storytellers from the clay villages, had been broadcast on BBC Radio Cornwall as part of 'White Mountains Week' and a selection of the material had been presented at various libraries to a wider public by both myself and local writer Alan Kent. At the time of writing, a third phase is planned for the project to produce a teachers' pack based upon the material to link into the English and History elements of the curriculum and also to feed into Cornish Studies. This has already received enthusiastic support from teachers and educationalists alike and is due to be published in Autumn 1996.

Notions of Tradition and Storytelling in the Clay Communities

It is now time to turn our attention to the stories which were collected as a result of the project, and in particular to identify aspects of tradition within local storytelling practices.

The clay villages could easily be described (and often are) as a traditional working-class community, in the sense that they form a community which still relies largely upon a single primary industry for a major part of its economy (although this is currently changing). The local population is also relatively settled and static and extended family networks, which have now largely been replaced by the nuclear unit in most of modern western society, are still not uncommon. We might, therefore, expect tradition to be prevalent in many aspects of life within the community, including its storytelling practices.

Indeed, storytelling within the clay villages can be said to be traditional in two ways, firstly the body of collected material contains a number of traditional narratives, which is to say narratives which have existed through oral circulation for a number of generations within that community, being constantly reinvented by each generation and, indeed, by each teller. Furthermore, these stories will often exist in variants in many other communities the world over. This material may range from old local legends, firmly rooted to a sense of place, such as the following examples about Roche Rock: [1]

Roche Rock is in the middle of Cornwall, in a village called Roche. There are many stories about Roche Rock. Mine is about how the Devil got into the edge and how he took revenge.

Many years ago when the monks were building a chapel on Roche Rock, the Devil was disturbed. The Devil got annoyed and took over the bodies of some of the monks. He made them sculpt a face into the side of the rock. When they had done this he returned them to normal, then he went into the face so he could see people coming up to the rock.

Years later an old woman came up to the rock. The Devil saw her and made a flower grow on the edge. The lady went to have a look at the flower and the Devil's hand came out of a hole and pushed the lady off the edge. The lady survived to tell what had happened to a passer-by, then she died.

That is how the edge became known as Devil's Edge.
   (Submitted in written form by Simon Martin. *More Tales from the White Mountains: 2.*)

and

There used to be a chap on the top of Roche Rock and there was a hermit who lived there and one day the chap fell down and the Devil came along and pushed him off the edge -- something like that.

If you stand on the edge you can see a witch on the bottom and the Devil on the side. You can see the faces in the rock.
   (Collected orally from Ann, Brannel School, April 1993. *Tales from the White Mountains: 7.*)

and

It is said that an old hermit used to live up at the Devil's Edge. One night his daughter brought his food up and they sat on the edge eating. Suddenly there was a tremor and the old hermit fell off the edge. His daughter was so distraught that she jumped off and killed herself. If you go up at about 1 a.m. it is said that you can hear her screaming.
   (Collected orally from an anonymous teller, Brannel School, April 1993.
   Tales from the White Mountains: 8.)

It may also include contemporary legends such as the following, which are well-documented throughout the world in local variant form, and whose traditional pedigree has been established by a large list of folklorists such as Jan Harold Brunvand (see especially Brunvand 1981). The following contemporary legend example is usually known as 'The Boyfriend's Death':

> There were these two people, husband and wife. They went on the moors one night and they stopped in the car because they had run out of petrol and the husband said that he would go down to the garage which was a few miles away.
>
> So he started walking to it and she heard something on the radio that there was a headless man on the moors and anybody who was on there should drive to their homes quickly. She didn't believe in anything like that so she ignored it.
>
> She was listening to the music on the radio when she heard banging on the roof so she thought it was on the radio, so she turned it off and the banging stopped and she turned it on and the banging started again. She turned the radio off and the banging kept on, so she looked out because the banging was coming from the roof.
>
> So she looked out of the door and she saw the headless man on the roof banging her husband's head, just his head, on the roof of the car.
> (Collected orally from Maria Docking, Brannel School, April 1993.
> Tales from the White Mountains: 5.)

What is particularly interesting is that the traditional stories are those that tend to be largely told by the teenage storytellers rather than the older members of the community, which, of course, undermines the stereotypical image of the teller of traditional tales as that of an older man or woman representing a rapidly fading former way of life. It is most heartening that the traditional stories are being kept alive by the very generation so often derided for their seeming obsession with technology and the consumer culture.

The older members of the clay villages tell largely personal stories which are therefore more innovative than traditional, although the traditionality of the stories increases as the stories are repeated. However, although these personal stories may not be traditional in themselves, the telling of them often is.

There are many stories, for example, which describe traditional activities, or at least, ways of doing things, which are fast disappearing (or perhaps have already disappeared) from contemporary life. These may be stories describing the baking of bread or the sequence of activities involved in wash day, or they may be like the following story from Alan Wilson of St Dennis, describing medical practice in the days before the National Health Service.

> My mother was in the village and if anyone was sick my grandmother used to go down the pit. There was this bloke that nearly lost his leg. They put him on a door and brought him home, sent for granny and they sent for a horse to

get a doctor. She got her little apron on and got her little knife out and cut away.

She was a very strong woman, my mother was the same. I had my teeth out when I was about fifteen or sixteen. That was done on the kitchen table with a bit of cloth with some chloroform on it. Tonsils were done that way too. If you can get them on the table, you did it there.

If somebody was bad, they would say go and see Annie or Granny Kent. They just did it if someone was bad. The only form of medicine they used to make themselves is sloe wine. If father had the scats my mother would give him a glassful. They had all sorts of old remedies.
(Collected orally from Alan Wilson, St. Dennis, May 1993. *Tales from the White Mountains:* 21.)

It is not surprising in a community so dominated by a single industry, that stories centred around work, which is a defining and unifying feature of that community, form a large part of the communal repertoire. The following story, told by Mrs Hardey, from the hamlet of Egypt, ⁀ about her brother who was afraid to finish work a minute early, is one of the most moving stories in the collection.

He went to work and when it was time to leave work the man said to him to come along because it was time to go off, but he hesitates because of being out of work for so long before. He had an accident.

He was put on a piece of board with a little sacking over him and carried by hand, a mile or more, and as he came over the road he was alive and when the men said, "Number six?", he said, "No, number nine." But it couldn't have been more than two or three minutes for him to get here. As he came in the hallway, he died.

He was dead, anyway, and when the doctor examined him   all that was wrong with him was a broken arm and shock. That was what killed him, whereas today he would have been in hospital, but there was nothing really for them back then, no help in any way.

That was all because he stayed on that extra minute because he didn't want to lose his job.
(Collected orally from Mrs. Hardey, Egypt, 23 June 1993. Unpublished.)

Communities are made up of people, and it is these individuals who give that community shape and definition. There will therefore be found a batch of stories in which the narrative, as such, plays a secondary role to the central character. That is to say that the action serves to define the central character who is being remembered and celebrated through the story.

Again many of these stories will focus on the amusing incidents which may affectionately poke fun at a particular person. The sub-text of these narrations is that the person is being remembered chiefly for their sociability, which enhances the quality of life within the community. The person in question was, in effect, 'a good sort' and even in times of austerity, there were enough 'good sorts' to pull you through.

However, the best stories are reserved for those people who showed a genuine compassion, especially for those who had met with misfortune. Time and time again the name of Dr Manson cropped up and praise was heaped on his memory. It seems that he was a local doctor who would only ever charge for his services what the patient could afford. In the days before free health care, he never withheld medical help for financial reasons. This earned him the enormous respect of the community and succeeding generations and a place in the community's folk memory as something of a folk hero. He also, it would seem, possessed certain roguish qualities, but these are now remembered with a degree of affection by the community and simply added to his humanity, proving his ability to relate effectively to the 'common people' and their experiences. The following is a typical example:

There was a marvellous doctor in St. Dennis where I lived called Dr. Manson and he would come and if you were poor he wouldn't charge you anything. But he used to like to kiss all the ladies. I used to be terrified of him. I had tonsilitis once and he said, "Come over to the window and open your mouth wide." I was a teenager and a bit shy. He said, "Open your mouth wide, then shut it." Then he kissed me and he said, "I've done it, haven't I?"

(Collected orally from Mary Treverna, June 1993. *Tales from the White Mountains*: 35.)

Finally, there are a significant number of stories which are described as tall tales and stories concerning practical jokes. This tradition of 'yarning', which has been closely analysed in a Texan context by Richard Bauman (33-53), would appear to be alive and well in the china clay communities of Cornwall, as the following examples illustrate:

This bloke went to Nance's to buy a new front door. He said, "I need a new front door, t'other's rotted through."

"Fine," said Nance, "I'll pop round in the afternoon and fit it."

"Oh don't bother," he said, "I'll do it myself."

"Are you sure?" said Nance. "It can be a tricky thing fitting a door."

Well, that afternoon the bloke comes back. "You know that door you sold me?" he said. "Well, 'tis no good?"

"What d'you mean?" said Nance. "What d'you mean, 'tis no good?"

"Well," he said, "the letter box is on the inside!"

(Collected orally from Alan Wilson, St. Dennis, June 1993. *Tales from the White Mountains*: 34.)

and

> *It was like the plumber. He wanted the doctor once. He phoned up and the doctor was ready to go out for the evening. "I'll tell you what," he said, "take a couple of aspirins and go to bed and I'll see you in the morning."*
>
> *Some weeks later the doctor phoned up. "Look, can 'ee, the toilet is blocked up," he said, "can you do anything?"*
>
> *"Well, the best thing you can do is drop in a couple of aspirins and I'll come and see 'ee in the morning!"*
>> (Collected orally from Tom Westlake, St. Dennis, June 1993. *Tales from the White Mountains*: 35.)

and

> *When I was a lad we had a chip shop in Roche. The proprietor was partially sighted, his step-daughter used to serve and he used to chop chips. He had this wooden box and when it got crowded we'd go up scrumping apples. We'd creep back with a few apples in our pockets, he'd pick them up and think they were potatoes!*
>> (Collected orally from Cedric Burden, Roche, September 1993. *Tales from the White Mountains*: 37.)

These four types of stories represent different storytelling traditions within the community, and so we can see that tradition plays an important role within the community. We have both story traditions and storytelling traditions that continue to develop across the generations.

Storytelling and 'The Community'

The project which has collected this wide range of material owes a lot to many different approaches. It is oral history. It is reminiscence. It is community arts. It is youth work. It is education. It is literacy development. It is folklore. It is multi-agency, cross-generational. It is all these things. It is, above all, about creating an awareness of existing storytelling cultures. It is about empowerment.

It is, unlike much of the work of the nineteenth century folklorists, not about reinventing a community's culture in language for an educated middle class readership, but about giving opportunity for people to tell those stories they want to tell in the way they want to tell them, and giving value to those stories as valid cultural expression, whilst recognising the verbal artistry of the individual. It is, in effect, about allowing a community and individuals within that community to set their own cultural agenda without one being imposed from outside. The job of the professional artsworker in all of this is to use his/her expertise to provide an appropriate context for this to happen.

Everybody tells stories -- all the time, because it is through our stories that we make sense of the world around us. It is by telling stories that we relate to our physical and social environment, because storytelling is an intrinsic element of human existence. As Harold Rosen would say, we all have the 'impulse to narrative'. (1988, 168)

Storytelling is fundamentally linked to place and community, because it is the means by which we celebrate and define our communities, however they be determined. Even within the clay villages where mobility is not great and extended families are still common, the community comprises people of all ages and backgrounds. There is no room for the purist here. Those in search of the authentic, timeless, ethnically-cleansed product had better look elsewhere. These stories are in celebration of the community as it exists today, warts and all.

The motivation behind recording and collecting these stories is not one of preservation, but one of celebration. We are not of the opinion that we had better get collecting quickly otherwise there'll soon be no folklore left. Folklorists and story collectors have always felt that they have been capturing the last vestiges of a fast-disappearing way of life. However, folklore and tradition are not specifically to do with the past, but are about deconstructing and defining the present, and to this end folklore and folk narrative constantly reinvent themselves to deal with the new realities. Contemporary folklore is a combination of tradition and innovation and by giving value to the oral narrative currently in circulation within a community, we create a snapshot of that community at a particular time of its development. This is something worth celebrating.

The professional storyteller and 'The Community'

For the professional arts practitioner, popular culture is not about numbers, it is not about bums on seats, but is about making connections. It is about giving voice to a community's own fund of cultural experiences. It is literally about 'speaking their language', or indeed allowing them to speak their own language.

This obviously has implications for us as we head towards the end of the twentieth century. It is not long ago that Margaret Thatcher was saying that there is no such thing as society and we are now (at the time of writing), we are told, living in John Major's 'classless society'. In reality we live in a society in which community is being constantly and systematically undermined and dismantled. Whole communities in the Welsh coalfields (and in other places) have been destroyed in recent years and large job losses are currently expected in the clay industry itself. Events like this cannot help but have a profound effect on these communities and perhaps the china clay villages themselves are about to undergo dramatic change. This is where community storytelling comes into its own, because in this sense, storytelling is the most inclusive form of popular culture. Everybody tells stories and so, by encouraging a storytelling culture, by giving people the time and the space to tell their stories, we are giving voice to that community's culture, whatever its state of growth or decline, and then giving it the opportunity to redefine itself in the light of ongoing change.

Evaluation of this kind of work is notoriously difficult. There are many people who, for a variety of reasons, will choose not to share their stories publicly and that in itself is a valid cultural statement. In any case, with limited resources projects such as this will never be able to reach every single person, and that has to be recognised. However, many of the most important benefits of this kind of work occur 'invisibly'.

I am reminded of an incident that happened during a similar community storytelling project on which I was engaged. During the course of the project stories were regularly posted on a bulletin board in the local library for all to read. One day, the librarian had unsuccessfully tried to persuade a couple of elderly residents to share their stories on tape, when she overheard them talking. They were standing by the bulletin board reading the stories and every sentence they read seemed to spark off another story within themselves, which they eagerly shared with each other. They were, of course, engaged in a vibrant and lively exchange of storytelling and, moreover, an exchange that may not have occurred had it not been for the work that was being done in the local community.

Of course, it is impossible to quantify how often this happens and much of the evidence is anecdotal rather than statistical, but I believe it is instances such as these that give community storytelling its real validity. For me, the most exciting development in the Restormel Arts Clay Stories Project has been a recent one. Two local inhabitants from the village of St. Dennis, who have been centrally involved in the project from its inception, responded to a request from a local group to go and talk to them about the project and to tell some stories from the collections. So successful was their venture that they are now in demand locally as storytellers. In turn, their presentations undoubtedly spark off much storytelling activity amongst their audiences and they are reaching many of the people in the community that we were unable to. And so the stone of community storytelling continues to roll, long after the professional catalysts have withdrawn, and that is as good a measure as any of ownership and success.

In his essay 'The Storyteller', Walter Benjamin describes the storyteller as a subversive. In our own small ways we too are subversives. By keeping storytelling off the pedestal of high art, we are giving value to people's real stories and trying to culturally empower communities at a time when they most need it.

NOTES

1 Roche Rock, a rocky outcrop just outside the village of Roche, is a popular local landmark. Upon its summit are the ruins of an old chapel/church, and its mysterious nature has made it a natural focal point for a number of local stories of the supernatural kind and it continues to attract such narratives -- a further aspect of the role of traditional storytelling.

2 Egypt is a small row of houses about one mile out of St. Dennis. It acquired its nickname from the stream that runs by it, thick and white with clay deposits, reminiscent of the rivers of milk in Egypt in the Old Testament. Or at least, that was the story I was told.

152

BIBLIOGRAPHY

Benjamin, Walter. 'The Storyteller' (1936). Ed. Hannah Arendt. Trans. Harry Zohn. *Illuminations*. New York: Schocken Books, 1969. 83-109.

Bauman, Richard. *Story, Performance and Event*. Cambridge University Press, 1986.

Bruner, Jerome. *Acts of Meaning*. Harvard University Press, 1990.

Brunvand, Jan Harold. *The Vanishing Hitchhiker: American urban legends and their meanings*. New York: W. W. Norton, 1981.

Restormel Arts Clay Stories Project. *Tales from the White Mountains*. St. Austell: Restormel Arts/Verbal Arts Cornwall, 1993.

_____. *More Tales from the White Mountains*. St. Austell: Restormel Arts/Verbal Arts Cornwall, 1994.

Rosen, Harold. *Stories and Meanings*. Sheffield: N.A.T.E., 1985.

_____. 'Postscript'. Betty Rosen. *And None of It Was Nonsense*. London: Mary Glasgow Publications, 1988. 163-172.

153

Regional Imaginations: an afterword

Philip Crang

In this afterword I want to float some reflections on this volume's interest in the cultural construction of place. Like many other contributors, I will be emphasising this notion of construction, casting place as a social and cultural process rather than an achieved state or a pre-social residue and refuge. But pulling back from the case of Cornwall, and indeed from particular imaginations of it or other places, I will be trying to do more than discuss the cultural constructions of these things called places and what meanings they are invested with. Instead I want to think about the construction of the whole idea of something called a 'place'; to consider, then, how we imagine a place or a region as an entity, how we 'figure' it out, what we think of it as being; and to reflect on how the form of those imaginations might have the potential both to draw us in and draw us out through them. More specifically, I am going to concentrate on how we imaginatively construct what has been termed, rather inelegantly, the 'spatiality' of place, [1] and in consequence on some quite geometrical questions of shape, reach, borders, and form.

I should say that I come to these questions as a (rather unprofessional) professional geographer. As this volume demonstrates, it would be ridiculous and myopic to fetishise that itinerary, to claim some privileged position for geographers in discussions of place. Geography has no monopoly on these matters, and indeed it has increasingly cultivated a very healthy disciplinary leakiness, encouraging borrowings from, and occasionally the odd gift to, a broad spectrum of the human sciences. But being a Geographer has, whether I like it or not, imprinted itself on me. For a start, it has meant that I work in a field where in many ways appeals to place, and the appeals of places, operate as disciplinary *raison d'etres*. To take a common external image of my discipline, that of the hairy-chested geography of explorers past and present, its 'discoveries' of and journeys to 'far-off' places and peoples are not only driven by and sometimes financed through the political and economic projects of western (neo)colonialisms but also stem from and promote a fascination with travel and the experiencing of different landscapes and cultures. [2] In turn this kind of geography is deeply implicated in the various cultural imaginings of non-western 'Others' established through discursive formations such as Orientalism, Primitivism or, indeed, contemporary post-modern consumerist globalisms with their trite celebrations of cultural diversity. [3] But the appeal of place is not limited to geographical concerns with 'distant' peoples and places. It equally permeates the more sensitive souls of the less rugged and more 'aesthetically masculinist' humanistic and cultural geographers who have sought to identify, evoke and often celebrate the sensuous, emotional attachments we have to

154

our 'near' places, our everyday spaces. [4] So, whether I look near or far, I live and work in an intellectual environment where it is almost taken as self-evident that place matters. [5] But, whilst I readily endorse that sentiment intellectually, I somehow, to my guilt and shame, do not feel it. I am not as obsessed about place and places as I feel I should be, being a geographer. I am left mostly unseduced by the romantic overtones of feminised comforting, relaxing homes or wild, exotic, untamed aways. I am much more ambivalent about, and even indifferent to, places than that. So, as a mild sort of therapy, I will be trying to write through that ambivalence here, and in turn by using some discussions over the character of academic geography I would like to open up a debate about the 'popular' geographical knowledges of regions that are produced and circulated much more generally.

I hope to do that by identifying a number of different, and admittedly rather crude, 'figures' through which place, and a regional place like Cornwall, can be imagined. Let me launch off from one of the most common, what I will term the 'regional mosaic'. By this I mean a constructed imagination of the world as being made up of a mosaic of bordering but distinct regions or areas, or perhaps more accurately, a number of such mosaics layered upon each other at different scales -- the continental, the national, the regional, the local, the neighbour-hood. These various places are in turn associated with spatially distinct peoples and their 'local cultures'. So there is a piece of the mosaic that is Cornwall, which sits next to other pieces (England, Devon), nestles within bigger cultural wholes (Europe), is in turn perhaps made up of smaller cultural areas, and which is home for something called Cornish culture and identity. In this imagination regional commentators and practitioners -- such as geographers, anthropologists, regional artists and novelists -- in part search for and are inspired by coherent, patterned cultural worlds enclosed within discrete landscapes, terri-tories, languages and customs. [6] More particularly, so-called 'regional geogra-phers' have often cast their craft as exploring the connections between peoples and places, their lives and their lands, hence framing geography as a study of the particularities of places, as 'the art of recognizing, describing and interpre-ting the *personalities* of regions'. [7]

This understanding of both geography and the region is noteworthy in a number of respects. I want to draw out three aspects in particular: its implicit theorisation of culture; its conception of the role of imagination in the produc-tion of regional geographies; and its interest in geographical or regional person-ality. [8] In terms of the first, the imagination of a mosaic of unique places and local cultures constructs those cultures, to quote Pam Shurmer-Smith and Kevin Hannam, as if they were 'the content of boxes placed alongside one another' and hence as 'things'. [9] Just what these cultural things are composed of might be debated -- for example in anthropological discussions over whether to conceive of culture as a way of life to be documented and/or a system of meaning to be interpreted [10] -- but what stays constant is a sense of culture as something held in common, something shared and coherent, a social glue. As the anthropologist Renato Rosaldo puts it, 'from this perspective [of the regional mosaic] to pursue a culture is to seek out its differences, and then to show how it makes sense, as they say, in its own terms'. [11] In turn, what is sidelined is any sense of culture not as a thing but as a process, and not as

155

coherent but as constantly contested. The noun 'culture', grounded in other nouns like 'region', 'place' or 'area', masks the verbs and adjectives of 'cultural processes'. Moreover, a chain of associations is set up from culture, to place, to atemporality, and on to tradition. Culture becomes something to do with inheritance and roots, roots which are nurtured from some sort of placed soil (for some it is the literal soil and land, for others it might be local customs or local cultural productions and arts). It becomes something which exists in opposition to the modern world. Culture survives on the margins of the contemporary, and is always under threat from its invasive and homogenizing incursions. [12] And regionalists cast themselves as documenters and defenders of cultures conceptualised as 'things' inherited from the past, and of meaningful places under threat from a sweeping placelessness.

This location of regional culture in the past, or at least in a timeless present, also positions the regionalist imagination in rather problematic ways. At its most extreme it can involve a denial of that imagination altogether, for example through literary tropes of objectivist realism which deny a subjective and involved commentator, or through taking refuge in a dry and dusty compendium of facts which bores the reader into the mistaken supposition that no imagination of any sort could have possibly entered into its production. [13] But more often the requirement for more than mere documentation is recognised, though the realm of imaginative operation remains quite tightly circumscribed. Academic geographers' praisings of non-academic geographical portraits illustrate this quite neatly. So, in an anthology of travel writings Margaret Anderson argues that 'no deadly accurate, purely technical description can bring vividly to life a mountain, a great river, or even a climate, can make it our own to love and remember, as an imaginative description by a great writer can do'. [14] And in a similar vein E.W. Gilbert encourages his academic colleagues to learn from the achievments of English regional novelists, arguing that:

English regional novelists display many merits that geographers can recognise and envy... Reality is faithfully shown; it is not lost in the dim twilight of modern geographical jargon... The regional novelists have been able to produce a synthesis, "a living picture of the unity of people and place".... The geographer often speaks of the "personality of the region" and this is exactly what some novelists have brought out so strongly... [15]

But the art here, the imaginative achievment, is one of evoking or giving expression to something that already exists, whether that be a regional landscape or culture. And as many of the contributions to this volume have highlighted that is a very partial account of the relationship between regions and regional imaginations as forged in art, literature and academy. Most importantly, it neglects the role that those imaginations play in constructing the region as a meaningful entity in the first place, instead focusing only on how they can 'encapsulate and crystallise regional values'. [16] Instead we need to recognise that regions are imaginative inventions, produced discursively and institutionally, and not just re-presented within literary, artistic and academic works. [17] Moreover, as Edward Said's work on 'imaginative geographies' has argued, this discursive production is not just a matter of content, of what places mean, of what fills the boxes of the regional mosaic; it is also about the production of that mosaic itself. So, in writing about the production of the 'Orient' Said is not only concerned with the characteristics attributed to the Orient and the Oriental but also with the psychic, affective and cultural economies embodied in the construction of a world divided into West and East, Self and Other. [18] It is not enough, then, just to acknowledge the imaginative character of regional geographies, mundanely by arguing that their boundaries are a matter of intuition, or more seriously by recognising them to be infused with and productive of a number of cultural meanings and normative values. Rather, we have to analyse the character of their imagination, and in particular the 'regionalizing technologies' they deploy. Crucially, the regional mosaic is one, and only one, of these imaginative technologies, and hence the mosaic is only one way of thinking of place.

A starting point in acknowledging this is to think about what the particular characteristics of the regional mosaic as a way of seeing are. Let me emphasise three. First, it suggests that places are bounded, and in consequence, lines of enclosure become crucial in creating the mosaic. In this vein Douglas Pocock, writing on the relations between place and the novelist, defines place in the following terms:

Place may refer to a variety of scales, in each of which, in experiential terms, there is a characteristic bounding with internal structure and identity, such that insideness is distinguished from outsidedness.... At its most obvious and familiar, it is wherever we feel "at home", where things "fall into place", beyond which we feel "out of place", intruders in someone else's domain. [19]

Less enthusiastically, and in one of a series of writings drawing attention to the forms of visual and mental cartography caught up with a bounded or what she terms an 'introverted' sense of place, the geographer Doreen Massey has 'reminisced' about some of her 'most painful times as a geographer... spent unwillingly struggling to think about how one could draw a boundary around somewhere like "the East Midlands"'. [20] Secondly, as Massey points out, this is not just a trivial technical fetish, but an expression of a much deeper logic in which divisions of inside and outside, here and there, and us and them are central. In consequence, a crucial 'problem' for regional writings and livings based upon appeals to the mosaic and a *defence* of the local are questions of purity and its corruption. Too much blurring of boundaries and borders, too much porosity, too much mixing, and the whole regionalization of difference disappears. In consequence, any such blurrings become a complicating 'noise', hiding or reducing regional and local differences. And searches for the truly distinctive region, and the truly different culture, tend to retreat into isolated margins or well insulated 'heartlands'. 'Englishness' is to be found in the Cotswolds, not the porous port cities of London or Bristol. The 'real' America is in the mid-west, not New York. The 'authentic' Spain is away from the tourist crowd.

So in this portrait the 'geographical personality' of a place is not only a question of specificity, but also of unity. As the focus on personality suggests, there are intriguing parallels here with accounts of the smaller region which is the individual human self. For example, John Shotter has examined the shifting vocabularies of semi-populist psychologies from the 1960s onwards, conceptualising them as resources or technologies that can be used in the authoring of our selves. [21] In the 1960s and 1970s he identifies a concern with 'personhood', and more specifically with the discovery of a deep, authentic set of personal powers from which individuals have been increasingly estranged through the invasions of modern disciplinary and bureaucratic social systems. The hope was, then, to recover a homogenous, ordered, unified and stable self by stripping away layers of distortions imposed from social systems external to the individual. The parallels with imaginations of the regional mosaic are clear. In both cases two competing options emerge: either to work at recovering some more authentic state seen to exist in some place not colonised by the connections that entity has into a wider world; or, to give oneself over to that world and live with inauthenticity. The latter would be typified at the scale of the self by the kinds of socially negotiated self-presentations documented so wonderfully by Erving Goffman, [22] and their association with an emphasis on a superficial 'personality' rather than any deeper 'character'; [23] and at the scale of the place or region by the booming practices of place promotion and their celebrations of the role of image in place identities. [24] But Shotter's argument is that these constructions of deep authenticity and superficial inauthenticities are not the only options open to us in the authoring of our selves. In particular, rather different understandings of the self have emerged with a shift away from questions of both personhood and personality, and towards questions of 'identity'. And by implication, then, these politics of identity also provide resources for thinking about the region in different ways than the regional mosaic; they provide alternative regionalizing technologies.

Rather than summarise Shotter's argument on the politics of identity here, I want instead to run it through materials more explicitly relevant to the question at hand, a variety of 'new' regional geographies which have emerged over the last fifteen years or so. [25] On the way I will construct some alternative regional figures than that of the mosaic: namely the *story*, the *tapestry*, the *circuitry*, and the *metropolis*. To reiterate, I do so because the mosaic, as a regional imagination, has two severe drawbacks: first, it operates with a spatial and political logic of inside and outside which depends upon a very particular point of view and has limiting political and imaginative possibilities; and second, it casts the region as a pre-existing 'thing' evoked, expressed or interpreted by the regionalist, rather than as an on-going process in which the regionalist is participating.

One way to deal with the latter problem in particular is to conceptualise the region as a process of *story-telling*, a narrative, a rhetorical construction. Here the region becomes a 'historically extended, socially embodied argument', [26] an argument in which inclusions and exclusions -- senses of local belonging and not belonging -- are constructed. And the argument is not over the content of something already in existence, but is a process in which something is created and recreated: 'the very activity of arguing about its various instantiations will work to establish patterns of relation between people that will be its instantiation'. [27] Here, then, if the region is about 'tradition' it is about a 'living tradition'.

And if it is about inclusion and exclusion, about belonging and not belonging, then these are not adjudications of fact ('you are Cornish, you are not Cornish'), but on-going constructions established in the process of argumentation as much as in any outcome ('I am not Cornish because my voice is not heard in the argument that is Cornwall', 'I am not Cornish because it is an argument whose words don't include me'). Hence, as an argued story Cornwall and other regional imaginations raise questions about the rhetorical politics and poetics of their argumentation. Politics over the voicings and mufflings of people who might contribute to the argument; and poetics over the structures through which that argument operates, its judgements on appropriate materials, and its conception of how those materials should be organised. Less abstractly, these politics and poetics are evidenced in debates within this volume over both the social institutionalisation and composition of regional cultural producers -- in terms of artists, promotionalists, political elites, academics, etc. -- and the ways of representing regional time-space that they deploy -- in terms of how they construct regional histories, how those histories are spatialised to allow for the configurational relations across space at any one time, and so on.[28]

But to view the region as a story, or perhaps better as an on-going argument, does run the risk of making it all too wordy, as somehow outside of much everyday life, and in turn of making the region too easily contained within the order of a narrative. One way to head these dangers off might be to see these regional arguments as one set of fibres woven into and through a *regional tapestry* which also includes threads made up of the routines of everyday life and the more widespread spatial connections on which they draw. This is the region as a process constantly being constructed and reconstructed through the times and spaces of everyday practices. Patterns of density and colour would be marked out by tight knots of routine interaction and co-presence, and the region would be seen as partly the product of these routinized 'time-space paths'.[29]

Regions emerge, then, from the spatial patterns of everyday life, and regional arguments operate within these spaces, and help shape them. But the times and spaces of our everyday lives are not only characterised by local routines and presences. Most obviously, our daily routines may well stretch well outside of our 'local' area. So yesterday, a fairly ordinary and typically boring day for me, I woke up in my council flat in East London and, like normal, caught the tube into Bloomsbury to begin writing this essay in my office. I saw people at work I see most days; even on the tube I saw some people I recognised because they often catch the train at the same time and 'place' as me (people tend to try to get in carriages that will stop nearest the exit at their destination station so have their regular places on the platform and in the train); and I got home in time to help cook and eat the evening meal I share with my partner most evenings. But I also rang my parents in Devon and a friend in west Wales which is where I used to work; I e.mailed someone in Australia; I flicked my office radio between national Radio 1, London News, and a north London pirate station playing what I think was 'jungle' (I'm not an expert) that kept mucking up my reception; and I watched one of my favourite TV programmes, NYPD Blue. My life was not neatly contained in a single place. What is more, all those boring routine things I did depended on a vast number of connections that I have, mostly without thinking or really knowing about them, with other people, places and times. For example, my enjoyment of NYPD Blue relied on the technical and commissioning staff at Channel 4; the producers, actors, script writers and so on in the US; as well as a fondness I have long had for the glamour of all things American, which I cannot explain exactly, but which I know relates to wider British imaginations of the 'absence' and 'away' that is American popular culture. [30] So both materially and imaginatively, my daily tapestry has threads that shoot off from the knots of daily spatial habits. Indeed these knots rely on threads that mark out much wider spaces of connection. More generally, Doreen Massey has argued that what picturing such a tapestry requires is therefore a 'global sense of the local, a global sense of place'. An imagination in which the particularity of place is not dependent on borders and boundaries cutting up space into heres and theres, but 'can come, in part, through the particularity of linkage to that "outside" which is therefore part of what constitutes the place'. [31] An imagination in which both presences and absences, the 'near' and the 'far', the local and the global are vital. [32] And thus an imagination less rooted in a 'possessive individualism', where particularity and difference depends upon properties held within the individual, and more routed through a 'social individuality' which emphasises relations to others. [33]

This shift from roots to routes is taken further if we refigure the region again through the metaphor of *regional circuitry*, an imagination in which the connections do not only make regions but also become them. Perhaps the best example of such an imagination is Paul Gilroy's ongoing work on what he calls the 'cultural circuitry' of the 'black Atlantic', defined as his 'own provisional attempt to figure a deterritorialised, multiplex, and anti-national basis for the affinity or 'identity of passions' between diverse black populations'. [34] Gilroy's work stems from a political project which opposes essentialising conceptions of race, culture and their relations to space. In understanding the diasporic cultures of the black Atlantic he argues against any simple territorial basis for culture, and hence against Black Nationalist attempts to view diaspora as a cultural weakness requiring a return to the territorial homelands of roots and origins. At the same time he is also unconvinced by more particularistic black nationalisms, for example those referring only to Black-Americans. Both conceptions, he suggests, betray an 'obsession with origins' and appeal to 'black absolutisms'. The spatiality of black Atlantic cultures are better understood in terms of the 'ex-centric communicative circuitry that has enabled dispersed populations to converse, interact and even synchronise', in terms then of routes of connection and disconnection rather than roots dug up from a place of origin. [35]

What we have here, then, is a regional imagination of the Atlantic as a complex of 'spaces of flows'. [36] Such an imagination could be worked out in a number of other directions as well. There could be regional geographies of particular flows, tracing through the cultural circuits of particular people and things, piecing together their multiple times and places. [37] There could be geographies of whole sets of flows; in that spirit David Morley and Kevin Robins write about the 'spaces of identity' forged within the new communications geographies of a globalizing and localizing set of mediascapes, arguing that 'the spaces of transmission defined by satellite footprints or radio signals... provid[e] the crucial, and permeable, boundaries of our age'. [38] Or there could be regional geographies marked more by what Edward Said has termed an integrative or contrapuntal orientation, devoted to juxtaposing and stitching together supposed heres and theres, [39] based on logics of causal or social connections, paradoxical and ironic effect, [40] or the re-insertion into presence of the shadowy but significant absences of those Others that the regional mosaic excludes and distances but of course still depends upon. Said argues in particular for the representation of the imperial connections that bring western and non-western experiences together, and cites C.LR. James's *The Black Jacobins* as a particularly stimulating example. For example he notes how:

James's Black Jacobins treats the Santo Domingo slave uprising as a process unfolding within the same history as that of the French Revolution, and Napoleon and Toussaint are the two great figures who dominate those turbulent years. Events in France and Haiti criss-cross and refer to one another like voices in a fugue. James's narrative is broken up as a history dispersed in geography, in archival sources, in emphases both Black and French. [41]

The contrapuntal historical geography James constructs is not the singular narrative of a unified place, securely bounded and anchored in historical traditions; it stages many voices, many times and places, is full of connections and inflections. For Said this allows an escape from 'the already charted and controlled narrative lanes' of colonialist discourse in favour of imaginative leaps that open up new possibilities and embody 'the energies of anti-imperialist liberation'. [42]

A slightly different viewpoint on, or immersion in, the circuitry of modern life is provided by the figure of the *metropolis,* perhaps most evocatively constructed in Iain Chambers' urban wanderings. [43] For Chambers urban geographies can no longer be grounded in the built landscape and its symbolisms. Instead they have become increasingly metropolitan in character, where 'the metropolis is, above all, a myth, a tale, a telling that helps some of us to locate our home in modernity'. The myth is constructed through an 'electronic topology... [of] visualscapes, soundscapes, and imaginaryscapes' that 'provide us with a city that is immaterial and transparent: a cinematic city, a telematic hyper-space...'. [44] Projects of belonging and home-making do not disappear in this environment, but become more a matter of 'being at home' than 'going home':

While "going home" recalls the nostalgic associations of a mythologized point of origins (our mothers and fathers), "being at home" in the world involves finding ourselves in a wider, shifting, but more flexible, framework in which our mothers and fathers, bonds and traditions, the myths we know to be myths yet continue to cling to, cherish and dream, exist alongside other stories, other fragments of memory and traces of time.... [45]

The metropolis, then, has a 'labyrinthine and contaminated quality', [46] and a malleability in and through which the relations between people and place are reflexively monitored, managed and experimented with. It does not mean the end of other sorts of geographical imaginations: mythical representations of the regional mosaic may well be served up within it as part of a metrocentric global culture in which metropolitans can sample a constructed diversity; and there will still be dreams of places and people that are not metropolitan but 'local' (indeed these constructions of the local are important in allowing the distinction of the 'cosmopolitan'[47]). But these are incorporated within a very different sort of spatiality. As a site of life and theory the metropolis is marked by travels rather than overviews, and logs rather than maps.

Chambers' provocative and sweeping urban scapes seem to have taken us a long way from Cornwall's regional geography. And it certainly is true that his vision is easier to deploy in certain settings and with certain cultural and economic resources than if distanced from both. We should also note that Chambers' concentration on the creative fusions of metropolitan youth cultures can lead to the downplaying of involvements in metropolitan flows and networks that are less positively initiated and experienced. But for all that, it would be too easy simply to locate the figure of the metropolis -- or indeed of the circuit, the tapestry and the argument -- as cosmopolitan conceits, largely irrelevant to Cornish places such as Truro or Penzance. Rather, what I have tried to work through here are a number of figures of the region all of which have the potential to operate as resources in our constructions of our places and our selves. And I have tried to show how they offer us different options for what those constructions look like, what shape they take, and what role they play in our meaningful engagements with the world around us. The issue then is what shapes we want to make, how we want our worlds to be, and what powers we have to carry out that shaping in a world that does not sit in our hands like plasticene. The metropolis is my end point here not because it offers a simple ideal to emulate but because I think there is more potential in regional imaginations that, to use John Shotter's terminology one final time, are less about the imagined -- the picturing of an order, an answer to our questions, a map of our locations -- than about the imaginary -- a figure of the possible, a question kept open, a terrain to explore. Others may not share my preference, but at least we might agree that it is in the field defined by the imagined and the imaginary, in a set of choices over what sort of regional imagination we find appropriate, useful and relevant to our lives, that the cultural politics of place construction should be argued through.

1 To that extent, I am going to write far too little about the articulations of regional imaginations with landscapes, environments and natures. For those who are interested, fascinating accounts of these can be found in the recently launched journal *Ecumene*. One of my personal favourites is: D. Matless, 1994, 'Moral geography in Broadland', *Ecumene: a journal of environment, culture and meaning*, 1(2), 127-55.

2 On Geography's implications with empire and exploration see: F. Driver, 1992, 'Geography's empire: histories of geographical knowledge', *Environment and Planning D: Society & Space*, 10, 23-40; B. Hudson, 1977, 'The new geography and the new imperialism: 1870-1918', *Antipode*, 9(2), 12--19; D. Livingstone, 1992, 'A "sternly practical" pursuit: Geography, race and empire', in *The Geographical Tradition: episodes in the history of a contested enterprise*, pp. 216-59. Oxford: Blackwell; D. Stoddart, 1986, *On Geography and its History*. Oxford: Blackwell.

3 For example take a look at Catherine Lutz and Jane Collins' wonderful account of the appeal of *National Geographic* magazine to US audiences: C. Lutz and J. Collins, 1993, *Reading National Geographic*. University of Chicago Press.

4 See G. Rose, 1993, *Feminism & Geography: the limits of geographical knowledge*. Cambridge: Polity Press.

5 I do not mean this to suggest that Geographers have been unthinking about what place is or why it matters. See for example: S. Daniels, 1992, 'Place and the geographical imagination', *Geography*, 77, 310-22; J.N. Entrikin, 1991, *The Betweeness of Place: towards a geography of modernity*. London: Macmillan; D. Livingstone, 1992, 'The regionalizing ritual: Geography, place and particularity', in *Op. cit.*, pp. 260-303. Oxford: Blackwell; D. Massey, 1995, 'The conceptualization of place', in D. Massey & P. Jess (eds.) *A Place in the World?: places, cultures and globalization*, pp. 45-85. Oxford University Press.

6 For parallel critical commentaries on the 'cultural mosaic' within anthropological writings see: J. Friedman, 1995, 'Global system, globalization, and the parameters of modernity' in M. Featherstone, S. Lash & R. Robertson (eds.) *Global Modernities*, pp. 69-90. London: Sage; U. Hannerz, 1992, *Cultural Complexity*. New York: Columbia University Press; J.N. Pieterse, 1995, 'Globalization as hybridization' in M. Featherstone, S. Lash & R. Robertson (eds.) *Global Modernities*, pp. 45-68. London: Sage; and R. Rosaldo, 1993, *Culture and Truth*. London: Routledge.

7 E.W. Gilbert, 1960, 'The idea of the region', *Geography*, 45(3), 157-75: p.158 (my emphasis).

8 For a general but illuminating review of the notion of 'geographical personality' within regional geographies from 1900-1970 see G. S. Dunbar, 1974, 'Geographical personality', *Geoscience and Man*, V, 25-33.

9 P. Shurmer-Smith & K. Hannam, 1994, *Worlds of Desire, Realms of Power: a cultural geography*. London: Arnold; p. 79.

10 See C. Geertz, 1973, *The Interpretation of Cultures*. New York: Basic Books.

11 R. Rosaldo *Op. Cit.*, p. 201.

12 See R. Peet, 1989, 'World capitalism and the destruction of regional cultures', in R.J. Johnston & P. Taylor (eds.) *The World in Crisis*, second edition, pp. 175-99. Oxford: Blackwell.

13 I should say that whilst this is a very common, and understandable, reaction to academic regional geographies and ethnographies I think it is a mistaken reading. Lurking behind even the driest regional geography is what David Matless has called a 'lively geographical imagination'. His discussion of Patrick Geddes and the Regional Survey movement, with the odd aside on

scouting and stamp collecting, demonstrates this admirably. See D. Matless, 1992, 'Regional surveys and local knowledges: the geographical imagination in Britain, 1918-39', *Transactions of the Institute of British Geographers*, 17, 464-80; quote p.464.

14 M.S. Anderson (ed.), 1954, *Splendour of the Earth*; cited in H.C. Darby, 1962, 'The problem of geographical description', *Transactions of the Institute of British Geographers*, 30, 1-14, p.3.

15 E.W. Gilbert, 1972, 'British regional novelists and geography', in *British Pioneers in Geography*, pp. 116-27. Newton Abbott: David and Charles; quote pp. 124-5. More generally on the role of imagination and artistry in geographical descriptions see: J. Leighly, 1937, 'Some comments on contemporary geographical method', *Annals of the Association of American Geographers*, 27, 131; H. Prince, 1962, 'The geographical imagination', *Landscape*, 11, 22-5.

16 J.R. Shortridge, 1991, 'The concept of the place-defining novel in American popular culture', *The Professional Geographer*, 43(3), 280-91; quote p. 290. As this quotation demonstrates, Shortridge's article is an intriguing example of how even attempts to give a more active role to the regionalist imagination, in this case as 'place-defining', often slip back into a more expressive conception of the relation between region and regional 'art'.

17 See for instance J. Donald, 1993, 'How English is it? Popular literature and national culture' in E. Carter, J. Donald & J. Squires (eds.) *Space & Place: theories of identity and location*, pp. 165-86. London: Lawrence and Wishart.

18 See E. Said, 1978, *Orientalism*. London: Routledge.

19 D.C.D. Pocock, 1994 (orig. 1981), 'Place and the novelist', in K.E. Foote, P.J. Hugill, K. Mathewson and J.M. Smith (eds.) *Re-Reading Cultural Geography*, pp. 363-73. Austin, Texas: University of Texas Press; quote p. 364.

20 D. Massey, 1993, 'Power-geometry and a progressive sense of place', in J. Bird *et al* (eds.) *Mapping the Futures: local cultures, global change*, pp. 59-69. London: Routledge; quote p. 64. See also: D. Massey, 1991, 'A global sense of place', *Marxism Today*, June, 24-9; D. Massey, 1992, 'A place called home?', *New Formations*, 17, 3-15; D. Massey, 1995, *Op. Cit.*

21 J. Shotter, 1993, 'The politics of identity and belonging' in *Cultural Politics of Everyday Life*, pp. 187-202. Milton Keynes: Open University Press.

22 See for example E. Goffman, 1956, *The Presentation of Self in Everyday Life*. Edinburgh: Social Sciences Research Centre, University of Edinburgh.

23 On this distinction between character and personality see B.S. Turner, 1986, 'Personhood and citizenship', *Theory, Culture & Society*, 3(1), 1-16.

24 For a critical review of place promotion see G. Kearns & C. Philo (eds.), 1993, *Selling Places: the city as cultural capital, past and present*. Oxford: Pergamon Press.

25 For general reviews see: A. Gilbert, 1988, 'The new regional geography in English and French speaking countries', *Progress in Human Geography*, 12, 208-28; M.B. Pudup, 1988, 'Arguments within regional geography', *Progress in Human Geography*, 12, 369-90.

26 J. Shotter, *Op. Cit.*, p. 193.

27 *Ibid.*, p.195.

28 For accounts of these poetics with reference to academic regional geographies see: H.C. Darby, *Op. cit.*; A. Sayer, 1989, 'The "new" regional geography and problems of narrative', *Environment and Planing D: Society & Space*, 7(3), 253-76. For an experiment in the poetics of the region see A. Pred, 1995, *Recognizing European Modernities: a montage of the present*. London: Routledge.

29 This attention to the ways people move through time and space -- that is their time-space paths -- and the 'bundles' they create when their paths come together comes out of a school of Geography known as 'time geography'. Not only influential within the new regional geography, time geography has also been drawn on by writers looking more generally at how society is

constituted, most notably the social theorist Anthony Giddens. See: A. Giddens, 1984, *The Constitution of Society*. Cambridge: Polity Press.

30 See D. Webster, 1988, *Looka Yonder! The imaginary America of populist culture*. London: Comedia.

31 D. Massey, 1991, *Op. Cit.*, p. 29.

32 See also A. Lipietz, 1993, 'The local and the global: regional individuality or interregionalism?', *Transactions of the Institute of British Geographers*, 18(1), 8-18.

33 For this distinction see J. Shotter, *Op. Cit.*, p. 175.

34 P. Gilroy, 1995, 'Route work: the black Atlantic and the politics of exile' in I. Chambers & L. Curti (eds.) *The Post-Colonial Question: common skies, divided horizons*, pp. 17-29. London: Routledge; quote p. 18. See also: P. Gilroy, 1992, 'Cultural studies and ethnic absolutism' in L. Grossberg, C. Nelson & P. Treichler (eds.) *Cultural Studies*, pp. 187-98. New York: Routledge; P. Gilroy, 1993, *The Black Atlantic*. London: Verso.

35 P. Gilroy, 1995, *Op. Cit.*, p. 22.

36 M. Castells & J. Henderson, 1987, 'Techno-economic restructuring, socio-political processes, and spatial transformations' in J. Henderson & M. Castells (eds.) *Global Restructuring and Territorial Development*, pp. 1-17. London: Sage; quote p. 7.

37 This approach has been particularly promoted in an emerging literature on 'multi-locale' ethnographies. See, for example, G. Marcus, 1995, 'Ethnography in/of the world system: the emergence of multi-sited ethnography', *Annual Review of Anthropology*, 24, 95-117.

38 D. Morley & K. Robins, 1995, *Spaces of Identity: global media, electronic landscapes and cultural boundaries*. London: Routledge; quote p. 1.

39 E. Said, 1993, *Culture and Imperialism*. London: Chatto and Windus; quote p. 337.

40 One of the more cited examples of ironic juxtaposition is Ed Soja's portrait of 1980's Los Angeles and its account of the 'Star Wars' in the local entertainment and defence industries. See E. Soja, 1989, 'Taking Los Angeles apart: towards a postmodern geography' in *Postmodern Geographies: the reassertion of space in critical social theory*, pp. 222-48. London: Verso. There is an interesting comparison to be made between this regional geography of LA with that written through in his preceding essay, 'It all comes together in Los Angeles', *Op. Cit.*, pp. 190-221.

41 E. Said, 1993, *Op. Cit.*, p.338.

42 *Ibid.*, p. 340.

43 See in particular I. Chambers, 1990, *Border Dialogues. Journeys in postmodernity*. London: Routledge.

44 *Ibid.*, p. 112, p. 60, and p. 54 respectively.

45 *Ibid.*, p. 104.

46 I. Chambers, 1993, 'Cities without maps' in Bird J. *et al.* (eds.) *Mapping the Futures: local cultures, global change*, pp. 188-98. London: Routledge; quote p. 190.

47 See U. Hannerz, 1990, 'Cosmopolitans and locals in world culture', *Theory, Culture & Society*, 7, 237-51.

NOTES ON CONTRIBUTORS

HAROLD BIRKS, who has lived in Cornwall for the past twelve years, is a lecturer in design history at Falmouth College of Arts. His research interests are heritage, tourism and representations of Cornwall.

PHILIP CRANG, a lecturer in cultural geography at University College London, grew up in Devon but spent too much time watching American TV programmes to venture over the Tamar very often. He is currently researching the global and local geographies of food in London.

BERNARD DEACON, born and bred in Cornwall, is an associate lecturer in social sciences with the Open University and a tutor with the University of Exeter in Cornwall. He specialises in historical and Cornish studies and is currently researching regional and class formation in Cornwall. He has been actively involved in the emergence of the 'New Cornish Studies'.

MIKE DUNSTAN is a professional storyteller who has worked extensively throughout Cornwall and published on various aspects of storytelling. He also teaches in the University of Exeter's Department of Drama, where he completed a doctorate on Narrative Traditions Amongst Teenagers in Britain and Ireland.

JUDITH HUBBACK is a semi-retired analytical psychologist, author of many professional papers. She has known many parts of Cornwall very well all her life, gardening there, walking and swimming. Her novel, *The Sea Has Many Voices*, won the 1991 Sagittarius prize, under the aegis of the Society of Authors.

HELEN HUGHES is a senior lecturer at Doncaster College, whose main area of research is popular fiction. Her interest in Cornwall lies in its use as a location for narratives in the Gothic and historical mode.

JOHN HURST is a senior tutor at the University of Exeter, based in the Cornwall office of the Department of Continuing and Adult Education. His main interests lie in the relationships between literature and religious thought and experience; he has also worked in recent years on literature written in and about Cornwall.

ALAN M. KENT was born in Cornwall in the heart of the china clay mining industry. He is a novelist, poet and teacher, currently completing a biography of the Hocking family of novelists and a doctorate at the Institute of Cornish Studies. He is a founding member of *Berdh Amowydh Kernewek/* Modern Cornish Poets.

NICKIANNE MOODY is a senior lecturer in media and cultural studies at Liverpool John Moores University. Her main research interests are popular fiction and cultural history. She is currently carrying out a national oral history survey into Boots Booklovers' Library.

PHILIP PAYTON is Reader in Cornish Studies and Director of the Institute of Cornish Studies at the University of Exeter. He has written extensively on modern and contemporary Cornwall, and is also interested in comparative issues of emigration, ethnicity and territorial identity.

SU REID is Deputy Director of the School of Law, Humanities and International Studies at the University of Teesside. She has taught English there and at the University of Aberdeen, but has recently been involved in the development of courses in a number of other areas, including cultural studies and law. She edited the *New Casebook on* Mrs Dalloway *and* To The Lighthouse, and is now writing a book about girls' schools and women's colleges in fiction. St Ives is where she escapes.

CHRIS THOMAS is a lecturer in geography at Staffordshire University with active research interests in the landscapes of labour and leisure. He is especially concerned with place, landscape and identity in Cornwall and Wales. He is currently writing a book on rural geography, completing a doctorate on some of the constructions and contestations of Cornwall and editing a volume based on the 'Industry, Identity and Landscape' conference held at Staffordshire University in 1996.

SIMON TREZISE is a lecturer at the University of Exeter, with research interests in the Victorian and modern periods. He is currently writing a book entitled *The West Country as a Literary Invention*. He has been a full-time programme organiser and teacher of mature students since 1982, working with the W.E.A., the Open University and the University of Exeter. His Welsh and Cornish origins mean that for him the 'Celtic Fringe' is at the centre.

ELLA WESTLAND is a lecturer at the University of Exeter and organises an academic programme in Cornwall. She publishes on Victorian literature, romantic fiction and the cultural study of place, and has begun work on a book on Dickens and the Sea. She lives on the Cornish coast near Mevagissey.